"The glory of God, celebrated by angels, but often lost on the church today, is here restored to our vision. This is a serious engagement with biblical truth and it asks the reader to engage with it seriously, too. When we climb a mountain, we know that however long is the ascent, it is all made worthwhile by the view from the top. So it is here."

David F. Wells, Distinguished Research Professor,
Gordon-Conwell Theological Seminary

"The Westminster Shorter Catechism rightly tells us that the chief end of man is to glorify God and to enjoy him forever. And yet, 'glorifying' God and living for 'the glory of God' can often seem mysterious and ultimately disconnected from day-to-day life. In this new installment in the Theology in Community series, Christopher Morgan and Robert Peterson have pulled together a team that not only teach about God's glory but in their very scholarship display 'the visible splendor and moral beauty of God's manifold perfections.' As I read this book, I wanted to sing, 'To God be the glory, great things he has done!'"

Sean Michael Lucas, Senior Minister,
The First Presbyterian Church, Hattiesburg, MS

"There is no theme more central to the message of Scripture than the glory of God. He created the world so that his name would be glorified in and by the things he made, and he has saved us so that we might glorify him in eternity. It is a focus that a self-centered generation badly needs to recover, and the contributors to this volume have given us a wonderful introduction on which to base our reflections and our worship."

Gerald Bray, Research Professor, Beeson Divinity School;
author, *Biblical Interpretation: Past and Present*

Christians often speak of the glory of God and living for the glory of God, but what is the glory of God? This work presents an excellent biblical study of God's glory. Not only does it provide a good doctrinal foundation for understanding the glory of God, but it also applies the subject practically to the Christian life. An understanding of God's glory affects every area of Christian living: the purpose of the Christian life, worship, ethics, evangelism, missions, pastoral ministry, and the study of theology. As a pastor, I highly recommend this work for the Christian who desires to understand more fully God's glory and what it means to live to the glory of God."

Van Lees, Pastor, Covenant of Grace Church, St. Charles, Missouri.

"Christopher Morgan and Robert Peterson have once again assembled a fine team of biblical, historical, and systematic theologians to shape the second volume in the Theology in Community series. This talented team of writers demonstrate how focusing on the all-encompassing theme of God's glory impacts our thinking about God, the self, and the world, including questions regarding meaning, purpose, and salvation. These explorations provide us with a more in-depth appreciation of how the glory of God has been emphasized in Scripture and how it has been interpreted in church history. In addition, we are presented with an overarching and powerful portrait of God's grandeur, beauty, and transcendence. I am pleased to recommend this outstanding volume to students, lay leaders, pastors, and theologians alike."

David S. Dockery, President, Union University

The Glory
of God

THEOLOGY IN COMMUNITY

A series edited by Christopher W. Morgan and Robert A. Peterson

Other titles in the Theology in Community Series:
Suffering and the Goodness of God (2008)

The Glory of God

Christopher W. Morgan
and Robert A. Peterson

EDITORS

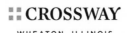 **CROSSWAY**

WHEATON, ILLINOIS

The Glory of God
Copyright © 2010 by Christopher W. Morgan and Robert A. Peterson
Published by Crossway
1300 Crescent Street
Wheaton, Illinois 60187

First printing 2010
Printed in the United States of America

Unless otherwise indicated, Scripture quotations are from the ESV® Bible (*The Holy Bible, English Standard Version*®), copyright © 2001 by Crossway. Used by permission. All rights reserved.

Scripture quotations marked AT are the author's translation.

Scripture quotations marked KJV are from the *King James Version* of the Bible.

Scripture quotations marked MESSAGE are from *The Message*. Copyright © by Eugene H. Peterson 1993, 1994, 1995, 1996, 2000, 2001, 2002. Used by permission of NavPress Publishing Group.

Scripture quotations marked NASB are from *The New American Standard Bible*®. Copyright © The Lockman Foundation 1960, 1962, 1963, 1968, 1971, 1972, 1973, 1975, 1977, 1995. Used by permission.

Scripture references marked NKJV are from *The New King James Version*. Copyright © 1982, Thomas Nelson, Inc. Used by permission.

Scripture references marked NIV are taken from the HOLY BIBLE, NEW INTERNATIONAL VERSION®. Copyright © 1973, 1978, 1984 Biblica. Used by permission of Zondervan. All rights reserved. The "NIV" and "New International Version" trademarks are registered in the United States Patent and Trademark Office by Biblica. Use of either trademark requires the permission of Biblica.

Scripture references marked NLT are from *The Holy Bible, New Living Translation*, copyright © 1996, 2004. Used by permission of Tyndale House Publishers, Inc., Wheaton, Ill., 60189. All rights reserved.

Scripture references marked NRSV are from *The New Revised Standard Version*. Copyright © 1989 by the Division of Christian Education of the National Council of the Churches of Christ in the U.S.A. Published by Thomas Nelson, Inc. Used by permission of the National Council of the Churches of Christ in the U.S.A.

Scripture references marked RSV are from *The Revised Standard Version*. Copyright © 1946, 1952, 1971, 1973 by the Division of Christian Education of the National Council of the Churches of Christ in the U.S.A.

All emphases in Scripture quotations have been added by the authors.

Hardcover ISBN: 978-1-58134-978-8

The glory of God / Christopher W. Morgan and Robert A. Peterson, editors.
    p. cm.—(Theology in community)
  Includes bibliographical references and indexes.
  ISBN 978-1-58134-978-8 (hc)
  1. Glory of God—Christianity. 2. Glory of God—Biblical teaching. I. Morgan, Christopher W., 1971–
II. Peterson, Robert A., 1948-
BT180.G6G66 2010
231.7—dc22
    2009053434

Crossway is a publishing ministry of Good News Publishers.

TS		21	20	19	18	17	16	15	14	13	12		11	10
14	13	12	11	10	9	8	7	6	5	4	3		2	1

To our colleagues at California Baptist University
and Covenant Theological Seminary, who faithfully teach
and lovingly shepherd students for the glory of God
and the good of his church

Contents

8. A Missional Theology of the Glory of God
   J. Nelson Jennings   209

List of Abbreviations

BECNT	Baker Exegetical Commentary on the New Testament
DJG	*Dictionary of Jesus and the Gospels*
DLNT	*Dictionary of the Later New Testament and Its Developments*
DPL	*Dictionary of Paul and His Letters*
EEC	*Encyclopedia of Early Christianity*
ISBE	*International Standard Bible Encyclopedia*
IDB	*The Interpreter's Dictionary of the Bible*
JBL	*Journal of Biblical Literature*
JETS	*Journal of the Evangelical Theological Society*
NAC	New American Commentary
NIDNTT	*New International Dictionary of New Testament Theology*
NIDOTTE	*New International Dictionary of Old Testament Theology and Exegesis*
NIGTC	New International Greek Testament Commentary
NTS	*New Testament Studies*
OTL	Old Testament Library
TDNT	*Theological Dictionary of the New Testament*
TynBul	*Tyndale Bulletin*
WC	Westminster Commentaries
WTJ	*Westminster Theological Journal*
WUNT	Wissenschaftliche Untersuchungen zum Neuen Testament
WBC	Word Biblical Commentary

Theology in Community

As the series name *Theology in Community* indicates, *theology* in community aims to promote clear thinking on and godly responses to historic and contemporary theological issues. The series examines issues central to the Christian faith, including traditional topics such as sin, the atonement, the church, and heaven, but also some which are more focused or contemporary, such as suffering and the goodness of God, the glory of God, the deity of Christ, and the kingdom of God. The series strives not only to follow a sound theological method but also to display it.

Chapters addressing the Old and New Testaments on the book's subject form the heart of each volume. Subsequent chapters synthesize the biblical teaching and link it to historical, philosophical, systematic, and pastoral concerns. Far from being mere collections of essays, the volumes are carefully crafted so that the voices of the various experts combine to proclaim a unified message.

Again, as the name suggests, theology *in community* also seeks to demonstrate that theology should be done in teams. The teachings of the Bible were forged in real-life situations by leaders in God's covenant communities. The biblical teachings addressed concerns of real people who needed the truth to guide their lives. Theology was formulated by the church and for the church. This series seeks to recapture that biblical reality. The volumes are written by scholars, from a variety of denominational backgrounds

13

and life experiences with academic credentials and significant expertise across the spectrum of theological disciplines, who collaborate with each other. They write from a high view of Scripture with robust evangelical conviction and in a gracious manner. They are not detached academics but are personally involved in ministry, serving as teachers, pastors, and missionaries. The contributors to these volumes stand in continuity with the historic church, care about the global church, share life together with other believers in local churches, and aim to write for the good of the church to strengthen its leaders, particularly pastors, teachers, missionaries, lay leaders, students, and professors.

> For the glory of God and the good of the church,
> Christopher W. Morgan and Robert A. Peterson

Acknowledgments

Allan Fisher, Jill Carter, Lydia Brownback, and the rest of the team at Crossway, for their expertise, helpfulness, and encouragement.

Beth Ann Brown and Rick Matt, for their careful editorial work. Jeremy Ruch, for compiling the bibliography.

Todd Bates, Tony Chute, Don Dunavant, Jeff Griffin, John Massey, Jeff Mooney, Roger Price, and Steve Wellum, for reading sections of the manuscript.

Steve Jamieson, reference and systems librarian, and James Pakala, library director, both of the J. Oliver Buswell Jr. Library at Covenant Theological Seminary, and Barry Parker, reference and serials librarian of California Baptist University, for invaluable assistance in research.

Contributors

Bryan Chapell (PhD, Southern Illinois University), President and Professor of Practical Theology, Covenant Theological Seminary

Richard B. Gaffin Jr. (ThD, Westminster Theological Seminary), Professor of Biblical and Systematic Theology, Westminster Theological Seminary, Philadelphia

J. Nelson Jennings (PhD, University of Edinburgh), Professor of World Mission, Covenant Theological Seminary

Andreas J. Köstenberger (PhD, Trinity Evangelical Divinity School), Professor of New Testament and Greek, Southeastern Baptist Theological Seminary

Tremper Longman III (PhD, Yale University), Professor of Biblical Studies, Westmont College

Richard R. Melick Jr. (PhD, Southwestern Baptist Theological Seminary), Professor of New Testament Studies, Golden Gate Baptist Theological Seminary

Christopher W. Morgan (PhD, Mid-America Baptist Theological Seminary), Professor of Theology, California Baptist University

Stephen J. Nichols (PhD, Westminster Theological Seminary), Research Professor of Christianity and Culture, Lancaster Bible College and Graduate School

Robert A. Peterson (PhD, Drew University), Professor of Systematic Theology, Covenant Theological Seminary

Introduction

I chabod" is one of the saddest words in all of Scripture. It means "Where is the glory?" It is the name given by the daughter-in-law of Eli, Israel's head priest, to her newborn baby in the time of Samuel. Here is the story:

> Now his daughter-in-law, the wife of Phinehas, was pregnant, about to give birth. And when she heard the news that the ark of God was captured, and that her father-in-law and her husband were dead, she bowed and gave birth, for her pains came upon her. And about the time of her death the women attending her said to her, "Do not be afraid, for you have borne a son." But she did not answer or pay attention. And she named the child Ichabod, saying, "The glory has departed from Israel!" because the ark of God had been captured and because of her father-in-law and her husband. And she said, "The glory has departed from Israel, for the ark of God has been captured." (1 Sam. 4:19–22)

The Philistines have captured Israel's ark; Eli's sons Hophni and Phinehas have been killed in battle; Eli drops dead when he hears the terrible news; his daughter-in-law, Phinehas's wife, dies in childbirth and names her infant Ichabod. Indeed, the glory has departed from God's Old Testament people Israel (for a season).

Similarly, many proclaim "Ichabod" today. They claim, and with good reason, that the glory of God has departed from the minds and hearts of many evangelical Christians.[1] But a recent book maintains that alongside this downward trend, another one is emerging. Journalist Collin Hansen took a two-year journey to conferences, seminaries, and churches and was

---

[1] So David F. Wells, *God in the Wasteland: The Reality of Truth in a World of Fading Dreams* (Grand Rapids, MI: Eerdmans, 1994).

startled to learn of a rapidly spreading majestic view of God. To write his book he interviewed many people, among them Joshua Harris:

> I do wonder if some of the appeal . . . and the trend isn't a reaction to the watered-down vision of God that's been portrayed in the evangelical seeker-oriented churches. . . . I just think that there's such a hunger for the transcendent and for a God who is not just sitting around waiting for us to show up so that the party can get started.[2]

Hansen also listened to Timothy George, dean of Beeson Divinity School:

> We live in a transcendence-starved culture and in a transcendence-starved evangelicalism. . . . We've so dumbed down the gospel and dumbed down worship in a good effort to reach as many people as we can that there's almost a backlash. It comes from this great hunger for a genuinely God-centered, transcendence-focused understanding of who God is and what God wants us to do and what God has given us in Jesus Christ.[3]

Hansen concludes, "Indeed, [the renewed view of God] puts much stock in transcendence, which draws out biblical themes such as God's holiness, glory, and majesty."[4] It would be foolish to think that a reemphasis on God's glory has swept the nation. But, as Hansen and others document, many are being captured by a renewed vision of God as almighty, gracious, and glorious.

It seems undeniable that a number of ministries are communicating effectively (especially to young people) that the purpose of their lives is to glorify God so that all they do is to be done for his glory.[5] We regard this as a positive development but must ask: Do all the young people involved really understand the words they are saying? Or will "the glory of God" become a cliché, much like "the love of God" to the previous generation, for whom too often love was reduced to sentimentality?

We sincerely hope and pray that the current good trends will be fanned into flame and produce a mighty fire that will blaze for God's glory. And we offer this volume as fuel for the fire. To that end we ask: What does the Bible actually teach about the glory of God?

---

[2] Collin Hansen, *Young, Restless, Reformed: A Journalist's Journey with the New Calvinists* (Wheaton, IL: Crossway, 2008), 21.

[3] Ibid.

[4] Ibid.

[5] Including those of John Piper, Timothy Keller, Gospel Coalition, and Mark Dever.

Few figures in church history have grasped the biblical teaching on God's glory as well as Jonathan Edwards, the great eighteenth-century American theologian of the glory of God. Edwards's words summarize the burden of this book: "God is glorified not only by His glory's being seen, but by its being rejoiced in."[6] Edwards is right—God's glory is promoted both in our minds and in our affections. This book is structured accordingly. While the entire volume aims to meet these two purposes, chapters 1 through 6 are particularly designed to help us glorify God in our minds by focusing on biblical and theological truths related to his glory. Chapters 7 and 8 help us rejoice in our hearts as they illuminate how these truths about God's glory shape our view and approach to the church, pastoral ministry, and missions.

The Glory of God begins with Stephen Nichols, who highlights important contemporary thinkers who address God's glory and points to their historic roots. Then Tremper Longman examines this pervasive theme in the Old Testament, expounding its major terms, passages, and ideas. Three New Testament chapters follow. Richard Melick covers the main passages on glory in the Synoptic Gospels, Acts, and the General Epistles. Andreas Köstenberger studies John's Gospel and Revelation to uncover John's distinctive teachings related to glory. Richard Gaffin opens up Paul's theology of glory and shows how it is linked to key themes such as the gospel, the image of God, and Jesus' resurrection. Christopher Morgan synthesizes and builds on the truths of the previous chapters and presents an overall theology of the glory of God. Bryan Chapell calls pastors to view their role in light of God's glory, showing how they function as representatives of Christ himself, especially in his three offices. Nelson Jennings concludes with a missional theology of God's glory, stripping away some of our Western myths about glory and clarifying our role in God's glorious mission of cosmic restoration.

To edit a book on the glory of God is daunting. But we make this modest attempt to fill a real need. In a nutshell, *The Glory of God* examines this oft-discussed but rarely understood biblical theme and develops a theology of God's glory that is historic and contemporary, explores Old and New Testaments, treats biblical and systematic theology, and adopts pastoral and missional perspectives.

Soli Deo Gloria

Christopher W. Morgan and Robert A. Peterson

---

[6] Jonathan Edwards, "The Glory of God," in *Our Great and Glorious God*, ed. Don Kistler (Morgan, PA: Soli Deo Gloria, 2003), 86.

1

The Glory of God Present and Past

STEPHEN J. NICHOLS

S peaking about God can be daunting. The author of Ecclesiastes sternly warns that we are to keep our words few as we approach God in worship. "God is in heaven," the author declares, "and you are on earth" (Eccles. 5:2). Theologians also are earthbound, and should take care to guard their steps and watch their words. We speak of the transcendent God, a rather humbling truth.

In light of the grandeur and transcendence of God, twentieth-century German theologian Wolfhart Pannenberg offers some helpful perspective on the theological task. Pannenberg explains, "Any intelligent attempt to talk about God—talk that is critically aware of its conditions and limitations—must begin and end with confession of the inconceivable majesty of God which transcends all our concepts."[1] Pannenberg is speaking, in glowing terms to be sure, of the distance between us and God, a distance that should be remembered as we begin the work of theology. We need to remember that when we do talk about God, we are entering into the realm of mystery. And we must keep this mystery in view even as we begin the

---

[1] Wolfhart Pannenberg, *Systematic Theology*, vol. 1, trans. Geoffrey W. Bromiley (Grand Rapids, MI: Eerdmans, 1991), 337.

23

task of theology. Pannenberg notes, the task of theology "must begin with this because the lofty mystery we call God is always close to the speaker and to all creatures, and prior to all our concepts it encloses and sustains all being, so that it is always the supreme condition of all reflection upon it and of all the resultant conceptualization."[2]

Before we start thinking and speaking of God, he is the "supreme condition" that makes any such reflection even possible. God is not only everywhere present as we begin the task of theology, but he is also everywhere present during it. Further, he is also everywhere present at the end or the goal of theology. Consequently, Pannenberg points out that the task of theology "must also end with God's inconceivable majesty because every statement about God, if there is in it any awareness of what is being said, points beyond itself."[3] God is so much bigger than our speaking or thinking of him. God is, in other words, so much bigger than our theology. He is before it, around it, at the end of it, and over it. Speaking and thinking about God can be daunting indeed.

Yet, and Pannenberg concedes this point quickly, no matter how majestic or how transcendent God may be, "it does not follow that we do better to be silent about God than to speak about him."[4] Rather, it is far better to speak. In fact, we must speak, for, as Pannenberg has duly noted, God's majesty is at the beginning, at the end, and also ever-present in the middle of theological discourse. The majesty of God permeates all our talking about God, serves as the focal point of all our worship of God, and grounds all our service to God. Or, at least it should.

Pannenberg's words, however insightful, also point to the problem. Speaking of the majesty of God is no easy task. Nevertheless, it is the theologian's task. Over the centuries of the Christian tradition, many theologians have spoken of the glory of God. They tend not to spend their energy on this topic defining it. Biblical scholars, in fact, may be better suited for the task. Where theologians do spend their energy, at least some theologians that is, is in thinking about how the glory of God functions in one's theology, how the glory of God functions methodologically in theological construction and discourse. In short, theologians who have a sense of the gravitas of the glory of God, who spend time and energy reflecting on the glory of God before they embark on their theological task, are better theologians. It may also be true that pastors who have a sense of the gravitas of the glory of God and spend their time reflecting on the glory of God are

---

[2] Ibid.
[3] Ibid.
[4] Ibid.

better pastors. And it may be further true that Christians, the faithful in the pew, who have a sense of the gravitas of the glory of God and spend time reflecting on the glory of God are better Christians. The glory of God is the compass that keeps all our theologizing, pastoring, and Christian living oriented in the right direction—toward God and not toward ourselves. The pull in the opposite direction is so strong that the psalmist repeats: "Not to us, O LORD, not to us, but to your name give glory" (Ps. 115:1).

This essay offers a foray into the history of the theological discussion of the glory of God by exploring the function of the glory of God in three contemporary theologians: Charles C. Ryrie, Hans Urs von Balthasar, and the pastor-theologian John Piper. It is likely a safe assumption that these three figures have never before been compared. All three, however, represent the end result of a number of significant lines of influence stretching back through the past two millennia of theology. And all three have the glory of God close to the center if not at the center of their theology. Like sampling a lake to determine the nature of the headwaters and tributaries of a watershed, their respective work will reveal these respective influences. A brief introduction of each of these three is in order before their work is examined in greater detail.

Hans Urs von Balthasar died on June 26, 1988, two days before his taking the position of cardinal in the Roman Catholic Church. Trained as a Jesuit, he left to form a secular institute. Drawing on his training in philosophy, literature, theology, and biblical studies, Balthasar published widely, embarking on a monumental project that would synthesize theology around the beautiful, the good, and the true—a theology that would synthesize the three fields of philosophy, namely, aesthetics, ethics, and logic or epistemology. The first undertaking was his seven-volume theo-aesthetics, appearing in English as *The Glory of the Lord*. Next came theo-drama, consisting of five volumes on theo-dramatics, exploring the grand drama of redemption. This was followed by the three-volume work on theo-logic, setting forth the truth that God has revealed of himself. A final volume, which he entitled simply *Epilogue*, offers a closing word on the project. In addition to these sixteen volumes, dozens more came from Balthasar's pen, earning him the title of the second "necessary theologian" of the twentieth century, standing in line behind Karl Barth. Like the Swiss Reformed neo-orthodox theologian, Balthasar, the Swiss Roman Catholic theologian, belonged to the twentieth century and continues to cast his shadow over the twenty-first.[5]

---

[5] For an Internet archive of sources on Hans Urs von Balthasar, see http://www.ratzingerfanclub/balthasar.

Charles C. Ryrie comes from a rather different and distant place on the theological map than Balthasar. Among his many publications, the eponymous Ryrie Study Bible and his single-volume systematic theology, *Basic Theology*, stand out. Ryrie also wrote a slimmer, less well-known volume entitled *Transformed by His Glory*. Considered the leading theologian of dispensationalism, Ryrie offered what to many has been the definitive word on the subject in his *Dispensationalism Today* in 1965, released as an expanded and revised work in 1995 simply titled *Dispensationalism*. In that work, Ryrie identified the glory of God as one of a trio of tenets he labeled the *sine qua non* of dispensationalism. Ryrie teased this out by declaring that Scripture is "God-centered because His glory is the center."[6] Ryrie, earning doctorates at both Dallas Theological Seminary and Edinburgh University, studying with Thomas Torrance among others, spent the larger share of his career as a systematics professor at Dallas Theological Seminary. He is an avid rare book collector, with a few medieval New Testament manuscripts among his collection. It is also quite safe to say that from his seminary post Ryrie has likely trained as many pastors theologically as any other person in the latter half of the twentieth century.[7]

The second of this trio of theologians, John Piper, would likely prefer to be designated a pastor, or at least a pastor-theologian. Credited with playing a key role in the recent Reformed resurgence, Piper also has introduced whole swaths of contemporary audiences to the Puritans, more specifically to the New England Puritan Jonathan Edwards.[8] Like Piper, Edwards was a pastor first and is better designated as a theologian-pastor. Piper finds within Edwards the material for his singular emphasis, the God-centeredness of God, which Piper expressed as "the supremacy of God in all things for the joy of all peoples through Jesus Christ." Piper studied at Fuller Seminary, then took a DTheol from the University of Munich. Having taught for six years at Bethel College, Piper then became pastor at Bethlehem Baptist Church, a post he has held for some thirty years. Piper has made many significant contributions; likely chief among them is that by example he has shown that Calvinists can indeed be both passionate and missional. No one can deny Piper's widespread influence today.[9]

---

[6] Charles C. Ryrie, *Dispensationalism* (Chicago: Moody, 1995), 40.

[7] For a brief biography of Ryrie, see Paul P. Enns, "Charles C. Ryrie," *Handbook of Evangelical Theologians*, ed. Walter A. Elwell (Grand Rapids, MI: Baker, 1993), 366–78.

[8] Hansen, *Young, Restless, Reformed: A Journalist's Journey with the New Calvinists* (Wheaton, IL: Crossway, 2009).

[9] For more resources on John Piper, see http://www.desiringgod.org.

As mentioned, one might be hard-pressed to find what connects these three figures, Balthasar, Ryrie, and Piper. All three, however, view the glory of God as the central and ultimate destination of theologizing. What is quite intriguing about them, however, is that all three get there via different routes. One of the tasks of historical theology is to listen to echoes. These echoes reflect the original voice, the Logos, the one who is not merely in the image of God, as we are, but the one who *is* the image of God (2 Cor. 4:4), the one who is the "radiance of the glory of God" (Heb. 1:3). The Logos echoes, as it were, through history and on to the present day. Examining the work of Balthasar, Ryrie, and Piper becomes then an exercise, and, I would argue, a rather healthy one, in listening. Below follows an attempt to listen not so much to the voices of Balthasar, Piper, and Ryrie, but to the voices they have listened to, to uncover the sources that they have drawn upon.

Glory and Beauty, Part 1: Hans Urs von Balthasar and the Church Fathers

Balthasar set out to develop a Christian theology in light of the true, the good, and the beautiful. But he started with the beautiful, a deliberate move. In his reading on the history of ideas, he had found that theologians had given up on aesthetics, abandoning the subject to philosophers, which in turn resulted in beauty becoming a topic of idle speculation and pure abstraction, an "aesthetic monism."[10] Neoplatonism, incubating in the church during the patristic period, came of full age in the medieval era.[11] This triumph of Neoplatonism distorted both God and beauty. Or, one could say, this was a doubly damning move, condemning both philosophy and theology. The former, philosophy, subjugated to lifeless abstraction and ethereal speculation, while the latter became lifeless logical pronouncements in artless expression. To put the matter more practically, in a world without beauty, Balthasar declares, "What remains is then a mere lump of existence," or conversely, a mere lump of ideas.[12]

In terms of theology, Balthasar, not surprisingly, faults Martin Luther for eliminating aesthetics from theology. Luther so distrusted Neoplatonic

---

[10] Hans Urs von Balthasar, *Seeing the Form (The Glory of the Lord: A Theological Aesthetics)*, trans. Erasmo Leiva-Merikakis, ed. Joseph Fessio and John Riches, 3 vols. (San Francisco: Ignatius Press; New York: Crossroad Publications, 1983–1991), I, 104.

[11] *Neoplatonism* technically refers to a school of thought founded by Plotinus (AD 204/5–270) in the third century, based on the thought of Plato. Its major tenet is that the world is monistic, with a transcendent Supreme Being (Plato's ideal) at the top of a great chain of being that extends down to lesser and lesser forms. It has little, if any, place for material beings or for matter. Neoplatonism wielded strong influence through the medieval era.

[12] Ibid., 19.

aesthetic metaphysics that he steered the church and theology clear of aesthetics altogether, according to Balthasar's reading of Luther. Balthasar also faults Calvin for overemphasizing the "actualistic," that which is solely and entirely concrete, over and against "the contemplative and aesthetic." Rushing in to fill this aesthetic vacuum came the pietists, in the church and in theology, and the German idealists, in the academy and in philosophy. These two strains of pietism and idealism, in Balthasar's estimation, are simply too abstract. They altogether lack the concrete. These two extremes of the singularly concrete or singularly abstract simply feed each other, causing both to go further and further afield.[13]

It is in light of this reading of the history of ideas—and it is duly noted that one can and should debate his reading of the Reformers—that Balthasar proposes his project, which may be summed up as setting forth a *theological aesthetics*. This encompasses two primary elements: *a theory of vision* and *a theory of rapture*. A theory of vision relates to how we perceive God, governed entirely by God's self-revelation and summed up by the expression "the glory of God." A theory of rapture has to do with ontology, in terms of both the nature of the divine being and of human beings. In the incarnation, Christ as the God-man is the revelation of God's glory, which is to say the revelation of being itself. And, according to Balthasar, through faith in the God-man, humanity participates in, is brought into communion (in the fullest sense of that term) with, God. The ultimate being is God, which Balthasar sees as nearly everywhere represented in Scripture as the glory of God. The end of human beings, then, is to be taken up (the term *rapture*) in fellowship and communion. The ultimate end of human beings is to be taken up entirely in participation in God. In speaking of Balthasar's theological style, Angelo Scola notes, "Its point of reference, in the final analysis, is the *Gloria Dei*, which is the absolutely free and enchanting irradiation of the Lordship of God on being, on every being—a glory from which irradiates a beauty capable of enrapturing whoever perceives it." The theory of vision and the theory of rapture come together around the concept of the glory of God.[14]

In Balthasar's theory of rapture, of being caught up in the glory of God, one clearly hears the resounding echoes of the Eastern Orthodox notion of theosis or deification. This concept may be summed up in the often quoted words of Athanasius, "God became man so that man might become God."[15] It

---

[13] Ibid., 45–57.
[14] Angelo Scola, *Hans Urs von Balthasar: A Theological Style* (Grand Rapids, MI: Eerdmans, 1995), 1.
[15] Athanasius, *On the Incarnation*, 54:3 (Migne PG 25:192B).

also, at least in a bare sense, seems to derive from such biblical texts as 2 Peter 1:4, in which Peter writes of the result of salvation, "by which he has granted to us his precious and very great promises, so that through them you may become partakers of the divine nature." For Balthasar, taking his cue from and following this text, the theory of vision and the theory of rapture are inseparable. At the center of God's revelation is glory. Glory then becomes a sort of theological shorthand to encompass and communicate all that he is. Glory is also the end goal of human beings. In the words of John, "When [Christ] appears we shall be like him" (1 John 3:2). And in the words of Paul, "We all, with unveiled face, beholding the glory of the Lord, are being transformed into the same image from one degree of glory to another" (2 Cor. 3:18). Theosis, however, is not exclusively an Eastern Orthodox notion. It is clearly evident in the teachings of Aquinas, in various Puritan writings, and, as will be seen, in the thought of Jonathan Edwards. Henry Scougal's classic work on the Christian life reveals the presence of the theosis doctrine in Puritan literature. Scougal's *The Life of God in the Soul of Man* wielded significant influence over British Puritans, as testified in its hold on John Bunyan. It was one of two books that comprised the entire dowry of his first wife. In this influential book, Scougal writes of "the image of the Almighty shining in the soul of man," which he further explains as a "real participation of his nature." Scougal adds, "It is a beam of the eternal light, a drop of that infinite ocean of goodness; and they who are endued with it, may be said to have 'God dwelling in their souls', and 'Christ formed within them.'"[16]

These Puritan sources, however, quite escaped Balthasar's notice. Instead, he looked to patristic sources. In short, what these patristic sources contribute to the church's understanding of the glory of God is absolutely crucial to any theology of the Godhead. They take the biblical phrase the "glory of God" to mean God in his being, as distinct from and superior to his creation. It is essential to any fundamental understanding of ontology. Once God is understood, then and only then human beings and all other kinds of being can be properly understood. But more, the early church fathers also infused their understanding of the glory of God with what they had learned from centuries of Greek philosophy, especially from Plato, namely, that understanding the biblical phrase "the glory of God" is enhanced by the philosophical discussions of excellence, of beauty. The key is not to be controlled by the Platonic discussions, which is exactly what happened in the case of Neoplatonism. This intersection of the theological and the

---

[16] Henry Scougal, *The Life of God in the Soul of Man: With the Methods of Attaining the Happiness Which It Proposes, Also an Account of the Beginnings and Advances of a Spiritual Life* (New York: Cosimo Classics, 2007), 13.

philosophical is what so intrigued Balthasar. It is precisely why he titled his theological aesthetics, which is another way of saying a theology of beauty, *The Glory of the Lord*. In other words, glory is beauty. Glory is that which is excellent, that which is extraordinary, that which is transcendent. And, Balthasar quickly points out, it is known only by revelation, which is to say it is known ultimately in Christ.

To simply speak of beauty and excellence and transcendence is not theology. That is, in Balthasar's estimation, the worst kind of philosophy, the kind that drifts off into pure romantic, idealistic, and ultimately anthropocentric abstractions. A theology that does not, however, make room for beauty, for the sheer transcendental luminosity of glory, also has its problems. And, in addition in Balthasar's estimation, it is of little appeal. The temptation for the early church fathers seemed to be strongest in the direction of philosophical speculation, given Plato's long shadow over Rome during the early centuries of the church's life. As Robert Grant observed in his article on God in the early church, "Patristic and medieval theologians often drew away from 'biblical realism' in favor of rational constructions."[17] Not all of them, however, succumbed to this temptation.

Many of the church fathers are well worth exploring on the theme of the glory of God. Ambrose of Milan once rather handily summarized the glory of the Godhead as being known by four marks. He declares: "God is known by these marks: either that he is without sin; or that he forgives sin; or that he is not a creature but the Creator; or that he does not give but receives worship."[18] While each one of these underscores the supremacy and uniqueness of God, they have a compounding effect. God's glory, according to Ambrose, is seen in what he is and what he does that is both unique and ultimate. It is of further interest that Ambrose concludes with worship, the response to God's glory. Glory is somewhat akin to fame, which is to say it is worthy and demanding of praise. God's glory calls forth, borrowing a line from a hymn writer, "songs of loudest praise." Ambrose himself wrote hymns of worship. Like the other church fathers, he uses the metaphor of light to express the glory of God, which is to say God himself. In one of these hymns, he speaks to God directly, "Light that you are, illumine our senses." In another he speaks of the creation as light, reflecting the Creator:

---

[17] Robert M. Grant, "God," *EEC* 1:475.

[18] Ambrose of Milan, *On the Holy Spirit*, in *A Select Library of Nicene and Post-Nicene Fathers of the Christian Church*, 2nd series, ed. Philip Schaff and Henry Wace (Grand Rapids, MI: Eerdmans, 1952–63), 10:154.

"God, Creator of all things and ruler of the heavens, fitting the day with beauteous light."[19]

The church fathers not only spoke of the glory of God to stress God's supremacy that results in his worship as the only adequate response, but they also consistently spoke of God's glory in the context of the Trinity. Discussions of the Trinity can be easily drawn away from "biblical realism" and toward "rational constructions," using Robert Grant's language. Ironically, though, it was precisely the Trinitarian formulas that kept the church fathers, at least those on the side of orthodoxy, tethered to biblical realism. These Trinitarian formulas, insisting as they did on the doctrine of the incarnation, kept the early church from running headlong in gnostic, Neoplatonic theologizing. Speaking of God's glory in the context of the Trinity kept them from having a God of abstraction, the God of the apophatic trajectory.

Apophatic theology, sometimes called "negative theology," derives from the Greek word *apophasis*, which means "denial." It refers to a method of arguing that argues for something by saying only what that thing is not, by offering a series of denials. Related to theology this means that we can say about God only that which we cannot say about God; we can say only what he is not. The idea here is that he is beyond his creation—so beyond, that is, that nothing positive or meaningful can be said of him. In short, this is the so-called god of Greek philosophy, the god of Plato, the god of Aristotle. To be sure, there is clearly a sense in which God is beyond his creation. Theologians speak of the hidden God (*Deus Absconditus*), or the incomprehensibility of God, to rightly express this truth of the nature of God. But God is not solely hidden. He has revealed himself. He is the *Deus Revelatus*, the revealed God. God has revealed himself in nature, in the various forms of special revelation, especially in the canon of Scripture. But God has revealed himself most clearly and distinctly in Christ, the One who is the radiance of God's glory (Heb. 1:1-4).[20]

When the church fathers spoke of the glory of God in the context of the Trinity, they were not only defending the Bible against the claims of the Arians or any other heretical group bent on defaming and distorting Christ. When the church fathers spoke of the glory of the Trinitarian God, they

---

[19] Ambrose, "Aeterne Rerum Conditor" and "Deus Creator Omnium," cited in Boniface Ramsey, O.P., *Ambrose* (London: Routledge, 1997), 167, 170.

[20] For a scholarly discussion of the apophatic tradition, see Deirdre Carabibe, *The Unknown God: Negative Theology in the Platonic Tradition: Plato to Eriugena* (Louvain: Peeters Press, 1995). Wolfhart Pannenberg is quite helpful on this discussion, not only in terms of the patristic period, but also in terms of twentieth-century developments in theology. See Iain Taylor, *Pannenberg on the Triune God* (London: Continuum/T & T Clark, 2007).

were saving themselves, saving theology, and ultimately saving the church from drifting off to a god of abstraction. This whole issue can be put rather directly. Would you rather pray to the God who not only hears our prayers but also entered into our world and took on flesh? Or would you prefer praying to Plato's Ideal or to Aristotle's Unmoved Mover?

One place where these questions have recently played out is in the openness of God debate. The two sides of this debate have been termed the openness view on the one side and the classical or traditional view on the other side. Those holding to the openness view have charged the classical side with overemphasizing the transcendence of God to the neglect of the immanence of God. God's transcendence refers to how God stands above and beyond his creation and created beings. God's immanence refers to God's intimate involvement with his creation and created beings. The openness side would actually prefer to speak of this involvement as God's partnership with created beings. Clark Pinnock, the leading proponent of open theism, titled one of his books *The Most Moved Mover* in a direct and purposeful move to make this claim.[21] One of the many respondents to the open theists, Bruce Ware, has artfully and persuasively expressed how one must hold to both the incompre- hensibility and comprehensibility of God, or to both the transcendence (that God is above and beyond his creation and created beings) and the immanence of God. His book titles on the subject are also worthy of note, both containing the word *glory*. In effect, Ware's work shows how the open theist position is guilty of relaxing the tension in the direction of immanence. An implication here is that the openness side of this debate misread the way that the position of classical or traditional the- ism maintained the tension.[22]

Returning to the church fathers, Gregory of Nyssa, one of the famed three Cappadocian fathers, is quite helpful in lodging the glory of God in the context of the Trinity. In his short piece "On the Faith," he points out that Hebrews 1:3 refers to Christ as "the brightness of glory" (KJV). Then Gregory explains why:

> That we may learn that as the light from the lamp is of the nature of that which sheds brightness. And is united with it (for as soon as the lamp appears the light that comes from it shines out simultaneously), so in this place the

[21] Clark Pinnock, *Most Moved Mover: A Theology of Openness* (Grand Rapids, MI: Baker, 2001).
[22] Bruce A. Ware, *God's Lesser Glory: The Diminished God of Open Theism* (Wheaton, IL: Crossway, 2000) and *God's Greater Glory: The Exalted God of Scripture and the Christian Faith* (Wheaton, IL: Crossway, 2004).

Apostle would have us consider both that the Son is of the Father, and that the Father is never without the Son; for it is impossible that glory should be without radiance, as it is impossible that the lamp should be without brightness.[23]

Gregory of Nyssa posits that the glory of God is known in the radiance of Christ, arguing that you cannot have one without the other. He further argues, "It is clear then that however great the Person of the Father is, so great also is the express image of that Person."[24] In his argument he is explicitly drawing from and quoting from John 1. It is Christ who reveals the Father, and that revelation, as summed up by John, is glory (John 1:14).

And then there is Augustine. Worthy of an essay all to himself, Augustine has much to contribute to this historical discussion of the glory of God. One particular citation, however, will have to suffice. In his monumental work *The City of God*, Augustine compares the city of God with the city of humanity, boiling down the difference between the two to who gets the glory. He is worth hearing at length:

Accordingly, two cities have been formed by two loves: the earthly by the love of self, even to the contempt of God; the heavenly by the love of God, even to the contempt of self. The former, in a word, glories in itself, the latter in the Lord. For the one seeks glory from men; but the greatest glory of the other is God, the witness of conscience. The one lifts up its head in its own glory; the other says to its God, "Thou art my glory, and the lifter up of mine head." In the one, the princes and the nations it subdues are ruled by the love of ruling; in the other, the princes and the subjects serve one another in love, the latter obeying, while the former take thought for all. The one delights in its own strength, represented in the persons of its rulers; the other says to its God, "I will love Thee, O Lord, my strength." And therefore the wise men of the one city, living according to man, have sought for profit to their own bodies or souls, or both, and those who have known God "glorified Him not as God, neither were thankful, but became vain in their imaginations, and their foolish heart was darkened; professing themselves to be wise"—that is, glorying in their own wisdom, and being possessed by pride—"they became fools, and changed the glory of the incorruptible God into an image made like to corruptible man, and to birds, and four-footed beasts, and creeping things." For they were either leaders or followers of the people in adoring images, "and worshipped and served the creature more than the Creator,

---

[23] Gregory of Nyssa, *On the Faith*, in *A Select Library of Nicene and Post-Nicene Fathers*, 2nd series, 5:338. He, following the typical view of most of the church fathers, attributes the writing of Hebrews to Paul.
[24] Ibid., 338.

who is blessed for ever." But in the other city there is no human wisdom, but only godliness, which offers due worship to the true God, and looks for its reward in the society of the saints, of holy angels as well as holy men, "that God may be all in all."[25]

Notice that, according to Augustine, everything flows from the question of glory. Once the question of glory is settled, where glory belongs and will reside, everything else flows from it. The purpose of life and the way one lives, which Augustine declares to be by love, all stem from glory. Notice, too, that glory must be positioned somewhere, either in the creation or in the Creator.

Balthasar offers a significant way of reading the Bible by seeing the Bible as first and foremost the revelation of the glory of God.[26] I would argue that Balthasar reads the Bible this way because he was so steeped in the church fathers. In them he found the same insistence as that of his own work, namely, the insistence on the centrality of the glory of God. The early church used the term *theologian* very carefully and very particularly to refer to those who speak for God, which is the literal translation of the word (*theos*, meaning God, and *logos*, meaning word). In fact, Moses was declared a theologian by the church fathers. And for them he was the model theologian. He stood as a salient reminder that anyone who wishes to be a theologian, who wishes to speak of and for God, must realize, like Moses, that he is standing on sacred soil and, again like Moses, must realize that he is coming into contact with the blinding and "irradiating" (to use Balthasar's term) glory of God. But the church fathers had a great advantage over Moses, for they had the clearest and fullest expression of the glory of God to draw upon for their work. As John puts it, "And the Word became flesh and dwelt among us, and we have seen his glory, glory as of the only Son from the Father, full of grace and truth" (John 1:14). This frames the christological controversy of the early church in a whole new light. Contesting for Christ's divinity was not a luxury. In short, the entire theological enterprise depended on it.

While Balthasar offers a substantial and worthy reading of Scripture and of the church fathers, I would contend that his reading of the Reformers and the post-Reformation Reformed trajectory is wide of the mark. He too quickly dismissed Luther and Calvin, while missing one theologian

---

[25] Augustine, *City of God*, bk. 14, chap. 28.
[26] See also the recent work of David Bentley Hart, *The Beauty of the Infinite: The Aesthetics of Christian Truth* (Grand Rapids, MI: Eerdmans, 2003). Though not as extensive as the work of Balthasar, Hart may very well offer the contemporary Eastern Orthodox counterpart to Balthasar.

altogether, Jonathan Edwards. It is not much of a surprise that Balthasar, a Roman Catholic theologian, overlooked Edwards. Jonathan Edwards did, after all, once refer to the pope as the antichrist. The next figure in our trio, however, fills that lacuna rather generously.

Glory and Beauty, Part 2: John Piper and the Contribution of Jonathan Edwards

For centuries, Jonathan Edwards's reputation languished, as did his work. To be sure, during the first decades after his death, Edwards continued to dominate New England theology. Even Charles Finney sought to be regarded as Edwards's true heir. Then Edwards fell out of favor among the Princetonians, in the academy, and in the public eye. He was reduced to playing the role of the caricature of all that was conceived to be evil in Puritanism. The lion's share of those who knew of him only knew of him as the mean-spirited preacher of hellfire and damnation, spouting forth "Sinners in the Hands of an Angry God." Then Perry Miller revived interest in him, correcting the caricature of Edwards and the New England Puritans in the academy. John Piper largely corrected the image of him in the church. Others, to be sure, played a role, but nobody's efforts served to resuscitate Jonathan Edwards in the church to the degree that Piper's efforts have done and continue to do. Piper found in Edwards not the foreboding and cajoling figure that many think of. Instead, Piper's Edwards is a purveyor of joy and delight. God is a wrathful God, an avenging God, to be sure. But he is also simultaneously and without contradiction the God of beauty who delights in himself and in his creation.

Piper's debt to Edwards may be seen in any number of his books. The central thesis to *Desiring God*, which serves for many as their introduction to Piper, derives from the thought of Jonathan Edwards.[27] In *The Pleasures of God*, Piper cites Edwards in every chapter.[28] Piper bookends his particular discussion of the pleasure God takes in his fame with writings of Edwards's protégé, the missionary David Brainerd, writings we have only because of the efforts of Jonathan Edwards in publishing them.[29] Additionally, one of Piper's works where the influence of Edwards can be seen quite clearly is his commentary on and reprinting of Edwards's text *Concerning the End for Which God Created the World*, published as *God's Passion for His Glory:*

---

[27] John Piper, *Desiring God: Meditations of a Christian Hedonist*, rev. and exp. ed. (Sisters, OR: Multnomah, 2003).

[28] John Piper, *The Pleasures of God: Meditations on God's Delight in Being God* (Sisters, OR: Multnomah, 1991).

[29] Ibid., 101–21.

Living the Vision of Jonathan Edwards.[30] Piper finds in "Edwards's relent-less God-centeredness" a great deal of both correction and hope for the misguided church of today, overly influenced by pragmatic concerns and numerical measures of success.[31] Edwards's God-centered vision serves as a necessary corrective to an overly human-centered vision.

Piper begins his commendation of Edwards by introducing readers to two lengthy quotes. The first of these reveals how Edwards takes the two propositions from the first question and answer from the Westminster Catechism to be in a symbiotic relationship:

Question: What is the chief end of man?
Answer: Man's chief end is to glorify God, and to enjoy him forever.

Here is how Edwards connects these two ideas of glorifying God and enjoy-ing him:

God in seeking his glory seeks the good of his creatures, because the emana-tion of his glory . . . implies the . . . happiness of his creatures. And in com-municating his fullness for them, he does it for himself, because their good, which he seeks, is so much in union and communion with himself. God is their good. Their excellency and happiness is nothing but the emanation and expression of God's glory. God, in seeking their glory and happiness, seeks himself, and in seeking himself, *i.e.* himself diffused . . . he seeks their glory and happiness.[32]

The next citation from Edwards that Piper uses to whet the appetites of his readers is equally instructive. Again Edwards:

Thus it is easy to conceive how God should seek the good of the creature . . . even his happiness, from a supreme regard to *himself*; as his happiness arises from . . . the creature's exercising a supreme regard to God . . . in beholding God's glory, in esteeming and loving it, and rejoicing in it. God's respect to the creature's good, and his respect to himself, is not a divided respect; but both are united in one, as the happiness of the creature aimed at is happiness in union with himself.[33]

---

[30] John Piper, *God's Passion for His Glory: Living the Vision of Jonathan Edwards, with the Complete Text of* The End for Which God Created the World (Wheaton, IL: Crossway, 1998).
[31] Ibid., *xiii*.
[32] Edwards, *Concerning the End for Which God Created the World*, as cited in Piper, *God's Passion for His Glory*, 33.
[33] Ibid.

Piper takes these opening quotes to get to the heart of what Edwards intended in his text. Piper then offers fifteen implications of this, all stemming from the idea that "the exhibition of God's glory and the deepest joy of human souls are one thing."[34] These fifteen implications concern first how we think about God and what his purposes are for the world and for us. Piper then addresses such wide-ranging issues as virtue and ethics, sin, evangelism, worship, missions, preaching, prayer, scholarship, death, and even heaven and eternal life.[35] In these fifteen implications, Piper stresses, in a way quite similar to Augustine's tack in *The City of God*, that everything in life, and even as here in death, stems from the glory of God. What Piper emphasizes, taking his cue from Edwards, is again the symbiotic relationship between God's glory and humanity's joy, happiness, and fulfillment. God-centeredness is, paradoxically, the only means to human fulfillment and human flourishing.

Following Piper's commendation, we now turn to further explorations of Edwards's text in the context of his thought and writings. Recent Edwards scholarship has drawn attention to the Trinitarian vision and theology of Edwards. Notable among this work is that of Amy Plantinga Pauw. She speaks of Edwards's Trinitarianism running "like a subterranean river throughout his career as a pastor and polemicist."[36] She adds, "I argue that Edwards's Trinitarianism provides an unusually wide view of his deepest philosophical, theological, and pastoral inclinations."[37] In other words, Edwards's Trinitarianism is key to his entire work. Pauw points out that it is not just that Edwards is Trinitarian; that much is or at least should be true of all Christian theologizing. It is also the way in which Edwards is Trinitarian that matters. Edwards's particular Trinitarianism, which draws heavily upon Augustine, sets Edwards's theology off in a remarkable way, especially Edwards's theology of the glory of God.

Pauw and other Edwards scholars such as Stephen Holmes, Robert Caldwell, and William Danaher have all engaged the question concerning the type of Trinitarian model Edwards espouses. Holmes takes Edwards to be "a child of Augustine," a line which Caldwell follows.[38] Danaher offers a

---

[34] Ibid.

[35] Ibid., 33–47.

[36] Amy Plantinga Pauw, *The Supreme Harmony of All: The Trinitarian Theology of Jonathan Edwards* (Grand Rapids, MI: Eerdmans, 2002), 3.

[37] Ibid.

[38] Stephen R. Holmes, *God of Grace and God of Glory: An Account of the Theology of Jonathan Edwards* (Grand Rapids, MI: Eerdmans, 2000), 69. See also Robert W. Caldwell III, *Communion in the Spirit: The Holy Spirit as the Bond of Union in the Theology of Jonathan Edwards* (Carlisle: Paternoster, 2006), 19–40.

slight corrective by claiming that while Edwards does indeed follow Augustine, Edwards also adds his own unique twist as he develops his thought. Pauw actually concludes that Edwards moves back and forth between a psychological model of the Trinity, as has been credited to Augustine, and a social model of the Trinity, as has been credited to Eastern church fathers.[39] It does seem that Edwards's Trinitarianism does reflect a wide array of sources and contours. Maybe the matter will never be fully settled. What does seem to be the case, though, is that when Edwards speaks of the glory of God, he is speaking of the glory of the Godhead, which is to say, he is everywhere and always speaking of the glory of the Trinitarian God. On this point, Edwards scholars would all agree. Regardless of how you parse his Trinitarian model, Trinitarianism both centers and permeates his thought.

It seems that Edwards does have a healthy dose of the social trinity model in his thought. Edwards begins his "Discourse on the Trinity" by pointing out that "when we speak of God's happiness, the account that we are wont to give of it is that God is infinitely happy in the enjoyment of himself, in perfectly beholding and infinitely loving, and rejoicing in, his own essence and perfections."[40] In *Concerning the End for Which God Created the World*, Edwards uses the glory of God interchangeably with the phrase "God's essence and perfections." God is ultimately obsessed with God. Edwards takes his cue from here. Edwards sees God as beauty and excellency. He further, borrowing an idea from Plato, sees harmony or symmetry as essential to the definition and nature of beauty. Applied to his Trinitarianism, Edwards sees Christ as the express mirror image of the Father. Christ is "the eternal, necessary, perfect, substantial and personal idea which God hath of himself." Edwards adds, "This seems also well to agree with Christ being called the brightness, effulgence or shining forth of God's glory."[41] Later in the essay, Edwards speaks of the Holy Spirit as the bond of union, a bond of love, within the Godhead.[42]

From this vantage point of Trinitarianism, Edwards raises the question of the purpose and meaning of humanity. God is complete in himself. Theologians use the term *aseity* to represent this idea. Aseity literally means "from

---

[39] William J. Danaher Jr., *The Trinitarian Ethics of Jonathan Edwards* (Louisville, KY: Westminster Press, 2004), 17.

[40] Jonathan Edwards, "Discourse on the Trinity," *The Works of Jonathan Edwards*, vol. 21: *Writings on the Trinity, Grace, and Faith*, ed. Sang Hyun Lee (New Haven: Yale University Press, 2003), 113.

[41] Ibid., 117, 119.

[42] For a further discussion of the Holy Spirit in Edwards's Trinitarianism, see Stephen J. Nichols, *An Absolute Sort of Certainty: The Holy Spirit and the Apologetics of Jonathan Edwards* (Phillipsburg, NJ: P&R, 2003), 24–27.

itself" (*a* meaning "from" and *se* meaning "self" in Latin). God is underived, not contingent for any other being or thing for his existence. Another way of saying this is that God does not need us. To suggest that he does is to say that God is incomplete in himself. Edwards steps in here to say that while God does not need us, he wants us, and that is far, far better. Ultimately God creates us to bring us into this circle of divine enjoyment and glorification. Adam and Eve were created to be God's image and were created for fellowship with him in love and harmony. But sin marred that image and fractured the harmonious relationship. Humanity, bent on self-fulfillment and self-glorification, continued in a downward spiral away from God and away, ultimately, from being fully and truly human. Consequently, Edwards writes *Concerning the End for Which God Created the World* with all the intention of a prophet, of one who points to a different way.

Edwards's *Concerning the End for Which God Created the World* was part of a two-part work, which Edwards entitled *The Two Dissertations*. *The End* took the position of the first dissertation, while the second belonged to his treatise *The Nature of True Virtue*. It was completed before Edwards's death in 1758 and published immediately thereafter. It is significant that Edwards pairs these two treatises. The second dissertation, as the title suggests, treats Edwards's ethics. The first dissertation treats the basis for his ethics. In other words, it is from the perspective of the glory of God that Edwards puts forth an ethic. That alone is instructive. It is even more instructive to take a closer, albeit brief look at the first dissertation. Edwards begins by discussing the different types of ends one may encounter. There are subordinate ends and then there are ultimate ends or, borrowing a word from the Westminster Catechism, *chief* ends. What concerns Edwards in this treatise is the latter, chief ends, which he actually then pinpoints to the chief end in the singular. The chief end is that which God aims all of his activity toward, his activities of creation and redemption—in short, everything God does.[43] Edwards then turns his attention at uncovering the chief end of God.

That chief end in the simplest and most direct terms is God himself. Edwards expands this by declaring it to be the glory of God: "All that is ever spoken of in the Scripture as an ultimate of God's works is included in that one phrase, 'the glory of God.'"[44] God created the world so that his name may be known, so that his purposes may be accomplished, and so that he

---

[43] Jonathan Edwards, "Concerning the End for Which God Created the World," in *Ethical Writings* The Works of Jonathan Edwards, vol. 8, ed. Paul Ramsey (New Haven: Yale University Press, 1989), 405–15.

[44] Ibid., 526.

may communicate himself to his creatures. These and others are ultimate or chief ends, but Edwards comes back to the glory of God as taking top rank among them.[45] Edwards then ends his first dissertation by attempting to define this term *glory of God*. He notes that the Hebrew noun *kavod* (sometimes *kabod*) "signifies gravity, heaviness, greatness, and abundance."[46] Edwards further looks to the biblical teaching to show that the glory of God speaks both to his internal glory, signifying what is inherent within God and to the external expression or communication of the internal glory.[47] Paul Ramsey contends that for Edwards, "'glory' came to be the one term for all" the biblical references to God's works.[48] There is more. Drawing upon his Trinitarianism, Edwards points out that the term *glory* is particularly applied to Christ, the chief exhibition of God's glory.[49]

Edwards finishes his treatise by speaking of the glory of God as both emanation and remanation (return). He explains, "The refulgence shines upon and into the creature, and is reflected back to the luminary. The beams of glory come from God, and are something of God, and are refunded back again to their original. So that the whole is *of* God, and *in* God, and *to* God; and God is the beginning, middle, and end in this affair."[50] This is Edwards's way of expressing what Balthasar speaks of as the theory of rapture. And, as Balthasar so well put it, those remanating the glory of God shine as the light of hope in a dark world. John Piper is correct, in other words, to draw out evangelism, missions, worship, and preaching as implications of Edwards's vision of the glory of God.

Edwards also links the glory of God to human fulfillment, joy, and happiness. Happiness is not only a modern infatuation. The topic of what constitutes happiness has a long and rich history. The Greeks spoke of *eudaimonia*, or living happily, and contended fiercely over what qualifies as such. While the term *eudaimonia* is not batted about much these days, certainly there is much discussion over what constitutes the good life. William Ames, a British Puritan theologian, argued that the good life (*euzoia*) is only found in the Godward life (*Theozoia*). We find our fulfillment not in pursuing our own ends but in living toward God.[51] Edwards could not agree more. God, Edwards reminds us, is our good. Humanity's "excellency and

---

[45] Ibid., 475–92.
[46] Ibid., 512.
[47] Ibid., 515.
[48] Ibid., 516, n. 2.
[49] Ibid., 519–25.
[50] Ibid., 531.
[51] William Ames, *The Marrow of Divinity* (Grand Rapids, MI: Baker, 1968), 78.

happiness is nothing but the emanation and expression of God's glory."[52] The pursuit of happiness, which some other American colonials codified as an inalienable right, is doomed from the outset if not oriented and aimed at, as well as driven by, the glory of God.

One other aspect of Edwards's thought should be mentioned. Reflecting the position of the Reformed tradition, Edwards gives plenty of space to the glory of God as revealed in creation and in what theologians term *common grace*. Susan Schreiner has well articulated this emphasis in John Calvin in *The Theater of His Glory: Nature and the Natural Order in the Thought of John Calvin*.[53] Richard Mouw has also recently pointed to the value of what he terms "commonness," calling for an updating of a theology of common grace that draws upon the riches of the past tradition that has had quite a bit to say of the natural order and common grace. Christ shines brightest, to be sure, but Mouw, taking a line from a hymn, also reminds us that God "shines in all that's fair."[54] If Edwards could see the glory of God in spiders, then maybe there is something to what Mouw commends.[55]

Piper has recently added a word of caution to his emphasis on God-centeredness. To counter a potential misstep, Piper speaks of "God's God-centeredness." Here is what he says in full: "I believe that if we are God-centered simply because we consciously or unconsciously believe God is man-centered, then our God-centeredness is in reality man-centeredness. Teaching God's God-centeredness forces the issue of whether we treasure God because of his excellence or mainly because he endorses ours."[56] It could be easy to be driven by God-centered means to accomplish human-centered ends. Piper, drawing heavily as he does on Edwards, reminds us that God-centered means lead to God-centered ends.

Glory and Transformation: Charles C. Ryrie and the Echo of Scripture
The last of the trio to consider is Charles C. Ryrie. Ryrie gives a prominent place to the glory of God in his theology by setting it among what he identifies as the *sine qua non* of dispensationalism. Ryrie lists three distinguishing criteria as the *sine qua non* of dispensationalism. The first is the consistent

---

[52] Edwards, *Concerning the End for Which God Created the World*, 459.
[53] Susan E. Schreiner, *The Theater of His Glory: Nature and the Natural Order in the Thought of John Calvin* (Grand Rapids, MI: Baker, 1991).
[54] Richard J. Mouw, *He Shines in All That's Fair: Culture and Common Grace* (Grand Rapids, MI: Eerdmans, 2001).
[55] Jonathan Edwards, "The Spider Letter," *Scientific and Philosophical Writings*, The Works of Jonathan Edwards, vol. 6, ed. Wallace E. Anderson (New Haven: Yale University Press, 1980), 163–69.
[56] John Piper, "Why God Is Not a Megalomaniac in Demanding to Be Worshipped," a paper presented to the Evangelical Theological Society National Meeting, Providence, RI, November 20, 2008.

distinction between Israel and the church. The second concerns a literal hermeneutic, especially of prophetic or apocalyptic texts. The third concerns the glory of God as the underlying purpose of God in the world. Ryrie posits this in light of what he takes to be a more human-centered approach in covenant theology to the underlying purpose of God's creating the world. Ryrie writes, "The covenant theologian, in practice, believes this purpose to be salvation (although covenant theologians strongly emphasize the glory of God in their theology), and the dispensationalist says the purpose is broader than that; namely, the glory of God."[57] Later, Ryrie adds, "The glory of God is the governing principle and overall purpose," of which God's soteriological purpose plays a subordinate role.[58] Ryrie cites fellow dispensationalist John Walvoord as offering a similar take. Walvoord declares, "All the events of the created world are designed to manifest the glory of God."[59]

Whether this is a fair reading of nondispensational theology is beyond the intention of this present essay. It has been debated and will continue to be debated. What is telling and what is of interest to this essay, however, is the insistence of Ryrie on the centrality of God's glory. Further, Ryrie insists on the centrality of God's glory for the exact same reasons that Piper and Edwards, both of whom are not dispensationalists, insist upon it. Ryrie's concern is to avoid a human-centered view, proclaiming a God-centered view instead. Sounding remarkably like Edwards, Ryrie concedes that there are many ways God manifests his glory, the plan of redemption chief among them, but that these manifestations are all subordinate to the central and chief purpose of God's glory itself. Even Scripture, Ryrie points out, "is not man-centered as though salvation were the main theme, but it is God-centered because His glory is at the center."[60] Ryrie makes a significant point in reminding us that Scripture is ultimately God-centered.

Ryrie further writes of the glory of God in *Transformed by His Glory*. Here he focuses on what may be learned from a close reading of Scripture on the glory of God, which he defines as "the character of God displayed."[61] In this approach, Ryrie reminds theologians of the necessity of grounding their work in Scripture. Ryrie presents the biblical teaching on the glory of God in all of its complexity. He notes that God is glorified both in judging and in blessing, something that is difficult at times to admit.[62] He also

---

[57] Ryrie, *Dispensationalism*, 40.

[58] Ibid., 93.

[59] Cited in ibid., 93; original may be found in John F. Walvoord, *The Millennial Kingdom* (Findley, OH: Dunham, 1959), 92.

[60] Ibid., 40.

[61] Charles C. Ryrie, *Transformed by His Glory* (Wheaton, IL: Victor Books, 1990), 45, cf. 17–19.

[62] Ibid., 45–53.

explains how God's revelation of himself in nature is a testimony to his glory.[63] Ryrie further reflects on how the glory of God is manifest in the life of Christ, pointing out that the incarnate Christ, who was the glory of God, also glorified God in various ways while on earth. Next he turns to the way the church and Christians glorify God in their obedience to Christ.

Along the way, Ryrie demystifies what can be sometimes a rather clouded topic for the person in the pew. The glory of God can stump even the brightest of thinkers. It is difficult in some ways to wrap one's mind around it. Ryrie's book reminds theologians that while they go about thinking through all of the various contours of the glory of God, there is an equal importance on remembering the various texts that call on the church to manifest the glory of God in their lives. He ends his book with a rather intriguing text, 1 Corinthians 10:31, Paul's answer to the communion controversy at Corinth.[64] The abuses of the Lord's Table at Corinth were bringing about the exact opposite of the intention of the Lord's Table. It was not bringing the Corinthian believers in closer communion with the triune God, but driving a wedge between them and God. In light of this, Paul issues a command. Mandating that whether the Corinthians eat or drink, which likely has specific reference to partaking of the elements of the Lord's Supper, they are to do so to the glory of God. But Paul inserts a curious phrase. The full text reads, "So, whether you eat or drink, *or whatever you do*, do all to the glory of God." Everything we do should be done for the glory of God. Ryrie ultimately reminds us that this discussion of the glory of God is to have a transformative effect. The glory of God should transform us.

Conclusion

The argument was made at the beginning of this essay that those theologians who give due place to the glory of God in their theological methodology are better theologians for doing so. No scientific metrics likely exist to measure this claim, but one can look at the content and implications of a given theologian's work to get some sense of both the validity of this claim and the importance of it for the life and health of the church. The glory of God directly impacts Trinitarian, christological, anthropological, soteriological, and even eschatological categories. To put the matter bluntly, the extent to which one makes room for the glory of God directly impacts thinking about God, the self, the world, and salvation. Ultimately, the glory of God impacts the way one answers the ultimate question of meaning

---

[63] Ibid., 57–63.
[64] Ibid., 129–35.

and purpose. Augustine well reminded us that everything stems from the question of where glory belongs and resides. Something other than a fully God-centered view of all things leaves too little room for God.

Hans Urs von Balthasar has shown as much in his massive project of laying out a "theology of the glory of the Living God." Aesthetics, ethics, logic, all of the categories philosophers work with, find their center in the glory of God. Balthasar was not ultimately concerned, however, about merely reading philosophy from the position of God's glory. He was focused on reading Scripture, church history, and theology from it. Balthasar also shows how the "*Theologia Gloriae*" is the church's proper and only response to the Glorious Word. The church then, having been drawn to the Glorious Word, reflects Christ in the world. Balthasar put it so well: "What she reflects back in the night is the hope of the world." Ambrose, Gregory of Nyssa, Augustine, not to mention many other church fathers worthy of inclusion, all in various ways revealed the importance of the glory of God for the enterprise of theology.

John Piper has also labored to set forth the God-centeredness of all things. In the process, he has drawn upon sources that escaped Balthasar's attention. Chief among these sources stands Jonathan Edwards. Recent Edwards scholarship has shown how Edwards draws from the same wells as Balthasar, not only from Augustine, but from a wide range of church fathers. Edwards's long-distance influences are, in my opinion, equally matched in those closer to him, the Reformed and Puritan constellations, leading stars of which include John Calvin and John Owen. All of these voices unite in the sermons and writings of Jonathan Edwards, as he proclaims the central song of God's glory.

God's glory points to his transcendence, his extraordinary nature, his beauty, his excellence—all of which set him apart from and far above all that he created. Yet, God's glory is known, revealed. It is revealed both in nature and in the Word, seen most conspicuously in Christ. Even in these revelations it is an unbounded glory; it cannot be contained. It spills out, as it were, to encompass that which it confronts and encounters. Moses shone after his time on Mount Sinai (Ex. 34:29 and 2 Cor. 3:13). Angels are repeatedly depicted as bright and shining beings, like stars reflecting a brilliant sun. The spectacle of Christ's glory terrified Peter, James, and John on the mountain at the time of Christ's transfiguration (Matthew 17).

This glory, Charles C. Ryrie reminds us, not only terrifies but transforms human beings. Ryrie points out that "the glory of God—God displayed—is a great gift to mankind in general and a munificent one to believers."[65] It is stupendous, even. But Ryrie also adds, "God particularly wants us to glorify him in the ordinary affairs of life."[66] "Do all to the glory of God," Paul tells us in 1 Corinthians 10:31. Ryrie concludes that it is in the "ordinary matters of life" that we glorify God.[67]

This essay has used the work of the unlikely trio of Balthasar, Piper, and Ryrie as a way to listen to the echoes from the past merely to sketch the glory of God in historical theology. The last word, however, comes from a literary scholar and a writer of children's books. Though the Narnia Chronicles have made C. S. Lewis a household name, I tend to see him at his best in his essays, with the essay "The Weight of Glory" taking top rank. Preached at Oxford's twelfth-century University Church of St. Mary the Virgin on June 8, 1941, Lewis addressed a nation at war on the topic of glory. Glory means, he points out, either fame or luminosity. At first glance, Lewis perceives fame "as a competitive passion and therefore of hell rather of heaven."[68] So he was "shocked" to find so many, like John Milton and Thomas Aquinas, taking glory to mean fame. He was even more shocked when, by his own admission, he found it to be scriptural. Lewis also finds plenty of scriptural warrant for the other meaning of glory, glory as luminosity. On this latter point, Lewis notes how glory breaks into our world through the beauty in nature, the bright morning star but a type of the Morning Star, and through the beauty in poetry, which represents the human activity of expressing this glory, this beauty. Lewis not only links glory to beauty, but also, like Edwards and Augustine, he links glory to joy. In this essay, Lewis writes with an Edwardsian accent, referring to drinking "joy from the fountain of joy."[69]

Up to this point in the essay, Lewis has been mostly ethereal in his treatment of the glory of God, so he asks the question that he assumes his listeners and readers are asking. "It may be asked," he writes, "what practical use there is in the speculations I have been indulging." He offers one, the way we think of fellow human beings. His well-cited passage follows:

> It may be possible for each to think too much of his own potential glory hereafter; it is hardly possible for him to think too often or too deeply about that of his neighbour. The load, or weight, or burden of my neighbor's glory

---

[65] Ryrie, *Transformed by His Glory*, 130.

[66] Ibid., 131.

[67] Ibid., 133.

[68] C. S. Lewis, "The Weight of Glory," in *The Weight of Glory and Other Addresses* (New York: HarperOne, 2001), 36.

[69] Ibid., 44.

should be laid on my back, a load so heavy that only humility can carry it, and the backs of the proud will be broken. It is a serious thing to live in a society of possible gods and goddesses. . . . There are no ordinary people. You have never talked to a mere mortal.[70]

Lewis is not indulging an anthropocentric vision. On the contrary, he is fully aware of the ramifications of a theocentric vision. A theocentric vision, arising as it does from coming to grips with the all-encompassing reality of the glory of God, lifts one from an anemic, shallow, and ultimately deadly anthropocentrism. But it is this theocentric vision that alone supplies the proper view of the self and of others. The extent to which one is committed to this theocentric vision, however, may be seen in how one lives and how one treats others. It was Christ who said, if you have done this to the least of these, the ones most unlikely to be perceived as beings of blinding glory, you have done it unto me (Matt. 25:31–46).

Perhaps there is a profound paradox here in the discussion of the glory of God, a paradox that many theologians and pastors in the history of theology seem to be acutely aware of. The glory of God, which is packed with the ideas of beauty, excellence, and transcendence, clearly speaks of the extraordinary. When Moses saw but a glimpse of God and when the disciples saw the glory of Christ break through even momentarily, these were extraordinary events. The angelic beings immersed in the presence of God's glory are terribly extraordinary. Yet, on the other hand, Scripture relates glory to the rather ordinary and common acts of eating and drinking. And, as Lewis reminds us, rather ordinary human beings conceal something rather extraordinary.

Thinking about the glory of God is seen in our theology, in our worship, and in our church practice and life. It is also seen in the everyday seemingly ordinary encounters we have with those around us. Do not be fooled, however, by appearances. Lewis offers the final word on the matter:

Next to the Blessed Sacrament itself, your neighbour is the holiest object presented to your senses. If he is your Christian neighbour, he is holy in almost the same way, for in him also Christ *vere latitat*—the glorifier and the glorified, Glory Himself, is truly hidden.[71]

---

[70] Ibid., 45–46.
[71] Ibid., 46.

2

The Glory of God in the Old Testament

TREMPER LONGMAN III

The Bible is God's self-revelation to humanity. Through its pages we learn about God's actions and his nature. Often the Bible describes God by means of metaphors of relationship. He is our king, our husband, our warrior, our father, our mother, our teacher, our shepherd, and the list goes on and on. Metaphors instruct us well by comparing God with something or someone we know from everyday experience. Metaphors also teach indirectly and thus preserve the mystery of God. Each metaphor casts a light on who God is, but not exhaustively. Indeed, all the metaphors of God in the Bible do not add up to a full description.

The Bible not only describes God through metaphor but also by narrating his actions in history. From the beginning (Genesis 1), we learn that God is both transcendent and immanent. He is not a part of creation, but he is involved with it. God's creation, his choice of Abraham, his rescue of Israel at the sea, his judgments on his rebellious people—all are parts of his great redemptive actions in space and time that culminate in the work of Jesus Christ.

Besides metaphors and descriptions of his actions, the Bible also uses key terms to inform us about the character of God. God is holy (Lev. 20:26), eternal (Rom. 16:26), unchangeable (Heb. 6:17), and much more. The following essay looks at one key term, *glory*. In particular, we will explore how the Old Testament reveals the glorious nature of God.

The Vocabulary of Glory

We begin by examining the key words that are used to refer to God's glory in the Old Testament.[1] The most important of these words is *kabod*, and the chapter will primarily focus on passages that use this word, but there are a number of closely related words that are often used alongside of or in a manner similar to *kabod*.

Kabod

By far, the most important Hebrew word that indicates "glory" is the noun *kabod*. To better understand what is meant by the glory of God, we should begin with an exploration of the meaning of this word in the Old Testament. Our attention in the following paragraphs will be on what might be called the "nontheological" use of *kabod*. In this way, we can come to a basic understanding of the meaning of the word, which will provide background to a study of the use of the word to describe God, which will be the subject of most of the essay.

Kabod's basic, literal sense is "heavy." The judge Eli, for instance, is described as "old and heavy [*kabed*]," when he falls off his seat and breaks his neck at the news of the loss of the ark to the Philistines (1 Sam. 4:18). Also, Absalom's long, luxurious hair is so heavy that his hair weighed "two hundred shekels by the king's weight" (2 Sam. 14:26).

The figurative use of *kabod* far outnumbers its literal use. Reluctant to heed God's commission to return to Egypt, Moses protests that he is "slow of speech and of tongue," literally "heavy of mouth and heavy of tongue" (Ex. 4:10). Pharaoh's stubborn heart is described as "hard," the Hebrew word being *kabed* (Ex. 8:15, 32; 9:34; 10:1). The plagues themselves are noted to be "heavy," that is, intense (Ex. 9:3). Battles may also be described as *kabod* when they are particularly fierce (Judg. 20:34).

Especially notable are those contexts in which *kabod* describes a person's wealth. English has a similar linguistic phenomenon when it refers to a person of wealth as a person of substance. Abraham, for example, is said to be "very rich (*kabed mᵉʿod*] in livestock, in silver, and in gold" (Gen. 13:2).

---

[1] The following comments are informed by the studies of G. H. Davies, "Glory," in *IDB* 2:401–3; C. C. Newman, "Glory, Glorify," *New Interpreter's Dictionary of the Bible*, vol. 2 (Nashville: Abingdon, 2007), 576–80; C. J. Collins, "*kabod*," *NIDOTTE* 2:577–87; E. F. Harrison, "Glory," in *ISBE* 2:477–83. See also Bernard Ramm, *Them He Glorified: A Systematic Doctrine of Glorification* (Grand Rapids, MI: Eerdmans, 1963), 9–11.

Being wealthy, that is, being heavy in possessions, is also connected to one's high reputation. Thus, we should not be surprised that the term *kabod* and its derivatives may also be used in connection with someone's prestige, reputation, or honor. Prince Shechem of Shechem is said to be "the most honored of all his father's house" (Gen. 34:19). When Saul cannot find his uncle's donkeys, his servant tells him about Samuel, "a man who is held in honor" (1 Sam. 9:6). Benaiah was "renowned [*kabed*] among the thirty" most distinguished of David's warriors.

Tip'eret (Beauty), Hod (Splendor), Hadar (Majesty), Sebi' (Beauty), and 'Addir (Excellent)

While the present chapter will focus on the word group associated with the noun *kabod*, we here take note of closely related vocabulary that often is found in context with "glory." These words too are used to refer to the overwhelming presence of Yahweh.

Psalm 96 is a prime example of a place where these words pile on top of each other to try to express the ineffable. The psalm is a hymn that extols God's greatness and calls on his people to praise him. In this, God is contrasted with empty idols. Verse 3 asks his worshipers to "declare his glory [*kebodi*] among the nations," and verse 8 demands that his followers "ascribe to the LORD the glory [*kebod*] due his name." Between these two passages the psalmist proclaims:

> Splendor [*hod*] and majesty [*hadar*] are before him;
> strength and beauty [*tip'eret*] are in his sanctuary.[2] (v. 6)

Another example of the combined use of this vocabulary appears in Psalm 145 where the psalmist speaks of the "majesty [*hadar*] of the glory [*kebod*] of your splendor [*hod*]."

It is impossible to make neat distinctions between the meanings of these words, and the English glosses that we (and the dictionaries) provide are just a means to differentiate the words and get something in the semantic ballpark. A good example may be seen by comparing Psalm 78:61 with 1 Samuel 4:21–22. In the former, the term *tip'eret* is used to refer to the ark when it was captured by the Philistines during the judgeship of Eli:

> He delivered his power to captivity,
> his beauty (*tip'eret*) to the foe. (AT)

---

[2] *Hod* and *hadar* often occur together (e.g., Job 40:10; Pss. 96:6; 104:1). *NIDOTTE* provides extremely helpful comments on these words. For *hod*, see 1:1016–17; for *hadar*, see 1:1013–15; for *tip'eret*, see 3:572–72.

When we turn back to the narrative in 1 Samuel 4, we see that there the ark is called Israel's "glory" (*kabod*), showing that the terms are interchangeable.

We turn next to a consideration of a number of the most important passages in the Old Testament that speak of God's glory.[3] In one sense, since God is inherently glorious, we might speak of God's glory whenever he appears or is described. Since he manifests glory, all of his works are glorious. The following study, however, focuses on a number of passages that explicitly speak of God's glory. In this section, we will exposit the texts with a focus on the concept of glory. In the final part of the essay, we will summarize our findings by addressing a number of key questions in an attempt to refine our understanding of God's glory.

The Glory of God in the Pentateuch

For many reasons, it makes sense to start with the Pentateuch, but most obviously because it is the foundation of the rest of the Bible. In the Pentateuch, we read about God's first revelations of himself to humanity, from the creation to the end of the wilderness wanderings.

God's Glory and the Exodus

Interestingly, Genesis never speaks of God's glory explicitly. Exodus first speaks of God's glory in connection with the climactic moment of Israel's release from Egyptian bondage, namely the crossing of the Sea of Reeds. Rather than helping Israel avoid a pursuing Pharaoh, God leads Israel into a trap from which it cannot escape. He, in essence, places their backs against a wall, telling them to encamp "in front of Pi-hahiroth between Migdol and the sea, in front of Baal-zephon" (Ex. 14:2). There will be no escape by human means from Egypt's fury. Pharaoh will think that the Israelites have foolishly trapped themselves, but God tells Moses that he has other plans in mind: "I will harden Pharaoh's heart, and he will pursue them, and I will get glory over Pharaoh and all his host, and the Egyptians shall know that I am the LORD" (Ex. 14:4). God reiterates this idea in 14:17–19, the moment he instructs Moses to extend his staff toward the sea.

What do we learn about God's glory from this account? What is it about the crossing of the Sea, the salvation of the Israelites and the destruction of the Egyptians, which lends itself to God's glory?

---

[3] In critical circles, studies of glory speak of the development of the idea of glory based on a hypothetical reconstruction of the growth of the literature of the OT. For instance, the more physical description of glory that we encounter in Ezekiel is said to be a later development along with the connection between the glory of God and fire in a putative postexilic P source.

As background, we need to recall who Pharaoh was. He was the most powerful human ruler in existence. He had the power of life and death. He was vastly wealthy with armies at his beck and call. With his wealth and power, he would have been considered glorious to human eyes. Let us also recall who Pharaoh and the Egyptians thought he was—god. Pharaoh was an important god in Egyptian religious thinking. So his glory, as thought of by the Egyptians, would have extended to his purported divinity.

In a word, the crossing of the sea was understood as the continuation and pinnacle of God's war against the Egyptian gods that began during the plagues (Ex. 12:12). Pharaoh's presumption (hard heart) would not allow him to surrender to Moses' demands, and so the conflict escalated until the point of the action at the sea. Indeed, this fit with God's plan. Not only did Pharaoh harden his heart, but God hardened it as well (Ex. 9:12). It was part of his plan to display his glory to the world (Ex. 9:16).

God's glory was thus displayed by shattering the pretentious glory of Egypt and its Pharaoh by the dramatic means of separating the sea to allow the Israelites to go through to safety and to close it in judgment on the Egyptians. God's saving and judging actions thus demonstrate his glory with the result that the Israelites worship him:

> I will sing to the LORD, for he has triumphed gloriously;
> the horse and his rider he has thrown into the sea. (Ex. 15:1)

Moses' Encounter with the Glory of God

In Exodus 33, we have one of the most remarkable passages in the Old Testament concerning God's glory, filled with as many enigmas as clarities.

The context of the passage is the sin with the golden calf. While Moses has been on the mountain receiving the law, the people, under Aaron's leadership, have indulged in false worship, either the worship of a false god or the worship of Yahweh in a false way. In either case, they break the first two commandments and deserve God's judgment. They have broken the covenant (as indicated by Moses' smashing the tablets of the law). The Levites respond to the call to come to "the LORD's side" (Ex. 32:26). They execute God's judgment on their brothers and sisters.[4] In his continuing anger, God also sends a plague on Israel (Ex. 32:35). In a word, the continuing covenant relationship between God and his people is thrown into question. Will God continue to be with his people as they travel toward

---

[4] And as a result secure their position as a priestly tribe. See Tremper Longman, *Immanuel in Our Place* (Phillipsburg, NJ: P&R, 2001), 134.

the Promised Land? This is the question that racked Moses' mind as he approached God in prayer.

In Exodus 33:17–23, Moses intercedes with the Lord on behalf of his people, seeking assurance that he will still travel with the Israelites. Moses knows only too well that if God does not go with them, their journey will be in vain.

In spite of God's assurances ("My presence will go with you," v. 14), Moses remains concerned and asks, "For how shall it be known that I have found favor in your sight, I and your people?" (v. 16). In other words, Moses wants a demonstration that God will indeed be present with the people as they travel on from here.[5] Out of love for Moses, God says that he will act in a way that will assure him of his continuing presence with the people. Moses then asks that God show him his glory (v. 18), his active and manifest presence,[6] so he knows for certain that God is still with them.

God's response is interesting, but not immediately clear. In response to the request that God show his glory, God says, "I will make all my goodness pass before you and will proclaim before you my name" (v. 19). So Moses will see God's goodness and hear his name. The name is presumably Yahweh; thus there are connections to Moses' call at the burning bush in Exodus 3. Peter Enns rightly points out that the force of these echoes is to show us that there is the need for a second commissioning after the disturbance in the Israel-Yahweh relationship in Exodus 32.[7] After saying what Moses will encounter ("goodness" and "name"), God announces that Moses will not see God's face. Why? Because people cannot see God's face and live. In other words, full exposure to the divine presence would overwhelm and destroy a human observer.

The same point is communicated by the language pertaining to God's "back." God says Moses cannot see his face but can see his back. Moses is to stand in the cleft of a rock. When God passes by, his hand will obscure Moses' vision from God's face, but then, after he passes by, Moses will be able to see his back. The language of "face," "hand," and "back" is boldly anthropomorphic. God is a spirit and does not literally have these body parts. That is not to say that Moses saw nothing, but we should acknowledge that this is metaphoric language that, in essence, points out that though

---

[5] J. I. Durham, *Exodus*, WBC (Dallas: Word, 1987), 452.

[6] "Glory, then, is a special term that depicts God's visible and active presence"; so Walter C. Kaiser Jr., *The Majesty of God in the Old Testament: A Guide for Preaching and Teaching* (Grand Rapids, MI: Baker, 2007), 120.

[7] Peter Enns, *Exodus*, NIV Application Commentary (Grand Rapids, MI: Zondervan, 2000), 583–84.

human beings, even Moses, cannot be exposed to God's full presence, his real, though partial, presence is impressive enough—indeed, so impressive that when Moses descended from the mountain with the new tablets of the law, his face shone, presumably with the reflective glory of God.

The Glory Cloud in the Wilderness

We are first introduced to the cloud that represents God's presence in Exodus 13:21–22, though the fire and smoke of the burning bush (Ex. 3:1–6) may very well anticipate the form of this theophany.[8] As they left Egypt, God made his presence and protection known to Israel in the form of a "pillar of cloud" during the day and the "pillar of fire" at night. Indeed, there is only one pillar, but the fire burning in the cloud becomes visible only during the evening and in this way remains a constant reminder of God's presence to the people.

A cloud, like smoke, serves well to represent God's presence and, as we will see, also his glory, because though it is visible, a cloud also obscures one's vision. People cannot see in it or through it; thus the cloud provides a sense of mystery and indirectness in the experience of God's presence. The presence of God is in the cloud (Ex. 13:21), protecting the people from a lethal dose of God's glory.

The cloud not only represents divine presence but also protection. This may be seen in Exodus 14:19–20 where the pillar of cloud moved from before the people to behind them, providing a buffer between the Egyptians and the Israelites. A third function of the cloud is guidance, since normally the cloud went in front in order to lead the way through the wilderness.

The cloud also is connected to God's provision in the wilderness. In response to the people's grumbling about their hunger, the glory of God announces the provision of manna and quail as "the LORD appeared in the cloud" (Ex. 16:10).

Perhaps the most dramatic occurrence of the cloud of glory is on Mount Sinai when God gave the law to Moses. The imagery of the cloud seems to have multiple connections and origins at Sinai. At first, the cloud, accompanied by thunder and lightning, is that of a storm. But then the cloud appears to emanate from the smoke produced by a volcano, where the smoke is accompanied by fire and goes up from the mountain like "the smoke of a kiln" (Ex. 19:18), and the trembling of the mountain suggests earthquakes.[9]

---

[8] Indeed, in Genesis God also made his presence known in the form of smoke and fire (Gen. 15:17–21).

[9] Note also the description given by Moses in Deut. 5:24 where God's glory and greatness is accompanied by fire on the day that he gave Israel the law.

It is in Exodus 24:15–18 that the cloud is specifically associated with the glory of God, again indicating a shroud that protects people from a full measure of what would overwhelm them. Moses, the prophet who, as we have seen, would have the most direct exposure to a direct revelation of God's presence, is the only one who could go into the cloud to meet with God on top of Sinai.

Glory and the Tabernacle

In the previous section, we observed how God's presence, and specifically his glory, was made manifest during the wilderness wanderings in the form of a cloud. To complete our look at the glory of God in the Pentateuch we can also observe the connection between the glory cloud and the tabernacle.

The tabernacle represented God's abiding, as opposed to his occasional, presence with his people. The tabernacle represented God's home on earth. Since the people were living in tents as they wandered in the wilderness, God's home was also in the form of a tent. The tabernacle was extremely ornate, since it represented the tent of the king. The materials used included the finest fabrics, gems, and metals. The interior curtain, the one visible from the inside (Ex. 26:1–6) was made from "fine twined linen and blue and purple and scarlet yarns" (Ex. 26:1). The representations of cherubim embroidered in this sky-colored fabric gave the impression of being in heaven on earth. The menorah (Ex. 25:31–40) is described as having branches and flowers on it. Thus, it is a tree image, representing the fact that the tabernacle was also Eden, the place where God and his human creatures enjoyed intimate fellowship.

The most holy part of the tabernacle was the back third of the structure, the Most Holy Place, where the ark of the covenant was kept. The ark was the most potent symbol of God's presence and represented the footstool of his royal throne (e.g., 1 Chron. 28:2). As such, one can detect gradations of holiness in the structure of the tabernacle. The structure of the tabernacle represents this also by virtue of the ascending value of the metals (bronze, silver, gold, pure gold) as one moves from the bases of the poles for the curtains of the courtyard in toward the Most Holy Place. Increasing holiness is also evidenced by the increasing difficulty of access as one moved from outside the camp (the realm of Gentiles and the unclean) to inside the camp (ritually clean Israelites), to the tabernacle area, where one had to be accompanied by Levites consecrated for service, to the Most Holy Place, accessible only to the high priest and to him only once a year (Leviticus 16).

How did God make his glorious presence known in the tabernacle? By the cloud. God announces this in Exodus 29:43 where he proclaims: "There I will meet with the people of Israel, and it shall be sanctified by my glory." Indeed, the book of Exodus dramatically ends after the lengthy description of the instructions for building the tabernacle (chaps. 25–31) followed by the detailed description of the actual building (chaps. 35–40)[10] with the cloud settling on the tabernacle:

> Then the cloud covered the tent of meeting, and the glory of the LORD filled the tabernacle. And Moses was not able to enter the tent of meeting because the cloud settled on it, and the glory of the LORD filled the tabernacle. Throughout all their journeys, whenever the cloud was taken up from over the tabernacle, the people of Israel would set out. But if the cloud was not taken up, then they did not set out till the day that it was taken up. For the cloud of the LORD was on the tabernacle by day, and fire was in it by night, in the sight of all the house of Israel throughout all their journeys. (Ex. 40:34–38)

But it was not only the tabernacle itself that was associated with God's glory. The items associated with the tabernacle were also connected to that glory. The book of Exodus in particular is explicit about the priestly garments. By virtue of their being set apart (or consecrated) for special service to God, the priests wore elaborate clothing that represented and reflected God's glory. Aaron's clothing is said to be made "for glory and for beauty" (Ex. 28:2, also v. 40).

Indeed, at the time of Aaron's and his sons' ordination, God made his glory manifest. First, Aaron had to prepare for the appearance of God's glory by offering sacrifices (Lev. 9:6–8), and then he had to prepare for the climactic moment when God's glory would appear in the form of fire and ignite the sacrifices on the altar. Not surprisingly, when the people saw this wonder, "they shouted and fell on their faces" (Lev. 9:24). Worship is the only proper response to God's glory.

Glory and Judgment

Already, at the crossing of the sea (see above), we may note a connection between the appearance of God in his glory and judgment. God is glorified when he judges, because his judgments proclaim that no one is powerful enough to resist him. God's glory is often accompanied by fire and storm thus indicating that he is dangerous, at least to his enemies. God shielded

---

[10] The instructions for building the tabernacle and their fulfillment are interrupted by the episode of the golden calf, which threatened the divine-human relationship (Exodus 32–34).

Moses from his glory because he did not wish him harm. In judgment God exposes his enemies to his intense glory, and they cannot survive. Though not explicitly connected to the theme of glory, the idea of judgment stands behind *herem* warfare. After battle (at least those that occurred within the Promised Land [Deut. 20:16–18]), all the prisoners were brought as an offering to the Lord. Since they were not holy, they were consumed by God's holiness.[11]

In the Pentateuch, God's glory is manifest in several judgment scenes. The first is narrated immediately following the ordination of Aaron and his sons (see above comments on Leviticus 9). Two of his sons, Nadab and Abihu, offered "strange" fire in their incense burners. What exactly was strange about the fire is not known, but it certainly is right to consider it (as the ESV translates the Hebrew) "unauthorized" (Lev. 10:1). During the ordination, fire came out and consumed the sacrifice (Lev. 9:22–24), which stood in the place of the sinners who were in God's presence, but here the fire comes out from the Lord and consumes Nadab and Abihu. Granted, the noun *glory* is not used in this context, but that glory is at issue is underlined by God's words that followed the execution of the wayward priests: "I will be sanctified, and before all the people I will be glorified" (Lev. 10:3).

The second example of glory and God's judgment is in the context of Israel's rebellion instigated by the report of the spies (Numbers 13–14). Ten of the twelve spies—Joshua and Caleb are the exceptions—came back with a disturbing report. Yes, the land was fertile beyond imagination, but the inhabitants were fearsome warriors. The Israelites responded with fear, showing their fundamental lack of faith in their warrior God. They were so upset that they wanted to kill Moses and Aaron. Before they could, though, God intervened when "the glory of the LORD appeared at the tent of meeting to all the people of Israel" (Num. 14:10). God was ready for judgment; he was ready to annihilate the people. As previously, during the sin with the golden calf (Exodus 32), Moses effectively interceded and warded off God's anger. Even though God pardoned the Israelites and did not destroy them as a nation, there were still horrible consequences. He condemned the adult generation, with the exception of Joshua and Caleb, to die in the wilderness. In this way, God's glory was to fill the earth (Num. 14:21), when none of those who saw his glory in Egypt were allowed to enter the Promised Land.

---

[11] See Tremper Longman and Dan G. Reid, *God Is a Warrior* (Grand Rapids, MI: Zondervan, 1995), 46–47.

Third is the story of Korah's rebellion, which has a similar pattern to both the golden calf and the spy incidents. It begins with sin. In this case a Levite, Korah, along with two laypeople from the tribe of Reuben named Dathan and Abiram, led a revolt against Moses' authority. Again, in response, God made his glory manifest and announced his intention to destroy them all (Num. 16:19–21). Moses and Aaron, though, again successfully interceded on behalf of the people so that only the sinners themselves would be destroyed. However, in this case, the people continued to grumble and even blamed Moses and Aaron for the death of "the people of the LORD" (Num. 16:41). Again, the glory of God appeared in the form of a cloud, and God intended to destroy the whole congregation. Once again, Moses and Aaron appeased God, though a number of people were killed in a plague.

The Glory of God in the Historical Books

The Historical Books narrate God's acts of salvation and judgment from the time of the conquest to the postexilic period. The Pentateuch and the Historical Books together narrate redemptive history through the Old Testament period.

The Ark as a Symbol of God's Glory

In the Pentateuch, we observed a close connection between God's glory and the tabernacle, the place where God made his presence known in the form of a cloud. We also noted that the ark was the most potent symbol of God's presence in the tabernacle, being lodged in the Most Holy Place and representing God's footstool. In the Historical Books, there is an even closer connection made between the ark and God's glory.

The ark was a mobile symbol of God's presence and was the only piece of sacred furniture that was taken out of the tabernacle even while it still stood. Of course, the ark was also taken out when the tabernacle was packed up for travel through the wilderness and actually led Israel through the wilderness. The language that Moses used at the beginning of the march indicates the military context of the ark: "Arise, O LORD, and let your enemies be scattered, and let those who hate you flee before you" (Num. 10:35). The ark represented God, the warrior king, who marched at the head of his army into battle.

In the Historical Books, the ark also was found on the battlefield and, as such, it represented God's presence, but not always in the way Israel expected. This is true particularly in a context where the ark is virtually identified with the glory of God.

The historical situation is a battle between the Philistines and Israel under the leadership of Samuel's wicked sons, Hophni and Phinehas (1 Samuel 4). After their initial defeat, the Israelite generals realized that they had neglected to bring the ark onto the battlefield. Their neglect and their general attitude indicate that when they did bring the ark to the battle-field, it was done not out of faith, but rather because they believed it was a magical source of power. The Philistines, on the other hand, were rightly fearful, since they knew the reputation of this God (1 Sam. 4:7–8), though they were spiritually confused in their description of him. In any case, they found courage to go out and fight the Israelites.

Israel was utterly routed by the Philistines, who captured the ark and took it back to one of their major cities, Ashdod, where they placed it in the temple of Dagon. Meanwhile, word reached Shiloh, the place where Eli officiated as priest-judge of Israel. He, along with his pregnant daughter-in-law, heard the news of the defeat. The text indicates that when Eli heard about the loss of the ark, he collapsed from his seat and broke his neck. The horrifying news and the death of Eli sent his daughter-in-law into labor. She died in childbirth, but not before naming her son Ichabod ("no glory" or perhaps "where is the glory?") and stating: "'The glory has departed from Israel!' because the ark of God had been captured and because of her father-in-law and her husband. And she said, 'The glory has departed from Israel, for the ark of God has been captured'" (1 Sam. 4:21–22).

The next chapter describes how the presence of the ark in Ashdod led to all kinds of problems for the Philistines. In the first place, the statue of Dagon kept falling down. By placing the ark at the feet of Dagon, the Philistines were illustrating their belief that their god had defeated Yahweh, the god of Israel, on his turf. Dagon, however, kept prostrating himself before the Lord. When the statue's hands and head broke off (perhaps symbolizing his death in battle), the Philistines got the message. In the second place, God caused a plague to hit the city. At first, the Philistines tried to avert the harm by sending the ark from city to city. Finally, as the disease followed the ark, they sent it back to Israel. They learned that Yahweh could have defeated the Philistines on the battlefield but chose not to in order to show that he is not a God that can be manipulated. This story shows a close connection between the ark and God's glory because the ark represents the presence of God.

Interestingly, at the time of David, we once again observe a close connection between the ark and the glory of God. David was not permitted to build the temple, but he was responsible for bringing the ark to Jerusalem and placing it in a sacred tent there. When that occurred, David composed a song that extolled God's glory. First Chronicles 16:8–36 presents the hymn, which, as a central theme, extols God's glory:

> Glory in his holy name;
> > let the hearts of those who seek the LORD rejoice! (v. 10)
>
> Declare his glory among the nations,
> > his marvelous works among all the peoples! (v. 24)
>
> Ascribe to the LORD, O clans of the peoples,
> > ascribe to the LORD glory and strength!
> Ascribe to the LORD the glory due his name;
> bring an offering and come before him!
> Worship the LORD in the splendor of holiness. (vv. 28–29)
>
> Save us, O God of our salvation,
> > and gather and deliver us from among the nations,
> that we may give thanks to your holy name,
> > and glory in your praise. (v. 35)

God's Glory and the Temple

The Historical Books also narrate the transition from the tabernacle to the temple. Above, we described the connection between God's glory and the tabernacle, so now we ask whether that connection continued in the temple.

Though David could not build the temple, he enthusiastically prepared for its construction. Indeed, it was the glory associated with the future temple and Solomon's inexperience that led David to make massive preparations for its construction (1 Chron. 22:1–7). Indeed, according to Chronicles, one of the last acts of David was to collect offerings for the construction of the temple, at the conclusion of which he prays:

> Yours, O LORD, is the greatness and the power and the glory and the victory and the majesty, for all that is in the heavens and in the earth is yours. Yours is the kingdom, O LORD, and you are exalted as head above all. Both riches and honor come from you, and you rule over all. In your hand are power and might, and in your hand it is to make great and to give strength to all. And now we thank you, our God, and praise your glorious name. (1 Chron. 29:11–13)

Now we turn to the temple itself and the glory of the Lord. The first questions we must ask are, "What is the relationship between the taber-

nacle and the temple? What is innovative about the temple?" As we follow
the theme of the place of worship in the Old Testament, we see that God
determined its shape. When David told Nathan of his intention to build the
temple, God reprimanded him for his initiative. That is God's prerogative.
The moment was not yet right for the construction of the temple, because
David was a man of blood (1 Chron. 22:8). This phrase does not indicate
that David was morally unqualified to build the temple; rather, it points
to the role that David played in redemptive history. He was the conquest
completer, the one who finally subdued all the internal enemies of Israel.
As a result, the law of centralization finally went into effect (Deut. 12:10).
Israel was now firmly established in the land and so a fixed abode, rather
than a mobile tent sanctuary, had become the appropriate venue for the
manifestation of the divine presence. Solomon, whose very name means
"Peaceful One," was divinely commissioned to construct the temple, the
architecture and the accoutrements of which (the pillars and the sea, 1
Kings 7:15–24) represented establishment in the land.

Since the temple replaced the tabernacle as the place where God made
his active and manifest presence known, and since it was the repository
of the ark of the covenant, we are not surprised that the Historical Books
speak of the temple as reflective of the glory of God.

Solomon made this abundantly clear at the dedication of the temple.
Upon its completion, the priests brought the ark into the Most Holy Place
of the temple. "And when the priests came out of the Holy Place, a cloud
filled the house of the LORD, so that the priests could not stand to minister because of the cloud, for the glory of the LORD filled the house of the
LORD" (1 Kings 8:10–11).

The Chronicler gives a slightly different or broader perspective on the
glory of God at the time of the temple dedication. While Chronicles, like
Kings, speaks of the glory cloud descending on the temple before Solomon's
dedicatory prayer and at the entry of the ark into the temple (2 Chron. 5:14),
the Chronicler also alerts the reader to the manifestation of God's glory
right after the prayer (2 Chron. 7:1–3).[12] He also speaks of the worshipful
response of the priests at the manifestation of his glory: "They bowed down
with their faces to the ground on the pavement and worshiped and gave
thanks to the LORD, saying, 'For he is good, for his steadfast love endures
forever'" (2 Chron. 7:3).

---

[12] Raymond Dillard, 2 Chronicles, WBC 15 (Dallas: Thomas Nelson, 1987), 56–57, suggests that
the manifestation of God's glory after the prayer may be the same as before, but narrated twice to
form a chiasm. He is open, however, to the suggestion that the first appearance of the glory cloud
was for the benefit of priests while the second was for all the people.

The temple thus replaced the tabernacle as the place where God made his glory known through the agency of the cloud. However, as we will see momentarily when we turn our attention to the prophets, the people allowed the privilege of God's glorious presence to turn into presumption.

The Glory of God in the Psalms

God's glory is the frequent object of the psalmists' hymnic attention. We should not be surprised. After all, we have already observed a close connection between God's glory and the sanctuary and its furniture, particularly the ark. The primary use of the Psalms during the Old Testament period was in corporate worship and was associated with the sanctuary, the place where God made his abiding presence known. The worshipers were in the very presence of God; thus it was natural that they would sing of his glory. Indeed, the theme of God's glory is so pervasive in the Psalms that we will have to be selective in our presentation and look at only a few of many examples. Rather than looking at the psalms in their present canonical order, we will begin with examples—psalms in which the theme of glory plays a major role—and then comment on some other notable psalms where glory is mentioned only once or twice but in striking ways.

Psalm 29: God's Glory in the Storm

Psalm 29 has received much attention in scholarship, particularly over the past eighty years. Since the recovery of Ugaritic literature, commentators have widely recognized that this psalm bears similarity to Canaanite writings.[13] The poetic style (repetitive parallelism and tricola) is more like Ugaritic poetry than typical Hebrew poetry; the geographical references (Lebanon and Kadesh) are north of Israel, and the description of God in the power of storm produces images that are similar to those used for the storm god Baal.[14]

These observations point to the conclusion that Psalm 29 is either a transformed Baal hymn or a Hebrew hymn written to intentionally mimic a hymn for Baal. The purpose of such a literary and theological strategy would have been to counter the urge to worship Baal. The psalm asserts that the power of the storm reveals Yahweh's power, not Baal's.

The storm not only reveals God's power, but also his glory. Thus, the faithful proclaim that glory in worship:

---

[13] H. L. Ginsberg, "A Phoenician Hymn in the Psalter," in *Atti del XIX Congresso Internazionale degli Orientalisti* (Rome, 1935); Peter C. Craigie, "Psalm XXIX in the Hebrew Poetic Tradition," *Vetus Testamentum* 22 (1972): 143–51; Frank M. Cross, "Notes on a Canaanite Psalm in the Old Testament," *Bulletin of the American Schools for Oriental Research* 117 (1950): 19–21.

[14] This includes the picture of God "enthroned over the flood" (v. 10).

Ascribe to the LORD, O heavenly beings,
  ascribe to the LORD glory and strength.
Ascribe to the LORD the glory due his name;
  worship the LORD in the splendor of holiness. (vv. 1–2)

Verses 3 through 8 extol the God of glory's voice. Verse 3b is a figurative reference to thunder. This thunder is accompanied by the fire of lightning, thus again combining cloud/smoke and fire in reference to God's glory.

Finally, mention should be made of the specific connection between God's glory and the worship in the temple, in verse 9. God's magnificent display of power in the storm leads those who worship in the temple to "all cry, 'Glory!'"

Psalm 24: God's Glory in Battle

Psalm 24 is well known in the Western world through the music of Handel's *Messiah*. The psalm begins with a proclamation that the whole world belongs to God by virtue of the fact that he created it. His creation is depicted as his placing the world on the waters: "He has founded it upon the seas and established it upon the rivers" (v. 2). The psalm then continues with what might be called an "entry liturgy" when the psalmist asks, "Who shall ascend the hill of the LORD? And who shall stand in his holy place?" (v. 3). The answer follows and describes a person of "clean hands and a pure heart" (v. 4; see also Psalm 15) before moving on to an enigmatic rendition of an interchange between two unidentified persons:

Lift up your heads, O gates!
  And be lifted up, O ancient doors,
    that the King of glory may come in.
Who is this King of glory?
The LORD, strong and mighty,
  the LORD, mighty in battle!
Lift up your heads, O gates!
  And lift them up, O ancient doors,
    that the King of glory may come in.
Who is this King of glory?
  The LORD of hosts,
  he is the King of glory! (vv. 7–10)

What is clear is that the King of glory seeks access through gates and that his representative requests entry from a gatekeeper. From the fact that God is here described in connection with battle and that the climactic verse gives him his warrior name ("the LORD of hosts," that is, the hosts of his heavenly and/or human army), we can confidently infer that the army has returned from battle with the ark of the covenant at its head, and it is seeking entry through either the city gates or the temple gates so that the ark might be placed back in the sanctuary.

God's glory here is associated with battle, as we have seen before in both the Pentateuch and the Historical Books, and linked with the ark and the sanctuary.

Psalm 8: God's Glory in Creation

While Psalm 29 proclaims God's glory in the storm and Psalm 24 in battle, Psalm 8 focuses on God as creator. The psalm opens and closes (vv. 1, 9) with the proclamation of God's excellence throughout the earth, using the word *'addir*, which is closely related to *glory* (*kabod*):

> O LORD, our Lord,
>   how majestic is your name in all the earth!

In verse 1, this praise is followed immediately by the statement, "You have set your glory above the heavens." The psalm goes on to describe the splendor of the creation, particularly the heavens (v. 3), and most climactically human beings, who are themselves crowned with glory and honor (v. 5b). As high and dignified a view of humanity as this psalm presents, it is clear from the fact that God "crowned them" that human glory is derivative and dependent on divine glory. God's glory is "above the heavens"; that is, the Creator's glory surpasses that of all his glorious creation and this realization evokes the worshiper's praise.[15]

The Glory of God in Lament

While most of the psalms that speak of God's glory are hymns of joy celebrating God's presence and power, God's glory is occasionally found in laments as well. While laments express disappointment in God, they often include a statement of confidence or praise that either indicates faith in the midst of turmoil or perhaps reflects the fact that the song was written after the resolution. No matter what the occasion of the composition of the lament, its effect on later worshipers who have similar though perhaps not identical circumstances to the composer's is to help them articulate their heartache before God, and also to move them toward a more positive attitude.

---

[15] Psalm 19 similarly begins with a connection between God's glory and creation when it says, "The heavens declare the glory of God, and the sky above proclaims his handiwork" (v. 1). The argument of this assertion is that the wonders of creation (e.g., the marvel of the sun) merely reflect the glory of the one who created it.

The title of Psalm 3 associates its composition with the time that David's son Absalom rebelled against his father (2 Samuel 15–18). However, David composed it in a way that later worshipers who feel beset by hostile people could use for their own prayer. In the midst of a cry for help against the attack of others ("O LORD, how many are my foes!"), the prayer proclaims, "But you, O LORD, are a shield about me, my glory, and the lifter of my head" (v. 3). God's glory provides protection to the besieged prayer, and in this way his confidence is renewed.

In Psalm 26, the poet has been falsely accused by enemies who are trying to take advantage of the situation. He appeals to God to "vindicate" him (v. 1), and he vigorously defends his integrity against their slander. As part of his defense he affirms:

> O LORD, I love the habitation of your house
> and the place where your glory dwells. (v. 8)

Thus, again we see the connection between God's glory and the temple. The poet's love of the temple is a result of his love of God because that is where God has made his presence manifest in a powerful way.

Psalm 57 is a third example of a lament psalm where the sufferer finds confidence in God's glory. The title of this psalm places its composition in association with David's flight from a murderous Saul. It specifies that David is in a cave, perhaps connected to 1 Samuel 22:1–5 where David sought refuge from Saul in the cave of Adullam. The psalmist makes no secret of his dire situation:

> My soul is in the midst of lions;
>   I lie down amid fiery beasts—
> the children of man, whose teeth are spears and arrows,
>   whose tongues are sharp swords. (v. 4)

In the next verse, as well as in the conclusion of the psalm (v. 11), the poet repeats his call for God to:

> Be exalted, O God, above the heavens!
>   Let your glory be over all the earth!

The psalmist praises God and his glory in the midst of his tribulation. He calls on God to display his glory. One manifestation of this glory would be the mercy God would render to the beleaguered prayer.

The Prophets and the Glory of God

We continue our survey of the Old Testament's depiction of the glory of God with the Prophets. Prophets are messengers of God and thus are sometimes summoned to the throne of God. We are not surprised, then, that many of them speak often of God's glory.

The Glory of God in Isaiah

It is appropriate to begin our exploration of the theme of glory in Isaiah with the account of Isaiah's prophetic commission in chapter 6, though five chapters precede it. The account does not follow chronology, with the oracles of the first five chapters coming later in time than his prophetic call. John Oswalt persuasively suggests that the placement is to show that Isaiah's experience can be the experience of the people of Israel; that is, a sinful person or people can have an experience of God that will lead to their atonement.[16]

In chapter 6, Isaiah has a vision of the throne room of God. The scene occurs in the temple (v. 1), but the vision reflects heavenly reality, since the temple is "heaven on earth."[17] Isaiah is in the presence of God, though his vision of God may only encompass "the train of his robe" (6:1). Spiritual powers, the seraphim, attend him, and even they may not experience a direct exposure to the divine presence. They are described as having six wings, two to cover their face, two their feet (likely a euphemism for their genitalia), leaving two with which to fly. The room shakes and is filled with smoke. We have already seen a connection between smoke and God's glorious presence, but the seraphim make God's glory explicit when they proclaim:

> Holy, holy, holy is the LORD of hosts;
>   the whole earth is full of his glory! (v. 3)

The thrice-repeated phrase "holy" (*qadosh*) emphasizes God's transcendence. He is "set apart" because he is the Creator, and everyone and everything else are creatures, including the magnificent seraphim. God is unique from Isaiah in his moral purity and thus is holy ("set apart") in that way too. Isaiah recognizes his sinfulness right away and believes he is doomed: "Woe is me! For I am lost; for I am a man of unclean lips, and I dwell in the midst of a people of unclean lips; for my eyes have seen the King, the LORD of hosts" (v. 5).

---

[16] John Oswalt, *Isaiah*, NIV Application Commentary (Grand Rapids, MI: Zondervan, 2003), 125.
[17] Longman, *Immanuel in Our Place*, 39–61.

Isaiah's concern is connected to God's glory, also proclaimed by the seraphim. We have seen how God's glory is a wonderful manifestation of his active presence, but to those who are sinful, it can mean death. However, Isaiah has not been brought to the throne room to be put to death but rather to be commissioned to his prophetic ministry, and thus a seraph brings a burning coal from the temple altar and touches his lips, symbolically purifying him and taking away his guilt.

Isaiah's vision of God on his throne fills him with awe. He does not speak face-to-face with God as Moses, the greatest prophet of all did (Num. 12:6–9; Deut. 18:15–22; 34:10–12). But he does have an overwhelming experience of God's holiness and glory that prepares him for his difficult prophetic task of calling sinful Israel back to a right relationship with God.

The Glory of God in Isaiah's Oracles (Isaiah 2)

From the above account of his commission as a prophet, we realize that when Isaiah spoke of God's glory in his oracles, he knew what he was talking about. In Isaiah 2, for instance, we read an oracle[18] that speaks of "the splendor of his [God's] majesty."[19] Indeed, this phrase occurs in a refrain that is repeated three times throughout the oracle (vv. 10, 19, 21). The oracle begins in 2:6 and continues to 4:1, though it may be composed of smaller units.[20] John Oswalt states well the theme of this oracle: Israel has turned away from the true source of glory to place their hope in the false glory of the nations (see below) and thus is ripe for humiliation.[21]

Israel has regarded "man in whose nostrils is breath" (2:22) and thus they had better seek shelter "from before the terror of the LORD, and from the splendor of his majesty" (vv. 10, 19, 21) in caves, holes, and the dust of the ground. Here the "splendor of his majesty" terrifies because the people have turned away from him to foreign allies and their false gods.

Isaiah 24

Isaiah 24 begins a new section of the book that continues through chapter 27. It is commonly referred to as the "Apocalypse of Isaiah" because it looks forward to the final judgment of the world. Whether it is apocalyptic is not important to our discussion, but it is germane to point out that these

---

[18] We cannot date this oracle, but for the reasons stated in the previous section, it is highly probable that it occurs after Isaiah's commission, which is dated in "the year that King Uzziah died" (Isa. 6:1; that is, 733 BC).

[19] Here the word *splendor* is not *kabod*, but rather *hadar*, one of the close synonyms we mentioned above.

[20] See Brevard S. Childs, *Isaiah*, OTL, 28–37.

[21] Oswalt, *Isaiah*, 95–96.

chapters follow well from the oracles against the nations in chapters 13 through 23 where individual nations receive oracles of judgment. Now the whole earth has become the object of God's wrath.

The oracle of chapter 24 begins by announcing the future judgment on the earth, which will devastate it: "The LORD will empty the earth and make it desolate" (v. 1). All celebration, including drinking and music, will come to an end (vv. 4–13). An enigmatic shift to the positive takes place in verses 14–16:

> They lift up their voices, they sing for joy;
>> over the majesty of the LORD they shout from the west.
> Therefore in the east give glory[22] to the LORD;
>> in the coastlands of the sea, give glory to the name of the LORD,
>> the God of Israel.
> From the ends of the earth we hear songs of praise,
>> of glory[23] to the Righteous One.

The enigma has to do with who is doing the singing. The music of the sinners of the earth has grown silent. Accordingly, these voices must be those of the righteous or perhaps the future remnant or perhaps even angels (or all of the above). The fact that they are scattered means that they are from all the nations of the world, or it anticipates the scattering of the people of God throughout the earth. They glorify God for his judgment, which cleanses the earth of sin.

The chapter ends with the statement that "his glory [*kabod*] will be before his elders." There are difficulties of understanding with this verse as well. The context again is the judgment upon the world leaders (v. 21). Does this include the elders? Probably so. The point is that God reigns from his temple (v. 23), and the glory that emanates from his presence is such that the "moon" and the "sun" will diminish in their splendor by comparison with God's glory.

The Glory of the Remnant

Isaiah's message is not just one of judgment but also of salvation. In the following passages, we learn that while God's glory is bad news for sinners, it is good news for the purified remnant:

> In that day the LORD of hosts will be a crown of glory,
>> and a diadem of beauty, to the remnant of his people. (28:5)

---

[22] This is the verbal form of *kbd*.
[23] This is a near synonym of *kabod*, namely *sebi'* (sometimes translated "beauty").

The wilderness and the dry land shall be glad;
   the desert shall rejoice and blossom like the crocus;
it shall blossom abundantly
   and rejoice with joy and singing.
The glory of Lebanon shall be given to it,
   the majesty of Carmel and Sharon.
They shall see the glory of the LORD,
   the majesty of our God. (35:1–2)

And finally, but not exhausting Isaiah's connection between restoration and God's glory,[24] we cite the most famous of all Isaiah's words of salvation:[25]

A voice cries:
"In the wilderness prepare the way of the LORD;
   make straight in the desert a highway for our God.
Every valley shall be lifted up,
   and every mountain and hill be made low;
the uneven ground shall become level,
   and the rough places a plain.
And the glory of the LORD shall be revealed,
   and all flesh shall see it together,
   for the mouth of the LORD has spoken." (40:3–5)

The Future Glory (Isaiah 60)

In the previous section, we cited passages that look at the glory of God that will come on God's people after their refinement through judgment of their sin. Isaiah 60 is just a dramatic example of this same theme.

God's glory is mentioned four times in this chapter (vv. 1, 2, 13, 19). The passage begins with a call for God's people to rise up because "their light" has come. This light is associated with God's glory that has "risen upon" them (v. 1). Darkness, though, will cover all the rest of the earth, but God's glory will be seen in the people of God (v. 2). John Oswalt suggests that the glory of God may be seen in the people because the divine warrior has conquered sin.[26] For that reason, the nations will come to God's people, since they are the source of light that they see out of their darkness. Indeed, the glory of God among the people of God, after their judgment, will mean that they will not need the light of the sun or the moon.

---

[24] See also 41:16; 42:12; 46:13; 58:8.
[25] Because it includes words that are cited at the beginning of Mark's Gospel as introduction to the saving work of Jesus (Mark 1:2–3).
[26] Oswalt, Isaiah, 642.

Furthermore, other passages in this last part of Isaiah suggest that the presence of God's glory will render the people of God glorious (see 62:2). What does it mean that the people will be glorious? After their purification by judgment, they can reflect God's glory. Their glory is not inherent to them but is reflected—as the moon reflects the light of the sun, so the people of God reflect the glory of their Lord. Thanks to the work of God, God's people are "heavy" with significance. God's people will be a "crown of beauty" and a "royal diadem" (62:3). They have substance and reputation ("you shall be called by a new name," 62:2). God's blessing will also bring them substance. Their glory primarily serves a missionary purpose, as the nations will see this glory and be attracted to it.

Casting Down the Glory of the Idols and the Nations

One of Isaiah's major concerns with Israel was their propensity to put their confidence not in the true God but in false gods and other powerful nations. God was their warrior, and Israel should know that God was all they needed for their security. Israel, however, would not trust God but instead turned to political alliances for aid against its enemies. Along with connections to foreign nations came the worship of those nations' false gods. Thus, Isaiah speaks against God's people for depending on the nations and their gods.

Relevant to the subject of this chapter, Isaiah will often pit the glory of the nations and of false gods against the glory of the Lord. Not surprisingly, the prophet announces that the glorious God of Israel destroys the glory of the nations and their idols, as the following passages illustrate:

> Therefore the Lord GOD of hosts
>   will send wasting sickness among his [that is, the king of Assyria's] stout warriors,
> and under his glory a burning will be kindled,
>   like the burning of fire.
> The light of Israel will become a fire,
>   and his Holy One a flame,
> and it will burn and devour
>   his thorns and briers in one day.
> The glory of his forest and of his fruitful land
>   the LORD will destroy, both soul and body,
>   and it will be as when a sick man wastes away.
> The remnant of the trees of his forest will be so few
>   that a child can write them down. (10:16–19)

Not only Assyria's glory, but also Babylon's will be destroyed:

And Babylon, the glory of kingdoms,
the splendor and pomp of the Chaldeans,
will be like Sodom and Gomorrah
when God overthrew them. (13:19)

Similar statements may be found concerning Moab (16:14), Syria (17:3), Judah (17:4), and the twin Phoenician cities of Tyre and Sidon (23:9).

God's people were also prone to put their trust in other gods represented by idols. In Isaiah 42:8, however, God makes it perfectly clear that he alone is glorious and he does not share his glory and its corresponding praise with these false gods:

I am the LORD; that is my name;
my glory I give to no other,
nor my praise to carved idols.

Conclusion

Isaiah was, in the first place, a prophet of judgment. Israel had put its confidence in other nations and in false gods. But these nations and gods had no glory; only God has glory. God will destroy the nations' and gods' pretensions to glory and will assert his own. Isaiah envisions salvation beyond the judgment. The refined remnant will emerge from the judgment with a new affirmation of the glory of God.

The Glory of God in Jeremiah and Ezekiel

While Isaiah is a prophet of the eighth-century BC crisis centered in the northern kingdom, Jeremiah and Ezekiel ministered in the seventh and sixth centuries BC with a focus on the southern kingdom of Judah.[27] Whereas Jeremiah prophesied from Judah, Ezekiel spoke from Babylon, where he had been exiled in 597 BC.

Jeremiah

The glory of God is not a major topic in Jeremiah. In an early but undated oracle, Jeremiah makes a point similar to Isaiah's, that God's people rebelled by putting their confidence in false gods rather than in the glory of the true God. He does this by asking a question that drips with sarcasm directed toward God's people: "Has a nation changed its gods, even though they are no gods?" (2:11a). He can hardly believe it when he answers his own

---

[27] For background information on Jeremiah and Ezekiel, consult Tremper Longman and Raymond Dillard, *An Introduction to the Old Testament*, 2nd ed. (Grand Rapids, MI: Zondervan, 2006), 323–28 and 356–62.

question: "But my people have changed their glory for that which does not profit" (v. 11b). Their glory is certainly the glory of God, which they have forfeited due to their worship of empty idols. Also similar to Isaiah, Jeremiah speaks of the downfall of the glory of the nations in which Judah put their trust. Unlike in Isaiah, however, this downfall happens in a single context, namely, that of Moab when it addresses the inhabitants of one of its prominent cities (Dibon) with the command, "Come down from your glory, and sit on the parched ground" (Jer. 48:18).

The only other passage where Jeremiah uses the term *glory* in reference to God is in a short oracle in 13:15–17:[28]

> Hear and give ear; be not proud,
>   for the LORD has spoken.
> Give glory to the LORD your God
>   before he brings darkness,
>   before your feet stumble on the twilight mountains,
> and while you look for light
>   he turns it into gloom
>   and makes it deep darkness.
> But if you will not listen,
>   my soul will weep in secret for your pride;
> my eyes will weep bitterly and run down with tears,
>   because the LORD's flock has been taken captive.

Here Jeremiah calls on God's people to repent by giving glory to God. However, there is a timeframe for this repentance; if they do not do so soon, God will bring darkness. The language of light connected with the glory of God, and darkness with judgment, is reminiscent of Isaiah 60.

Ezekiel

While Jeremiah speaks sparingly of God's glory, Ezekiel says much about it. Rather than an exhaustive survey of all the occurrences of God's glory in the book, we will look at three particularly significant moments of the appearance of the glory of God. These three moments are at strategic places within the book. Ezekiel 1 shows the initial encounter between Ezekiel and the glory of God. Ezekiel 9 through 11 describes the time when God's glory abandons the temple, while chapters 40 through 43 speak of the future day when God's glory will again fill the temple.[29]

---

[28] For a fuller treatment of this passage, see Tremper Longman, *Jeremiah/Lamentations* (Peabody, MA: Hendrickson, 2008), 112–13.

[29] See Ian Duguid, *Ezekiel*, NIV Application Commentary (Grand Rapids, MI: Zondervan, 1999), 47.

Ezekiel's Commission (Ezekiel 1). Few biblical texts are as dramatic as the introduction to Ezekiel's prophetic call. Ian Duguid helpfully contrasts Ezekiel's commission with that of Isaiah's (Isaiah 6).[30] Both prophets gaze into the very throne room of God. Isaiah's call is magnificent, but it does not have the "movement" of Ezekiel's. As described in Ezekiel 1, the movement is so fast that it is hard to keep pace with it, and some of the details of the narrative are hard to envision with precision.

The introduction to Ezekiel's commission is in chapter 1, while chapters 2 and 3 record the call itself. Ezekiel begins by saying that he saw "a stormy wind" come "out of the north, and a great cloud, with brightness around it, and fire flashing forth continually, and in the midst of the fire, as it were gleaming metal" (1:4). Though the word *glory* is not used until the very end of the chapter, the description here anticipates the connection. Our study going back to the book of Exodus indicates that the bright cloud with fire is often a sign of the glory of God. But before Ezekiel turns attention to the appearance of God, he gives a lengthy description of the chariot that God rides, powered by four cherubim. The description of the chariot connects the appearance of God here with the divine warrior theme and anticipates the judgment to come.[31] The cherubim are mighty angelic beings, those responsible for guarding God's holiness. Their four faces represent the apex of wild animals (lion), domesticated animals (ox), birds (eagle), and the most dignified of all creatures (human).[32] Above the cherubim and the wheels of the chariot is an "expanse" (1:22) on which is the divine throne on which is seated "a likeness with a human appearance" (v. 26). The chapter concludes, "Such was the appearance of the likeness of the glory of the LORD" (v. 28). Ezekiel then responds appropriately by falling on his face in worship.

The next two chapters narrate his prophetic call. God blessed Ezekiel as he did Isaiah with a wonderful vision of his glory, and in pagan Babylon, at that, far away from the temple. Such a gracious vision surely bolstered Ezekiel before he began his difficult ministry of proclaiming to the people of Judah.

The Departure of the Glory of God (Ezekiel 8–11). As Jeremiah (in chapter 7) states, the people were presumptuous in their relationship with God because they thought he would never let his temple be destroyed. In their minds, God lived in Jerusalem, so they could not imagine that city falling. Thus, they felt they could live with impunity, sinning and worshiping other gods. Jeremiah reminded them what Solomon had stated in his temple

---

[30] Duguid, *Ezekiel*, 56–58.

[31] For an exposition of the divine warrior theme, see Longman and Reid, *God Is a Warrior.*

[32] It is interesting to observe that hybrids or mixtures are normally considered "unclean" and monstrous (Dan. 7:1–9) but here are considered of the utmost holiness.

dedication service (1 Kings 8:27), that God did not really live in his temple. Jeremiah also reminded them of previous times when God in his judgment had destroyed the place where he was thought to dwell on earth (Jer. 7:12, for instance, where he cites the destruction of the tabernacle at Shiloh at the time of Eli).

Ezekiel addresses this presumption through a prophetic vision that describes the departure of the "glory of the LORD" from the temple. This divine abandonment of the temple thus becomes the preparation for its destruction by the Babylonians who are led by none other than the Lord himself. The extraordinary vision of Ezekiel 8–11 tells of God's departure from the temple.[33]

The vision begins in chapter 8 when a "form that had the appearance of a man" (v. 2) came and grabbed Ezekiel and took him to Jerusalem and specifically to the "entrance of the gateway of the inner court that faces north" (v. 3). Here he came into the presence of the "glory of God," which he connects with what he saw earlier in the Kebar Valley (chap. 1).

God then took him on a tour of the temple. He visited four parts of the temple and witnessed the horrible goings-on there. First, in the entrance, north of the altar gate was an "image of jealousy." The exact identification of this image is left unspecified (perhaps it is Asherah), but the jealousy it provokes is God's. After all, the temple should be dedicated completely to the worship of Yahweh, yet here was an idol. The effect of this and the following abominations will be to "drive me [God] far away from my sanctuary" (v. 6). After this, God brought Ezekiel to the "entrance of the court" (v. 7). Here there was a hole that led to a den where there were vile engravings of unclean animals and idols. Seventy elders of Israel were offering incense to these abominations (v. 11). Yahweh then took Ezekiel to a third location, "the entrance of the north gate of the house of the LORD" (v. 14). Here they encountered women who were weeping for Tammuz, an ancient Mesopotamian deity. Finally, they went to the "entrance of the temple of the LORD, between the porch and the altar" (v. 16). Here they found twenty-five men who were worshiping the sun. For these reasons, Yahweh told Ezekiel that he will judge the city. Before judgment, though, comes divine abandonment. The next three chapters narrate Yahweh's withdrawal from the city.

In chapters 9 through 11, we read of God's response to Judah's sacrilegious behavior. He will severely punish the city of Jerusalem. But before the

---

[33] That these chapters are a unified vision is clear from the fact that Ezek. 8:1–3 speaks of Ezekiel's being taken in the vision to Jerusalem, and 11:24–25 describes his return by the Spirit to Babylon.

judgment comes, God himself will abandon his temple. In these chapters, God's glory is treated in an anthropomorphic fashion so that the glory stands and walks. This way of talking about God's glory gives Ezekiel's message a strong measure of vividness as well as concreteness.

The movement begins in 9:3 where we learn that "the glory of the God of Israel had gone up from the cherub on which it rested to the threshold of the house." The cherub is a reference to the fact that two cherub figures were placed above the ark of the covenant with their heads faced down so as not to be consumed by God's glory above them. Thus, we learn that God had arisen from his throne and moved to the threshold of the temple. At this time, he also commissioned the devastation of the city.

Chapter 10 notes that the cherub-driven chariot that Ezekiel saw in chapter 1 is waiting for God on the south side of the house. As the glory of God moves out into the courtyard of the temple, the temple and the courtyard are filled with the cloud that represents his glorious presence. By the end of this chapter God's glory has mounted the chariot: "the glory of the LORD went out from the threshold of the house, and stood over the cherubim" (v. 18). At the end of the vision, God's glory mounted on the chariot was last seen hovering over the "mountain that is on the east side of the city"[34] (11:23). God is heading east toward the land of Babylonia. The temple is now abandoned, ripe for its destruction.

The Eschatological Temple (Ezekiel 40–43). Like most prophets, Ezekiel's message does not end with judgment, but it looks ahead to the restoration that comes after. Chapters 40 through 43 are a case in point. The judgment that God brought on Judah would culminate with the destruction of the temple by the Babylonians in 586/7 BC. However, Ezekiel's prophetic imagination extended beyond that time to a future time when there would be another temple. In chapters 40 through 42 Ezekiel is given a tour of this future temple, the description of which climaxes when it is filled with God's glory:

> Then he led me to the gate, the gate facing east. And behold, the glory of the God of Israel was coming from the east. And the sound of his coming was like the sound of many waters, and the earth shone with his glory. And the vision I saw was just like the vision that I had seen when he came to destroy the city, and just like the vision that I had seen by the Chebar canal. And I fell on my face. As the glory of the LORD entered the temple by the gate facing east, the Spirit lifted me up and brought me into the inner court; and behold, the glory of the LORD filled the temple. (43:1–5)

---

[34] Presumably this is the Mount of Olives.

Ezekiel 9 through 11 pictures the glory of God leaving the temple to the east, and this passage speaks of the glory returning from the east. The glory of God here is also connected to the vision in Ezekiel 1 at the Chebar canal.

The glory of God in this instance comes quickly as opposed to its slow departure in Ezekiel 9 through 11. God's glory here, though, while filling the temple is also said to make the whole earth shine (43:2). Ezekiel's response is the appropriate one, as we have seen—worship.[35]

The Glory of God in the Minor Prophets

Only four Minor Prophets speak of the glory (*kabod*) of God: Hosea, Habakkuk, Haggai, and Zechariah. Of these, Hosea makes the most extensive use of the term as he condemns the people for glorifying false gods rather than the true God. Similarly to Isaiah, Hosea announces the destruction and shaming of the glory that Israel attributed to their false gods. Illustrative is Hosea 10:5–6, which speaks of the departed glory of the calf idol at Bethel:[36]

> The inhabitants of Samaria tremble
>   for the calf of Beth-aven.
> Its people mourn for it, and so do its idolatrous priests—
>   those who rejoiced over it and over its glory—
>   for it has departed from them.
> The thing itself shall be carried to Assyria
>   as tribute to the great king.
> Ephraim shall be put to shame,
>   and Israel shall be ashamed of his idol.

Habakkuk was a prophet who spoke into the chaos that preceded and included the fall of Jerusalem at the beginning of the sixth century BC. He was disturbed by the evil in Judah, only to hear that they would be destroyed by an equally evil Babylonia. However, God would ultimately judge the Babylonians and deliver a series of woes directed toward those who built themselves up through violence. In the midst of these woes, Habakkuk expressed the future day when people all around the world will learn about God's glory:

> For the earth will be filled
>   with the knowledge of the glory of the LORD
>   as the waters cover the sea. (Hab. 2:14)

---

[35] The manner in which this eschatological vision is fulfilled is highly debated but irrelevant to this study. For more, see Duguid, *Ezekiel*, 464–97.

[36] Here it is derisively called Beth-aven ("house of iniquity").

However, the wicked will experience only God's judgment. They will not revel in God's glory but rather "utter shame will come upon your glory" (2:16). Finally, in Habakkuk's response to God's answer concerning the prophet's question about justice, he prays a prayer that includes a dramatic depiction of God's power and might, introduced by the phrase "His splendor [*hod*] covered the heavens, and the earth was full of his praise" (3:3).

Haggai and Zechariah were prophets of the early postexilic period. God called them to instruct those who returned to Jerusalem after the exile to complete the rebuilding of the temple. In these historical circumstances, it is not surprising that Haggai spoke of glory in connection with the temple. He challenged those who were old enough to remember the glory of the first temple not to be discouraged as they see the new, presumably less ornate, second temple (Hag. 2:3). Zechariah too spoke of God's glory in a way that gave hope to the returnees who may well have been discouraged at the difficult task of rebuilding they faced. In one of his night visions, Zechariah saw a "man with a measuring line in his hand" (2:1). He was taking measurements of the city, presumably to rebuild it. The vision then gives the hopeful message that God himself "will be to her a wall of fire all around . . . and I will be the glory in her midst" (v. 5).

The Glory of God in Apocalyptic Literature (Daniel)

Apocalyptic literature is similar but not identical to prophetic literature. In prophetic literature God speaks to prophets who then proclaim God's message to the people in order to elicit repentance and the avoidance of judgment. In an apocalyptic book, God never speaks to the seer. He communicates through visions, which are then interpreted by an angel.[37] The seer is not sent to the people, and the message is not intended to elicit repentance. The message is typically judgment on the evil oppressors of God's people, and its effect on God's people is comfort in the midst of oppression.

Daniel is the only undisputed example of apocalyptic in the Old Testament. The theological use of glory occurs only one time, but at an extremely significant moment in the book. Daniel 7 begins with a vision of four beasts arising from the sea, each representing an evil human kingdom. The second part of the vision occurs in a courtroom, where the Ancient of Days, clearly God, is about to pronounce judgment. Into his presence arrives one "like a son of man." In the Old Testament, the "son of man"

---

[37] In some extrabiblical apocalyptic literature like Enoch, the seer goes on an otherworldly journey.

always indicates a human being. But this is one "like a son of man." He is riding the cloud, which in the ancient Near East is the prerogative of God. The New Testament takes notice of this passage and quotes it often (Matt. 24:30; Mark 13:26; 14:62; Luke 21:27; Rev. 1:13) in reference to Jesus Christ. It is this "one like a son of man" to whom is given dominion, and glory and a kingdom (7:13–14).

Summary: The Glory of God in the Old Testament

God's glory is the subject of all the major sections of the Old Testament: Pentateuch, Historical Books, Poetical Books, Prophets, and Apocalyptic.[38] Our approach up to now has been an exegetical survey of many of the passages that speak explicitly about God's glory. We conclude by summarizing many of the most important aspects of the concept of the glory of God.

First, the nontheological use of the vocabulary of glory gives us a helpful background to its theological use. The word *kabod*, for instance, means "weight" and in a metaphorical sense refers to someone who is "of substance," or "wealthy." The word can also be used less concretely in terms of reputation. A person with *kabod* is a person of substance in terms of character and accomplishments, not necessarily because of material wealth. The passages that we surveyed with reference to God's glory thus point to God as a person of great and weighty reputation.

Second, God's weighty presence is often accompanied by fire and smoke or a cloud that illuminates at night. On the one hand, the smoke and cloud obscure, reminding people that direct exposure to the presence of God is overwhelming. Fire, on the other hand, is both beneficial and destructive. Fire warms but also burns. Fire attracts our attention (cf. Moses at the burning bush), but accompanied by smoke does not allow one's gaze to penetrate behind it. Fire is dangerous and powerful.[39] One important connection between fire and the glory of God is summarized in our next point.

Third, God's glory is manifested in judgment. It is impossible for sinners to be fully exposed to God's glorious presence and live. God's judgment

---

[38] Brief mention should be made concerning the ancient Near Eastern background of the "glory of God." From Sumerian times in the third millennium BC and into Babylonian and Assyrian periods, Mesopotamians wrote concerning the luminous aura that surrounded their gods and adhered to people and things that were associated with them. The vocabulary of glory in Akkadian is represented most clearly by the term *melammu*. Most recently, S. Z. Aster, "The Phenomenon of Divine and Human Radiance in the Hebrew Bible and in Northwest Semitic and Mesopotamian Literature: A Philological and Comparative Study," PhD dissertation, The University of Pennsylvania (2006).

[39] Similarly, the "glory of God is unapproachable and dangerous and may not be seen by people or even Moses," so J. Gordon McConville, "God's 'Name' and God's 'Glory,'" *TynBul* 30 (1979): 156.

often takes the form of burning, as in Leviticus 10:2 with the execution of Nadab and Abihu.

Fourth, glory elicits praise.[40] Indeed, the verb related to the noun *kabod* may be translated "praised." In other words, to "glorify" someone is to attribute weight or substance to him. Indeed, our English word *worship* indicates the ascription of worth to someone. As we have seen, many psalms attribute glory to God in the context of worship.

The fifth point is related to the previous ones, particularly the fourth. God's glory is associated with objects that represent his presence and are also associated with the worship of God. In particular, as we have seen, the tabernacle, temple, and ark are connected with God's glory.

Sixth, the Old Testament acknowledges that sinful human beings attribute glory to other deities, people, things, and even themselves rather than the true God. The prophets in particular point out that these false objects of glory will ultimately be destroyed and become the occasion of shame.

Lastly, it must be admitted that in the final analysis the "glory of God" is not reducible to a simple definition. John Piper is surely correct when he says that though "the term 'glory of God' in the Bible generally refers to the visible splendor or moral beauty of God's manifold perfections, . . . [i]t is an attempt to put into words what cannot be contained in words—what God is like in his unveiled magnificence and excellence."[41]

---

[40] See the excellent study by Allen P. Ross, *Recalling the Hope of Glory: Biblical Worship from the Garden to the New Creation* (Grand Rapids, MI: Kregel, 2006).

[41] John Piper, *Desiring God: Meditations of a Christian Hedonist*, 2nd ed. (Sisters, OR: Multnomah, 1986), 227.

3

. . . .

The Glory of God in the Synoptic Gospels, Acts, and the General Epistles

RICHARD R. MELICK JR.

. . . .

Understanding the glory of God challenges all readers. Its meaning is at once both blatantly obvious and mysteriously vague. The most naive reader of the Bible seems to understand the phrase, yet the most experienced interpreter ponders the depths of its meaning. Myriads of questions arise. What does *glory* mean? What is distinctive about God's glory? How do people relate to God's glory? Why does God's glory seem to have a unique power about it, power to accomplish God's work? What happens when human beings come into contact with God's glory? Can we, as creatures, enhance God's glory?

Answers to these questions come primarily from a survey of the portrayal and use of God's glory in Scripture. Biblical definitions begin with exegesis then move to systematic categorizations. Often glory is defined by synonyms, many of which are as vague as the original term. Language requires synonymous comparisons, but accuracy also demands functional considerations. Thus it is imperative to see what glory "does" in order to understand its meaning. This chapter surveys the occurrences of God's glory in the Synoptic Gospels, Acts, and the General Epistles. At times it will also be necessary to consider the Bible's use of *glory* that is separate from direct references to God.

At first glance, the material is overwhelming. There are at least seven different authors who treat God's glory: Matthew, Mark, Luke, the author of Hebrews, Peter, James, and Jude.

For practical purposes, we survey Matthew and Mark together. This represents more a matter of synoptic parallels than biblical theology. Luke is grouped with Acts, although it is a Synoptic Gospel and therefore could be grouped with Matthew and Mark. Current scholarship, however, increasingly recognizes the unique contribution that the author Luke made to the theology of the early church. Hebrews remains alone. First and 2 Peter are considered together, although many contemporary scholars resist this traditional grouping. Finally, James and Jude are also considered separately.

Each of the following sections follows a pattern. First, we will provide a general survey of data regarding the word *glory* and specifically the glory of God. This will reflect all the uses of the Greek root word for *glory*, *dok*. Second, we will examine significant texts that express the author's use of *glory*. Generally, these texts will be less numerous with each new section, since there is no need to repeat the previous discussions of God's glory. Finally, we will summarize findings and suggest meanings from the author's expressions.

This chapter obviously connects with the other chapters in this book. In the New Testament more references to God's glory occur in the Johannine and Pauline materials than outside them. Additionally, the New Testament presentation of glory depends on the Old Testament. The New Testament use of the words for glory, those built on the *dok* root, relies on the Septuagint translation of the Hebrew *kabod* more than the classical use of the Greek words.[1]

The glory of God is the self-revelation of his character (being) and the visible and energetic (power) presence of God. For the New Testament writers, therefore, God's glory reveals the fact that God exists, that he is superior to human life, that he reveals himself through his presence, and that by his presence he is ready to engage in a relationship with those to whom his glory is revealed. God's glory, then, is always dynamic. It produces a response from those who witness it.

---

[1] Most scholars accept this conclusion. E.g., "Its main use in the NT is shaped by the OT; it thus becomes a biblical term rather than a Greek one." *TDNT* 2:180. For more recent works see Gary M. Burge, "Glory," *DJG*, 269; or Richard B. Gaffin Jr., "glory," in *New Dictionary of Biblical Theology*, ed. T. Desmond Alexander and Brian S. Rosner (Downers Grove, IL: InterVarsity, 2000), 509.

Matthew and Mark

Though written to different audiences and in different circumstances, both Matthew and Mark use the *dok* words similarly (with 10 and 4 occurrences, respectively). The infrequent use of the words is striking when compared with the frequency of the words in Luke-Acts.

Scholars generally observe that in the life of Jesus explicit references to the glory of the Lord predominate in the birth narratives and transfiguration. This observation is based, linguistically at least, on Luke. That begs the question as to why Matthew and Mark chose alternate terminology. Without question they were aware of the significance of Jesus' birth and transfiguration, but their narratives of these events do not employ the words for glory.

Both Matthew and Mark demonstrate a similar pattern in their selection of words. The noun *doxa* predominates (it comprises six of the ten occurrences of the *dok* words in Matthew and three of the four occurrences in Mark). The noun expresses an objective idea and may usually be translated by words like "splendor" or "majesty." Thus Matthew speaks of the "glory" of the kingdoms of the world offered to Jesus in his temptation (4:8), and he compares the lily to Solomon's glory (6:29). These two references contain a basic use of the word. They describe the totality of an object's characteristics. Thus, the world's glory is the attractiveness of its character, and Solomon's glory was the attractive character of his kingdom.

The other four references to glory in Matthew refer to the second coming of Jesus. Only one (16:27) speaks directly of the glory of God. Jesus will come in the "glory of his Father." Clearly, this remarkable claim combines two elements: the Glorious One, whom all Jews would understand as God, was actually Jesus' Father, and when Jesus comes again he will come in God's glory. Thus God the Father uniquely shares his character (glory) with Jesus, his Son.

The other references follow and depend on this one. Jesus can refer to his coming as a time accompanied by his own glory (rather than his Father's). Those who see him at the parousia will be able to see him on his own glorious throne (16:27; 19:28; 24:30; 25:31). Again two elements predominate in these statements. First, Jesus' return reveals his glory along with that of his Father. Second, in eternity Jesus has glorious power (a throne). The throne imagery communicates sovereignty and, in particular, the judgment of his enemies.[2]

---

[2] This seems to be alluding to Dan. 7:9 and reflecting Dan. 7:13, which describe the throne and the coming Son of Man.

The noun *doxa* in Mark consistently describes a characteristic of the second coming. The three Markan references parallel Matthew's exactly. When Jesus comes, he shares the glory of the Father (8:38), participating in God's glory and revealing it to earth. Twice Mark speaks of Jesus' own glory at the parousia. One instance is a question from the disciples regarding Jesus' glory (10:37); the other is Jesus' statement of his own "power and glory" (13:26).

The use of the noun in Matthew and Mark suggests several points. First, Matthew uses *glory* to indicate real, rather than perceived, characteristics of the object of glory. Second, Matthew speaks of Jesus' sharing in the Father's glory and, in fact, revealing it when he returns. He, therefore, not only has a unique relationship to God, but, as his Son, participates in God's glory. Yet Jesus described himself as having his own glory and sitting on a glorious throne. Thus both he and the Father share the divine glory.

Third, the glory is eschatological. Most of the references refer to the parousia and/or Jesus' eternal throne of victory. Perhaps Matthew's pattern reveals a latent theology: Jesus has a veiled glory on earth but a visible glory in heaven. Certainly other words describe Jesus' divine nature, but the word *glory* communicates the visible expression of that nature.

Both Matthew and Mark use the verb *glorify* similarly. In Matthew (5:16; 9:8; 15:31) and Mark (2:12) the crowds glorify God. Matthew 5:16 urges Jesus' followers to do good works themselves so that others may glorify God. Matthew 9:8, 15:31, and Mark 2:12 record the people's responses to Jesus' miracles. Genuinely good works are revelatory. They demonstrate God's presence and working in the world. Through them, people acknowledge his superior character and nature. He is the ultimate source of all good.

There are also counterfeit activities that misplace glory. The hypocrites *perform* before crowds to elicit glory (Matt. 6:2). Given the way Matthew carefully uses the words for glory, we are to assume that hypocrites deflect glory from God, whose true nature is seen in genuinely spiritual acts done on earth. In this, they impede the proper flow of appreciation for God's goodness by taking glory for themselves. They also set themselves as candidates for destruction. Their glory is now—in time. This contrasts with Jesus' eternal glory.

In Matthew and Mark the noun *glory* involves a revelation of true character, while the verb involves acknowledging that character. People "glorify" by appreciating the character observed. Thus in seeing genuinely good works, spiritually minded people acknowledge them as God's character revealed in a world of selfishness and evil. In glorifying him, they participate in spreading the glory of God.

In summary, the *dok* words in Matthew and Mark have four character-istics. (1) The noun identifies the true character someone or something possesses. God's glory points people to the true and uniquely attractive character of God. (2) It is possible to participate in God's glory by acknowl-edging it. Praising God for his actions contributes to the spread of his glory. People can hardly increase God's glory. They can, however, participate in spreading the awareness of God's true character and thereby enhance the perception of God and his character. (3) Matthew and Mark clearly present the eschatological reality of God's glory. The world sees the true glory of the Father and the Son only at the end of the age. Here Matthew's presentation reflects the commitments of the Old Testament, that the revelation of God's glory ultimately awaits the coming kingdom. (4) Jesus shares God's glory. Through him people see God's glory on earth. The Son inherited God's glory rather than God's delegating it to him. Jesus has divine glory and is legitimately surrounded by the glory of God. Where he is, God's glory is also.

Other concepts express the glory of God. For example, earlier we observed that Matthew uses *glory/glorify* sparingly compared to some of the other writers. One parallel passage provides insight. Mark 10:37 records the dis-ciples' request, "Grant us to sit, one at your right hand and one at your left, in your glory." Matthew uses alternate terminology in 20:21, stating, ". . . your right hand and . . . your left, in your kingdom." In Matthew, kingdom terminology often expresses the same idea as glory terminology in Mark. The kingdom is future, as Jews expected. The kingdom is God's kingdom, as Jesus taught them to pray (Matt. 6:10). Further, as its king, Jesus brings the kingdom establishing God's visible rule on earth. It is the time antic-ipated throughout all ages, when God will conquer evil and bring peace on earth. Therefore, Matthew's kingdom language is glory language.[3] This greatly enlarges our understanding of the effectiveness of God's glory on earth and throughout the universe.

Luke-Acts

Luke has the preponderance of references to glory (thirteen as a noun; nine as a verb). The Gospel of Luke will be surveyed before Acts.

---

[3] This is also reflected in the spurious ending to the Lord's Prayer (See Matt. 6:13), "Yours is the kingdom and the power and the glory forever. Amen." The early church combined "kingdom," "power," and "glory" as though each intersected the others. The manuscript witnesses to this read-ing suggest a combining of these three into characteristics of the one reign of God.

Luke

As a Synoptic Gospel, Luke has parallels to Matthew and Mark. The similar texts for the most part present the same material. While they may represent separate incidents in Jesus' life, the sayings and the responses to good works are the same. These include, with the noun form of *glory*, the temptation (4:6), Solomon's glory (12:27), and the eschatological aspects of Jesus' coming in his glory (9:26; 21:27; 24:26). When the verb occurs, it, like its occurrences in Matthew and Mark, involves a response of ascribing glory to God (4:15; 5:25, 26; 7:16; 13:13; 18:43; 23:47). One significant difference, however, is that glory is directed to Jesus while he is on earth (4:15). This is rare and in the Synoptics occurs only in Luke.

Another occurrence is unusual. Speaking in a parable to those who clamor for the best seats at dinner (14:10), Jesus tells them to take the lowest seats in hope that they will be elevated. If you are asked to move to better seats, people are "glorifying" you.[4] Jesus teaches that genuine humility displays true godlike character; it will be recognized and appreciated by people on earth. Translating the word *dokimazo* as "glory" recognizes the nature of parables. They teach godlike character. Genuine humility reflects the servant aspect of God's glory.

Two primary texts add to the biblical presentation of God's glory.

The Birth Narrative

The birth narrative has three occurrences of glory in quick succession (Luke 2:9, 14, 32). They stand in striking contrast to Matthew, who tells the same story without using the word *glory*.

The familiar story demonstrates the reactions and interactions of people who observe God's glory. God reveals his glory to the most unlikely of people. Indeed, shepherds saw and heard angels, and Jesus' earthly family accepted the lofty praise the shepherds brought in response to God's message.

Luke 2:9 presents the first use of *glory*. The "angel of the Lord" parallels "the glory of the Lord" structurally.[5] In this unique instance, an angel brought

---

[4] For obvious reasons, this is usually translated by something like "honor you." That preserves the almost consistent translation of *glory* to refer only to God or Jesus. The unusual nature of this text prompted some to retranslate from the Aramaic or later Syriac versions in attempts to understand something other than the Greek word *glory (doxa)*. "Glory" no doubt reflects the breadth with which Luke can use the word. See I. Howard Marshall, *The Gospel of Luke: A Commentary on the Greek Text*, NIGTC, 582.

[5] Both are simple genitives of description, syntactically parallel.

the glory.[6] Significantly, however, the glory of the Lord surrounded him and the other angels. Most artists depict the glory of the Lord as light since the Greek word for "shone around" suggests illumination.[7] The shepherds could obviously see and hear the angels speak, but the glory contributed tangibly to the impact of the scene and the importance of the message.

Furthermore, the shepherds were terrified. Fear is a common reaction to God's glory (see 1:12). The sudden appearance of glory is strikingly uncommon and unnatural. Shepherds expected various kinds of dangers in nature, from animals and humans. Yet none of these experiences prepares them to see and feel God's glory. God's glory should bring comfort, not fear, to those who acknowledge him, and thus the angel's first words are "fear not" (2:10).

At this stage, an important observation is in order. God's glory is more than his character. It extends beyond God himself into an environment of godlike presence.[8] Understanding this, the passages surveyed thus far that speak to the eschatological nature of God's glory make better sense. When Jesus returns in future glory, he brings more than the "character" (personality) that judges and shows mercy. He brings with him an aura, an environmental presence that no one can escape. Along with his vindicating actions, the power of his might and the fear of his presence cause his enemies to turn in flight. Alternatively, the righteous, who eagerly anticipate his glory, connect with him and the glorious environment in a positive and peaceful way. This text reveals the visible and existential power of God's glory not observed elsewhere in the Synoptics.

The second use of *glory* in the birth narrative (Luke 2:14) explicitly states the theme of this book: "glory to God." Like most doxologies, the cryptic language needs elucidation. The noun *glory* implies a statement and thus requires a verb to complete its thought. Following normal Greek patterns, we should supply either an indicative or an optative form of "to be." The statement literally reads either "there is glory to God in the highest" (indicative) or "let there be glory to God in the highest" (optative). While either will

---

[6] He is, of course, an "angel of the Lord," a technical title. Most believe he was the angel Gabriel, consistently the Lord's messenger in the birth narrative. His title reveals both his stature and the trust God placed in him. Nevertheless, significantly, an intermediary brings God's glory to earth.

[7] The word is *perilampein*, "to shine around." This occurs only one other time in the NT, in Acts 26:13, when Paul explained the light that surrounded him on the Damascus road.

[8] Glory as God's empirical presence goes beyond explanation. *Environment* is too weak a term and too easily misunderstood. On the other hand, this Scripture reveals a real presence of God's glory even when God is absent (he has not focused his visible presence here as he did at other places and times in history). Thus, with some misgivings, I have chosen the word "environment" to contrast with a purely spiritual or ideological presence.

fit grammatically, this context calls for the indicative. The angels proclaim "what is" because of the incarnation, not what can be.

The angels' message contains two significant contrasts. First, it contrasts "glory," which inspires fear, and "peace" (*"glory* to God in the highest, and on earth *peace* . . . "). The two belong together, as the angel already demonstrated in 2:10 by calming the fears of those who witnessed God's glory empirically. Fear turned to peace once they realized the significance of the angels' visit: peace, joy, a Savior (2:10–11).

Second, the angels contrast "in the highest" with "on earth" ("glory to God *in the highest* and *on earth* peace. . . . "). Both the syntax and the semantics require this contrast. The phrase "in the highest" can refer to either the location of God, heaven, or the position of God, the highest degree. However, the contrast with earth naturally shows location, "heaven and earth."[9] Thus we should understand this as an angelic description of what is happening "in heaven" and simultaneously "on earth" because of the incarnation.

Scripture seldom provides a glimpse of heaven. Revelation gives the most explicit views, but even the pictures there come veiled through apocalyptic imagery. Jesus sometimes spoke about heaven, such as the occupants of heaven rejoicing over the salvation of each sinner (Luke 15:10), and heaven being a place of genuine order and happiness because God's will is done perfectly there (Matt. 6:10). Here the angels reveal that "in the highest" there is "glory to God." "The heavenly visitors indicate that heaven is impressed by what God has achieved."[10] Heaven's long-awaited moment of triumph has begun. The fullness of time has come (Gal. 4:4). In the highest they are congratulating God for the incarnation. The citizens of heaven anticipate the final victory, realizing it has begun in the incarnation.[11]

At the same time, there is peace on earth. Peace suggests the fullness of the Hebrew *shalom,* a general term implying comprehensive well-being. Because of Jesus' birth, people are to have tranquility, an inner sense of rightness that comes partly by looking within to the changes brought by the Messiah, and partly by looking ahead to the fullness of peace because of Jesus' incarnation.

Who are those to receive God's peace? There are multiple interpretations. Generally they fall into two groupings. First, the traditional interpretation

---

9 "These terms are often contrasted in the NT and have OT roots (Matt. 6:10, 19; 16:19; 18:18; 23:9; Heb. 8:1–5; Hermann Sasse, *Theological Dictionary of the New Testament* 1:679; Helmut Traub, ibid., 5:513, nn. 118–19)." Darrell L. Bock, *Luke, Volume 1: 1:1–9:50,* BECNT (Grand Rapids, MI: Baker, 1994), 220.

10 John Nolland, *Luke 1:1–9:20,* vol. 35A, WBC (Dallas, TX: Word, 1989), 108.

11 It should be noted that at the triumphal entry the people exclaim, "Glory in the highest" (Luke 19:38), which is also coupled with peace and the rule of the Lord.

as found in the Received Text translations says "good will to men." Second, most contemporary scholars follow the interpretation that the peace is reserved for those who are objects of God's pleasure, translated something like "to men of [God's] good will." The second fits the general biblical use and this context better. It suggests that a particular chosen group receives peace.[12]

The angels' message reflects God's plan of redemption. The long-awaited deliverance from evil has come. While the New Testament in particular reveals that the deliverance occurs in two stages, a first and a second coming, the incarnation signals the beginning of the event with its later complete fulfillment.[13] This unusual revelation of glory, and the congratulatory response in heaven, focuses on God's plan of salvation. It is a salvation in the fullest sense, including the natural world,[14] the human world, and the supernatural world.[15] In this text, God's glory has a unique revelation in and relationship to redemption.

The third birth narrative text is Luke 2:32. Simeon, blessing God for the incarnation, states that Jesus is the "glory to your people Israel." Again the syntax is ambiguous. Here "glory" may be in apposition to "light," making the text read "light, unto the revelation to the Gentiles, and glory to your people Israel."[16] It may also be that "glory" is in apposition to "revelation,"

---

[12] This is much discussed. Two brief articles that put the issues into perspective are: Albert M. Wolters, "Anthropoi Eudokias (Luke 2:14) and 'Nšy Rswn (4Q416)," *JBL* 113 (Summer 1994): 291–92, who advocates "men on whom favor rests"; and Ross S. Kilpatrick, "The Greek Syntax of Luke 2:14," *NTS* 34 (July 1988): 472–75, who seems to conclude in favor of "good will to men." These, along with the exegetical commentaries, provide ample data for the discussion. If this is a universal promise of peace, it is not a promise of universal salvation. Rather, it implies that the eschatological order taught by Scripture will be fulfilled because of the incarnation. This order includes the vindication of the righteous and the judgment of the wicked, both universal in establishing an order of peace.

[13] The "two stages" found in OT texts lack the clarity of development found in the NT. Most devout Jews in the first century, like the disciples, seemed to expect one climactic event to usher in the kingdom (so Acts 1:6).

[14] Evidenced in such texts as Rom. 8:18–22 and Col. 1:15–20.

[15] The scope of God's salvation is given in multiple places in Scripture but is celebrated poetically in Col. 1:15–20, which includes "all things in heaven and on earth."

[16] Stein, representing probably most scholars, says this "is better due to the parallels in Isa. 60:1, 19; 58:8 so that our text should be translated 'light for revelation to the Gentiles and glory to your people Israel.' Thus the salvation Jesus brings is light (to give revelation) to the Gentiles and glory to Israel. (The Jews already had the divine revelation but awaited the manifestation of the glory God had promised.) This verse goes a step further than the angelic song found in Luke 2:14 and is the clearest indication so far of the universal dimension of Jesus' redemptive work." Robert H. Stein, *Luke*, NAC 24:116. See also Bock, *Luke, Volume 1: 1:1–9:50*, 257, and Nolland, *Luke 1:1–9:20*, 120, who says "'Glory for . . . Israel,' but 'light for revelation to the Gentiles' recognizes that the Gentiles come to the light from pagan darkness while Israel is already God's people and by God's gracious commitment destined for glory.'"

making the statement read "light, unto revelation to Gentiles and glory to your people Israel." The parallel to Isaiah 60:1–3, where light and glory are combined, speaks to the twofold aspects of salvation: light to Gentiles, glory to Israel. The former interpretation is correct.

Consistent with the angels' message, Simeon recognizes the uniqueness of the incarnation. Jesus is at once a revelation to the entire world and the epitome of Israel's hopes for salvation. Since all salvation is through the Jewish Messiah, in the incarnation Israel's glory reaches its zenith. Jesus, then, is what Israel is about. In him, her hopes and dreams come to fulfillment.

The Transfiguration

The second major passage in Luke is the transfiguration of Jesus. Luke alone uses the word *glory* in describing the event, though the other Synoptics surely intend for the reader to grasp what Luke makes explicit. The word *glory* appears twice in this narrative, in 9:31 and 32. The scene challenges the reader for many reasons, not the least of which is the appearance of glory. Here the disciples see Moses and Elijah "in glory," and they subsequently witness Jesus' glory along with the two Old Testament saints.

The first use of *glory* refers to the two Old Testament witnesses, Moses and Elijah.[17] Significantly, they appear "in glory." This is the first use of *glory* associated with human characters, other than warnings about those who assume false glory (Matt. 6:2). Yet, clearly, they are no longer alive in the body, both having died centuries earlier. Thus, their glory is derived from their situation after death. Visible glory evidences their relationship with God.[18] These two stand as visible proof of the afterlife and of the blessings God's faithful inherit in it. Furthermore, Luke's writings reveal that all persons who come from heaven have glory.[19] These two Old Testament greats join the angels in that regard (Luke 2:14).

The second use of *glory* refers to Jesus' glory (9:32). This glory may have been the same, although in separating the two Luke seems to be making a distinction. First, Luke singles out the glory of the two men (v. 31) then

---

[17] The purpose of the appearance of Moses and Elijah is much discussed in the literature. Most agree that they appear because they represent the lawgiver and the greatest preaching (but not writing) prophet. Some disagree over the specifics. The resolution of this problem is not essential to the purpose of this chapter, a study of glory.

[18] Stein notes, "By this addition Luke emphasized that Moses and Elijah brought *with* them the glorious splendor that came from their presence with God," *Luke*, 284.

[19] "These figures appear in glory because they appear from heaven. All the figures of the heavenly court have glory (cf. v. 26)." Nolland, *Luke 1:1–9:20*, 499.

refers to Jesus' own glory and the two men with him.[20] Jesus has "his glory"; they are "in glory."

What was "his glory" that they saw? Some point to the preexistent glory of Jesus, the visible aspects having been somehow covered in, and perhaps due to, his incarnation.[21] Most refer it to Jesus' glory of the parousia.[22] Yet Jesus had neither died nor been glorified at this time. The text suggests nothing of a future glory. It is thus necessary to understand that this is a present glory to be revealed in full at the parousia but able to be revealed at the present because it is a present reality.[23] Jesus' divine nature shone through the limitations voluntarily imposed in the incarnation. The three disciples actually saw who Jesus *is*, not only who he *was* or *will be*. The transfiguration was "a revelation of the glory which Jesus possessed continually but not openly."[24]

Before leaving this text, it is important to note that the parties at the transfiguration discussed Jesus' exodus. Often interpreted as Jesus' death, the Greek word is *exodus*, which calls Israel's exodus to mind. The passage is often discussed in terms of (1) whether Jesus is compared to Moses here, and (2) whether the exodus is his death or resurrection/glorification.[25] Regardless of the details, since Jesus' mission was to redeem, his exodus points to a salvation motif. Jesus' exodus occurs only through his death or only after his death. Significantly, with this cluster of uses of the word *glory*, the theme again relates to salvation. Luke consistently suggests God's greatest revealed glory is in the salvation of his people.

---

[20] The Greek does not state that Moses and Elijah had an independent glory; only that they appeared "in glory." Furthermore, Luke says "the glory of him" (Jesus' glory) "and the two men." Could this be a way of distinguishing the glory of Jesus from that of Moses and Elijah?

[21] Walter A. Elwell and Philip Wesley Comfort, *Tyndale Bible Dictionary* (Carol Stream, IL: Tyndale, 2001), 1271. The author (unidentified in this article) recalls the preincarnate and future glory of Jesus, but not his present glory.

[22] For example, Marshall, *The Gospel of Luke*, 380. Strangely, Marshall says, "His face and clothes underwent a transformation to *give the impression* of heavenly light and glory, such as might be associated with his heavenly exaltation or his appearance at the parousia" (italics added). This runs counter to the natural meaning of the text that Jesus actually possessed glory, not merely gave that impression.

[23] "For Luke, Jesus' eschatological glory was not just future but could be assumed under unique circumstances during his life on earth." Burge, "Glory" in *DJG*, 269.

[24] Sverre Aalen, *NIDNNT* 2:48.

[25] Though somewhat dated, Kasemann's suggestion that Luke was in a process of changing the "theology of the cross" to a "theology of glory" still stimulates thought. Ernst Kasemann, "Ministry and Community in the New Testament" in *Essays on New Testament Themes* (Philadelphia: Fortress, 1982), 92. One should also note that Luke 24:26 states that after the Christ suffers he will enter his glory. The return to permanent, visible glory should not replace the emphasis on a present but unseen glory.

Summary of Luke

Luke uses the noun *glory* and the verb *glorify* more than the other Synoptics. He uses them in a patterned way, first following the distinction between the noun and the verb. The noun refers to a characteristic of an individual. It challenges the reader to define glory and to think in terms of the revelatory power of God's glory.

Luke also uses *glory* to describe visible and recognizable elements of God's character. His glory is manifest as "light," the illuminating truth that God is and that he is radically different from his creation. He also depicts God's glory as an attribute of Jesus. The world awaits the parousia to see it and thereby understand that Jesus is, in fact, an independent possessor of God's glory. While Luke shares the eschatological emphasis of Jesus' glory at the parousia and in eternity, Luke also reveals that Jesus always possesses uniquely divine glory. The transfiguration reveals his true identity. His glory stands in contrast to those who, after death, find themselves in God's presence and glory (Moses and Elijah). Jesus has come from God and, therefore, has independent glory, yet the glory of God himself.

Finally, for Luke the most common and at the same time ultimate revelation of God's glory occurs in his salvation. The clustering of references to glory at Jesus' birth and parousia attests to that. At the transfiguration, the three glorified individuals speak of Jesus' death and movement back to a place of his glory. Thus, Jesus' glory is revealed in connection with his ultimate reason to be incarnate: he is the Savior.

Acts

Although Acts is one of the longest books of the New Testament, it contains only nine direct references to glory: four of them the noun and five the verb. The noun *glory* refers to a divine attribute only twice: Acts 7:2 and 7:55, both in connection with Stephen's stoning. Once each the noun is used to refer to a misunderstood glory (12:23) and a glorious light (22:11).

Stephen referred to "the God of glory [who] appeared to our father Abraham" (7:2). In this longest speech in Acts, Stephen corrects the typical Jewish approach to their history. Interestingly, the God of glory appeared to Abraham in Mesopotamia. The Jews understood that the unique and visible presence of God awaited the land of Canaan, the tabernacle with its *shekinah*, and the powerful manifestations of glory attendant to Israel's early years as a nation. Stephen preached that the full manifestation of God—the true God and Israel's God—occurred in a foreign land, Haran. "In fact, it was to this landless Abraham that God gave the promises to Israel."[26]

---

[26] John B. Polhill, *Acts*, NAC 26:190.

Luke's use of *glory* here, following Stephen's speech, presents the fullness of character of the God Israel came to appreciate as theirs. While there were times when the "glory departed" and times when the "glory came," the Israelites identified themselves with the God of glory. In their minds, God's was a unique glory associated with a people, a land, and a temple. Stephen reveals that God never has been located in a specific people, land, or temple. His appellation of God unites all the attributes of Israel's God into one simple statement: he is the God of glory. His glory is beyond that of any person or nation.

Later in Luke's account, Stephen faced death by stoning. About to die, he looked up into heaven and saw "the glory of God" and Jesus (7:55). This beatific sight allowed Stephen to understand his own destiny and the presence of the glorious God, and also to pray for mercy for his persecutors. Often people praise Stephen for his Christlike attitude of forgiveness. Notably, after Stephen saw God's glory, he asked God to forgive his persecutors. Without doubt God's glory manifested his power: perhaps it also manifested his grace. As noted in the survey of Luke, God's glory usually accompanies his acts of salvation.

This represents a change from Luke's vocabulary in the Gospel of Luke. There the preponderance of references refers to Jesus' glory, at times also to the glory of God that surrounded significant events in Jesus' life. These two references in Acts, however, have little to do with Jesus' glory directly.[27] Moreover, they also challenge definitions. Little in these contexts enables the reader to define God's glory with precision. It is, again, something everyone knows enough about to recognize when it is present but something very difficult to define.

A third reference to glory in Acts occurs in 22:11, where Paul rehearsed his conversion experience. Among the unique elements of his account, the most notable was that Paul saw the "light's glory" (author's translation). Usually this is understandably translated as "brightness," "splendor," or some other physical characteristic of light. Yet when Paul saw the light, he was impressed with a person and engaged in conversation with him. As in Luke 2:32, light and glory often occur together (see also Isa. 60:1–3). The reference to the light's glory may be a cryptic reference to the specific revelation contained in this light rather than simply the characteristics of its brightness. If Luke intends such a reference, the light was like that at the

---

[27] It should be noted that this is the one reference to Jesus standing at the right hand of God. Since normally he is seated, the change of posture obviously demonstrates the interest Jesus took in Stephen's witness. The primary point here, however, is that at this time Stephen focused on God's glory. Jesus' glory, so often the theme of Luke's Gospel, is not mentioned in Acts.

birth of Jesus—the glory of the Lord. Like the birth narratives, this glory is empirical and "environmental." These are the only two references in the New Testament to a combination of glory and light.

One further occurrence of the noun appears in Acts 12:23, where Luke records Herod's death. Herod died because he accepted worship rather than giving glory to God. The text has overtones of Matthew 6:2 (and perhaps also of Luke 14:10), when Jesus warned about the glory-seeking hypocrites. It assumes that the duty of all persons, whether religious or not, is to recognize their responsibility to give praise to God for the good things he gives them. In this way God jealously guards his glory.

The verb for *glory* occurs five times in Acts. Four of these instances describe people glorifying God or his Word (4:21; 11:18; 13:48 [the Word of the Lord]; 21:20). Consistent with other verbal occurrences, these describe people recognizing and acknowledging God's glorious character and seeking to promote his interests through their praise. At a deeper level, Luke records that others observed them glorifying God. Some were converted (cf. 13:48) and others escaped persecution (4:21). These texts speak to the power of God's glory in that those who acknowledge his glory somehow demonstrate the same power, though to a lesser degree. Once again, God's glory is more than an abstract characteristic. It is a dynamic and powerful reality.

One time Luke states that Peter and John attributed their miracles to God's glorifying his servant Jesus (3:13). After the lame man was healed on the temple steps, Peter deflected the praise the people gave him. He stated that the miracle occurred because in it God chose to glorify Jesus. His response was instinctive, not contrived. The apostles recognized that their miracles pointed to Jesus' power, not their own.

This account reveals two aspects of God's glory. First, miracles are not an end in themselves. They point others to Jesus.[28] Miracles bring the glory of God into the human sphere. God's glory has power to change circumstances, correcting evil and evidencing heaven's completeness. Miracles do not simply point people to God; they bring God to people, allowing them to receive and acknowledge his glory.

Second, God is glorified when Jesus is glorified. Describing God as the "God of Abraham, the God of Isaac, and the God of Jacob, the God of our fathers" demonstrates the continuity between the God the Israelites knew

---

[28] In this Peter agrees with his partner John who later wrote that the miracles were "signs" that lead to an understanding of Jesus so that all who believe in him might have life (John 20:30–31). Specifically, signs point to the fact that Jesus is both Messiah and God's Son (his work and his character). The disciples realized this in their experience as recorded in John 2:11.

through the Old Testament and the God they were to acknowledge because of the incarnation and resurrection. Jesus worked in harmony with the God of their fathers. Even more specifically, God the Father chose to allow his Son, Jesus, and his glory, to be the way to God himself.

While there is a paucity of references to God's glory in Acts, Luke writes from the perspective of God's glory without always using the specific words. God is glorified in the universal nature of the gospel. Every phase of Gentile salvation is a tribute to God's salvation. The gospel of Luke reveals God's glory primarily in his redemption, and Acts continues this theme. The Gentiles acknowledge the one true God. Although the word *glory* occurs only once in developing this particular theme, after Peter retells the conversion of Cornelius (11:18), every Gentile conversion brings glory to God. This is seen specifically when the Jerusalem Christians give glory to God for Gentile repentance. In the larger sense, the entire book of Acts is about the glory of God. It records the spread of the gospel into ever new vistas as God is saving the world through Christ.

Summary of Acts

Compared to the Synoptic Gospels, Acts makes a threefold contribution to understanding the glory of God. First, Stephen is allowed to participate in promoting God's glory. He sees God's glory as he faces martyrdom. The vision comforts him and prompts him to forgive his persecutors. Second, Luke makes clear the continuity between the God of the Old Testament, affirmed by the Jewish community, and Jesus, acknowledged by the Christian community. God the Father and Jesus share glory, a clear confirmation of Jesus' deity. Third, the salvation begun in glory in the birth narratives of Luke continues in the church's spreading the gospel to the nations. Every Gentile conversion is based on and contributes to the glory of God.[29]

Hebrews

Direct references to glory occur eight times in Hebrews. Once glory refers to God (1:3), once to the glorification of Christians (2:10), once to the cherubim (9:5), and five times to Jesus (2:7, 9; 3:3; 5:5; 13:21). Since Hebrews is about the supremacy of the Son, Jesus, the five references to Jesus seem quite natural. Jesus' glory surpasses that of angels (2:7, 9), Moses (3:3), and the priests (5:5).

---

[29] Schreiner states, "God's glory constitutes an important theme in Acts" and outlines the same theme of Gentile salvation. Thomas R. Schreiner, *New Testament Theology: Magnifying God in Christ* (Grand Rapids, MI: Baker Academic, 2008), 143.

The most distinctive texts occur in the prologue (1:3), in the quotation of Psalm 2:7–8 (1:5; 2:5), and in the doxology (13:21). The prologue contains some of the more challenging and developed Christology of the entire New Testament. It appropriately introduces the epistle and its Christological focus.[30]

Hebrews 1:3

The significant expression in Hebrews 1:3 is "the radiance of His glory" (NASB). The word "his" refers to God, who is the subject of this section. It is God's glory that is seen in Christ, who is God's final word of revelation. Glory is again ambiguous, though the writer assumes his readers' understanding. God's glory is clearly revealed in Jesus, the "radiance." The close association of Jesus with God's glory, especially as a revelation of God's nature to us, demands an understanding of "radiance" and its structural parallel in this verse, "exact expression." Furthermore, in this text "glory" parallels "nature."[31]

The word *radiance* does not occur elsewhere in the New Testament and occurs only once in the Septuagint.[32] Because it occurs only once, there are no parallels for translation, and the word is capable of being either active or passive.[33] Those who consider it passive usually translate it as "reflection"; thus Jesus receives God's glory and passes it on.

On the other hand, the word may be active. The majority of the early Greek fathers understood it this way,[34] suggesting that Christ has his own glory. While it is difficult to decide on linguistic and syntactical grounds, the fact that Hebrews favors Christ's having personal glory suggests an active meaning here.[35] This being the case, Jesus has independent glory, which can be expressed correctly as God's glory. He shares the divine attributes,

---

[30] Major questions arise in the literature, particularly concerning the nature of this text (hymn or not), age of the text (pre-Hebrews or not), and its structure. Though interesting, none of these has a bearing on the subject of glory, which is more semantic and syntactical. For a good discussion of these issues, see Paul Ellingworth, *The Epistle to the Hebrews: A Commentary on the Greek Text* (Grand Rapids, MI: Eerdmans, 1993), 98, and William L. Lane, *Hebrews 1–8*, vol. 47a, WBC (Dallas: Word, 1991), 7–8.

[31] The two go together: "He is the radiance of His glory, and the exact expression of His nature" (HCSB). The Greek words are *apaugasma* and *character*, respectively.

[32] Lane, *Hebrews 1–8*, 13.

[33] It contains a *-ma* ending in Greek, indicating the results of an action and is parallel to "exact expression," almost of necessity a passive idea.

[34] For some of the evidence for this see Ellingworth, *The Epistle to the Hebrews*, 98. He surveys the issues but fails to take a position.

[35] As an illustration in teaching, I often use celestial language. The passive would be like the moon, a reflected glory. The active is like the sun, the rays of which are in essence the sun, but they are the sun making its way into our world of perception. The rays, therefore, are distinct from the body of the sun, but of the same material and move dynamically toward the earth.

and he is the one who brings them into the realm of human perception. Therefore, in seeing him, people are confronted with God himself. While they do not see all of God, they do see God.

The structural parallel to radiance is translated "exact expression" (*charakter*). In the Septuagint it is used of leprosy scars (Lev. 13:28). Philo uses it in a spiritual sense to speak of impressions made on the soul by God.[36] Along with its parallel, radiance, this phrase describes "the essential unity and exact resemblance between God and his Son."[37]

Finally, the other two parallel words in the statement illuminate each other. God's glory is further explained as his nature.[38] The word *hypostasis* occurs again in Hebrews 11:1, where it is often translated "confidence" rather than "substance." Both texts should have the same meaning, that of substance. Here the writer makes the strongest possible statement that Jesus shares the divine nature. He is God himself. God's nature (substance) is, in fact, his glory. Everything that makes his nature what it is combines in his glory. On any specific occasion, one aspect or another of his nature may become the dominant and visible attribute and thus become the focus of his glory. Individuals who witness his glory inevitably see only certain aspects of it because his glory is greater than any particular expression of it.

As the writer of Hebrews affirms, everything that God is, the Son is. Everything God's glory is, the glory of the Son is as well. This strong statement affirms a shared glory. Both Jesus and God demonstrate their character, their nature. What is true of one is true of the other.

Hebrews 2:7, 9

The word *glory* occurs twice in these verses, once in a quotation of Psalm 8:4–6. Imbedded in a larger section revealing Jesus' superiority, this text solves a puzzle long hidden in the Old Testament. God created humanity a little lower than the angels, but crowned them with glory and honor. The riddle is how can people be lower than the angels, yet possess a unique glory and honor that subordinates all things to them?[39] People have neither the power nor the honor angels have.

The answer to the puzzle is Jesus. He, too, was created human—a little lower than the angels—yet he was crowned with glory beyond all other created beings. In this, Jesus elevated humanity to a position intended in cre-

---

[36] Ellingworth, *The Epistle to the Hebrews*, 99.
[37] Ibid.
[38] The Greek word is *hypostasis*, a term much debated in the christological controversies of the early centuries.
[39] It is a clear reference to Ps. 110:1, which the early church joined to this psalm. The two were part of an early compilation of OT texts used apologetically and evangelistically to prove Jesus' divinity.

ation but now possible only through redemption. In Jesus, humanity rules over all. The focus on Jesus clarifies how the psalm can be fulfilled.

This text builds on what we have seen so far. Jesus shares the divine glory and reveals God the Father to us. Because of Jesus' human nature, he also enables humanity to share in the glory of God by identifying with Jesus' power and position. Redeemed people do not become divine; neither do they share God's glory as Jesus does. Nevertheless, our relationship to Jesus brings a new understanding and experience of glory.

Hebrews 13:21

The concluding doxology of Hebrews has a familiar ring. Its structure is similar to doxologies both within and outside the New Testament.[40] In the New Testament, most doxologies are Pauline (eight of thirteen) and most of the Pauline doxologies refer to God rather than Jesus. Three times this structure occurs outside the Pauline materials with a reference to God (Jude 25; Rev. 5:13; 7:12). There is only one clear Pauline reference in which a doxology with this structure refers to Christ (2 Tim. 4:18). Second Peter 3:18 and Revelation 1:6 also refer to Christ.

The grammar of the Hebrews passage is unclear. The subject of the sentence is "God" (13:20) and the verb is "equip" (13:21). The subordinate clause introduced by "to him" (*ho* in Greek) is masculine singular and may refer to the subject of the sentence, adding another subordinate idea in praise of God, or it may refer to the most immediate masculine reference, Christ, who is the immediate occasion of praising God.

The context of Hebrews does not clearly decide. In 1:3 Jesus is God's radiance (possessing his own glory), while in 2:7–8 God chose to give Jesus (and humanity) great glory. Thus the question is, does the "natural" grammar of the sentence rule or does the immediate reference rule? Without doubt the primary content of the doxology is about Jesus. It fittingly concludes and summarizes the epistle as a whole.

While difficult to decide, the more natural reading is to take God as the subject of the doxology.[41] Understood this way, the writer expresses his praise to God for how he worked in and through Jesus. This combines the two persons of the Trinity in a functional unity. The glories of Christ, unfathomable in themselves, are an occasion for praising God.

[40] Similar doxologies are addressed both to God (4 Macc. 18:24; Rom. 11:36; 16:27; Gal. 1:5; Eph. 3:21; Phil. 4:20; 1 Tim. 1:17; Jude 25; Rev. 5:13; 7:12) and to Christ (2 Tim. 4:18; 2 Pet. 3:18; Rev. 1:6; *1 Clem.* 20:12); Ellingworth, *The Epistle to the Hebrews*, 731.
[41] On the contrary, see *TDNT*, 2:248.

This interpretation encapsulates the focus of glory in Hebrews. The general biblical pattern is that God the Father plans and ultimately determines the course of history. Jesus, the Son, accomplishes God's plans and thus, in harmony with the Father, participates in directing the course of history.

Doxologies always speak of glory. They are based on recognition of God's nature and character and, in turn, speak of it in the presence of others so as to encourage their understanding and participation in such praise. Here the three typical elements are combined. First, there is the object of praise, God. Second, there is the blessing pronounced, glory. Third, there is the extent of the blessing, forever and ever. The writer expects his readers will understand and agree with his conclusion. Humans see God's splendor in Christ. We see it in his superior person and his surpassing work. Those who see it, in return, express the hope that God's splendor will be seen and appreciated eternally. There is none greater and none more worthy.

The doxology praises God's positive action in sending Christ. Hebrews clearly warns of the dangers of rejecting Christ, but the thrust of Hebrews is the magnificence of Christ and his qualifications as Savior. Thus the glory seen in Hebrews is the glory of God's salvation rather than the punitive glory of God's judgment. Vindicating righteousness is necessary, but providing redemption brings greater praise.

Summary of Hebrews

Like the epistle itself, God's glory in Hebrews intertwines the person and work of his Son. Jesus is God's radiance (1:3), possessing shared but independent splendor. Jesus' person and work surpass that of previous revelations of God's character (e.g., Moses, 3:3), and thus Jesus' glory is greater. Finally, the two combine in a concluding doxology expressing appreciation for the shared work of the Father and the Son and attributing glory to God forever. Once again, the primary focus of glory is redemption.

James

Glory occurs only one time in James (2:1). Its use significantly identifies James as a Christian document, and thus its unique content occasions considerable debate as to the integrity of this text. At issue is whether the phrase "the Lord of glory," referring to Jesus, represents a later interpolation by Christians. Peter Davids surveys the issue well and concludes, "Certainly the phrase reads awkwardly, but this solution [regarding it as a later interpolation] appears extreme."[42] This conclusion seems best, and thus we accept the authenticity of the passage.

For this study, the question is the use of the word *glorious*. Four possibilities exist, of which two are grammatically most likely.[43] The genitive construction may be in apposition to "Lord Jesus Christ," resulting in a description of him as "the Glory." Supporting this, the early Christians probably assumed that Jesus was often equated with the *shekinah* of the Old Testament. Those who accept this view consider James a strongly Jewish document in which this would fit well. Alternatively, the genitive may be adjectival, resulting in a translation like "the glorious Lord Jesus Christ." This is preferred and fits James's grammar well (cf. 1:25).[44]

The text warns about favoritism. Literally, the word used to define the problem means "accepting the face," that is, basing relationships on external matters.[45] It occurs only four times in the New Testament, once in James 2:1 and three times in Paul (Rom. 2:11; Eph. 6:9; Col. 3:25). Each refers to God, whose judging eye penetrates beyond external characteristics.[46] Significantly, because of Jesus, James warns his readers not to give preferential treatment to those with economic and social power. He attributes to Jesus the same judging eye as God the Father.

The passage assumes equity because of the transformation that takes place among those who recognize the glory residing in God and Christ. "If the glory of God has not remained high and removed from his people but has come among them and delivered them from death and sin, there is no room for favoritism toward the rich."[47] Favoritism results in judgment, and judgment comes from the Lord Jesus, whose glory opposes such action.

---

[42] Davids presents the arguments succinctly. Peter H. Davids, *The Epistle of James: A Commentary on the Greek Text*, The New International Greek Text Commentary (Grand Rapids, MI: Eerdmans, 1982), 106.

[43] Ralph Martin provides a good survey of the options. Ralph P. Martin, *James*, WBC (Waco, TX: Word, 1988), 59–60.

[44] Both Davids, *The Epistle of James*, 106–7, and Martin, *James*, 60, opt for this solution. They represent many, if not the majority, of modern scholars in this matter.

[45] The Greek word is *prosopolempsia*.

[46] The most illustrative of the passages are Eph. 6:9 and Col. 4:1, which warn that the God of heaven notices when masters treat slaves based on external matters (the economy of slavery).

[47] Kurt A. Richardson, *James*, vol. 36, New American Commentary (Nashville: Broadman, 1997), 109. Peter Davids comments: "God shows no partiality (Dt. 10:17), so neither should human judges. This theme is repeated in the NT (Gal. 2:6), and the coined expression for favoritism, προσωπολημψία, entered the NT tradition first as a characteristic of God's judgment (Col. 3:25; Eph. 6:9; Rom. 2:11; Acts 10:34; cf. 1 Pet. 1:17) and then (as in the OT) as a mandate for human justice. This meaning naturally continues in church tradition (cf. E. Lohse, *TDNT* 6:779–780; Mayor, 78–79)." *The Epistle of James*, 106.

James makes two contributions to the biblical teaching of glory. First, Jesus is himself glorious. His glory is capable of revealing and judging in the same way as God's glory. Second, those who understand Jesus' glory, by faith, are called to act according to what they have seen. They represent God's glory on earth by the values they hold as well as by their actions.

1 and 2 Peter

Peter uses *glory* proportionately more than the other writers surveyed in this chapter. The word occurs twelve times total, eight times in 1 Peter and four in 2 Peter. There is a clear pattern to the way he uses it, with only a couple of references requiring comment.

1 Peter

In his first epistle, Peter combines the major themes of suffering and Christian pilgrimage. Writing in light of potential persecution, Peter reminds his readers how to suffer as Christians and that those who suffer will receive glory. Similarly, they are not to be surprised at the suffering here on earth. They are pilgrims and strangers, looking for a permanent home.

Not surprisingly, therefore, Peter relates glory to these two themes. He moves almost systematically between Jesus as the great example and his followers as the privileged who, in their identification with him, will share in his glory. Since those who suffer and those who are aliens have no visible glory in the eyes of society, Peter reminds his readers of true glory. It is a greater glory than can be found on earth. Christians share in the glory of Jesus himself.

Several references, therefore, speak of Jesus' life and experience as the proper model for Christian success. Peter writes that the prophets spoke of Jesus' sufferings and the glories (plural) that would follow (1:11). The plural noun indicates the fullness and greatness of the glory ahead. Similarly, the suffering of Jesus was a necessary prerequisite for the experience of glory (1:21). Jesus remains the model for all.

Identifying with Jesus brings both its own suffering and reward. The believers' reward is glory. It is a glory received when Jesus' glory is revealed, at the second coming (1:7; 4:13; 5:1, 4). Both Jesus' glory and that of believers are in this sense eschatological: both will be glorified at the parousia. Yet Jesus' glory is ever present. The second coming only reveals his glory. God gave Jesus glory in the resurrection (1:21). Peter's language implies that the resurrection restored Jesus to a state of glory previously unseen. It was a glory that triumphed over and contrasted with suffering.

Both Jesus and his followers, therefore, bring glory to God by their proper attitudes and actions. Believers encourage the glory of God through the proper exercise of their gifts and opportunities (4:11), and their ultimate destiny is to contribute to God's glory (5:10). These two texts reveal that when Christians live like Christ they enhance God's reputation among those who observe them, thereby spreading and encouraging his glory. It is the human perception of God's glory that believers spread, not the glory itself that is ever present.

Twice in 4:11 glory occurs. First, it is the intended result of the exercise of spiritual gifts in the church (4:10) that "God may be glorified through Jesus Christ." The other occurrence is in the doxology at the end of verse 11.

The church bears the responsibility for glorifying God through spiritual gifts (4:11). The list of gifts resembles the Pauline list of Romans 12. The proper exercise of these gifts comes "by the strength that God supplies" and "through Jesus Christ." The combination of these three—God, Jesus, and the church—cooperates in expressing how God is glorified. Spiritual gifts come to those who are in Christ, and thus the proper exercise of the gifts occurs in connection with Christ. They are the direct product of grace (4:10). The church alone glorifies God in this sense, and it does so because of the redemption in Jesus. The church and Jesus maintain the closest of relationships evidenced in a common mission: to glorify God.

The glory God receives comes from speaking and serving. Representing the entirety of life's activities, these suggest that the primary concern of Christian people is furthering God's reputation. As they speak and serve Christianly, they do so in the name of Christ and bring honor to God.

The section ends with a doxology. The doxology begins with a relative pronoun, "to whom" (NASB),[48] which can refer to either God or Christ. Karen Jobes observes that "most of the sixteen doxologies in the New Testament are offered to God, but some of these also seem ambiguous."[49] Scholars are divided. Those who understand the antecedent is Christ point to (1) the natural proximity of the word order; (2) the parallel in Revelation 1:6 with its identical phrase; and (3) the similarity to *1 Clement* 20:11–12; 50:7.[50] Those who understand the antecedent as God point out the difficulty of glorifying God "through Jesus Christ" and then ascribing glory "to Christ."[51]

---

[48] The Greek is *ho*. The masculine dative pronoun may refer to the masculine "Christ" or "God." As is the case in some of the other doxologies, this causes the ambiguity.

[49] Karen Jobes, *1 Peter*, BECNT (Grand Rapids, MI: Baker Academic, 2005), 283.

[50] Outlined from E. G. Selwyn, *The First Epistle of Peter* (London: MacMillan, 1947), 220.

[51] See, e.g., J. N. D. Kelly, *A Commentary on the Epistles of Peter and of Jude*, Harper New Testament Commentary (New York: Harper and Row, 1969), 181–82.

While difficult to decide, the most likely reading is to take Christ as the antecedent.[52] Peter, then, ascribes to Christ independent glory in a manner typically ascribed to God. He reinforces the earlier statement that God is glorified through Christ, who has independent glory ascribed to him.[53]

2 Peter

Second Peter has four occurrences of glory. One is an adjective ("glorious ones," 2:10); another is in a doxology (3:18). The doxology clearly attributes glory to Jesus Christ. Typical of doxologies, the writer exhorts readers to contribute to Jesus' glory by recognizing its present and future manifestations. In so doing, they will enhance Jesus' reputation on earth and bring him the praise he deserves.

In 1:3, Peter states that Christians are called by "his own glory and goodness" (NIV). Each of the pronouns in this verse is problematic,[54] and the section is introduced without any prior clear references to determine their antecedents. The antecedent of "him" is particularly important in the statement "him who called us by his own glory and goodness." Generally speaking, calling is an activity of God. However, Peter's common references to Christ suggest to many that he describes Christ as the caller. The general pattern of Scripture, that God calls, and the fact that in this paragraph Peter identifies Christ specifically by name in order to clear ambiguity (1:8, 11), suggest that the reference is to God rather than Christ.[55]

Calling occurs "by" God's glory and virtue. The combination of glory and virtue parallels the earlier "divine power" (v. 3) but is hardly completely synonymous. Power represents only one aspect of God's glory, the particular characteristic necessary to develop Peter's thought here. Even so, power and glory share one important quality: they effect change. God's glory is more than a static personal characteristic. It is an energy ever seeking to bring people into conformity to God and, though not explicit in Peter, ever confronting and judging what is contrary to God. Here Peter Christianizes

---

[52] So J. Ramsey Michaels, *1 Peter*, WBC (Nashville, TN: Word, 1988), 253: "These considerations, especially the word order, make Selwyn's view the more plausible." However, Arichea and Nida state: "To whom refers most probably to God and not to Jesus Christ . . . although the word order in Greek favors Jesus Christ rather than God." Daniel C. Arichea and Eugene Albert Nida, *A Translator's Handbook on the First Letter from Peter* (New York: United Bible Societies, 1994), 143.

[53] This is consistent with the doxology of 2 Pet. 3:18, which clearly attributes glory to Christ.

[54] A helpful, concise, and nontechnical description of the options is found in Daniel C. Arichea and Howard Hatton, *A Handbook on the Letter from Jude and the Second Letter from Peter*, UBS Handbook Series: Helps for Translators (New York: United Bible Societies, 1993), 73.

[55] Compare also 1 Pet. 1:1 where God is described as the one who elects.

a common expression that unites these two words (*glory* and *virtue*). Glory is an effective activity of God's nature.[56]

For this study, two significant points occur. First, God's glory has energy, effectively accomplishing his purposes. Thus there is a synergy between God's person and his activity. Second, this synergy is directed at least in part to the redemption of humanity. It is the power by which God calls people to salvation.

The fourth text in which glory occurs is 1:17, in which Peter recalls the glory of Jesus' transfiguration. Apparently some whom Peter addressed questioned the reality of the second coming of Christ. Peter calls their position a "myth," using the very word that they had used to promote their false teaching. The issue involved the "power and coming" of the Lord. These two words in parallel apparently describe the "power expressed in his coming." The first answer to the myth was the reality of what Peter saw at the transfiguration of Jesus.[57] Describing this experience, he used the word *glory* twice.

The first occurrence of *glory* in 1:17 describes Jesus' glory: "He received honor and glory from God the Father." While some have sought to distinguish between the meanings of "honor" and "glory,"[58] they are indistinguishable here and hence emphatic.[59] It is quite likely that Peter relies on the Septuagint of Psalm 8:6, which predicts the glorious reign of the coming Messiah. Like the Synoptic Gospels, Peter understands the transfiguration to be a preface to the parousia rather than to the resurrection. It is an unveiling and prefiguring of Jesus' glory at that time. Those who witnessed it personally—Peter, James, and John—saw Jesus' true and, in some sense, complete character. The voice from the Father clearly affirmed his Son's worthiness (honor) and splendor. Consistent with Luke's account, Peter was allowed to see the reality of Jesus' exalted person—the person who will return in glory.

---

[56] Although Bauckham understands this section to refer to Christ, he handles this text well. He states that this "presumably refers to the incarnate life, ministry and resurrection of Christ as a manifestation of divine power by means of which he called men and women to be Christians." Richard J. Bauckham, *2 Peter, Jude*, WBC (Waco, TX: Word, 1983), 179.

[57] There is considerable discussion as to whether this is a firsthand account or one dependent on the synoptic tradition. Richard Bauckham contends it is independent (ibid., 205ff.). A good counterargument that contends that Peter is based on Matthew is Robert J. Miller, "Is There Independent Attestation for the Transfiguration in 2 Peter?" *NTS* 42 (October 1996): 620–25.

[58] Perhaps "honour—in the voice that spake to Him, glory—in the light which shone around Him." Robert Jamieson, A. R. Fausset et al., *A Commentary, Critical, Explanatory, and Practical on the Old and New Testaments* (Grand Rapids, MI: Eerdmans, 1945), 621.

[59] Bauckham, *2 Peter, Jude*, 218.

The second use of *glory* in 1:17 describes God. God is called "the Majestic Glory." *Majesty* was a common term for God, though not exclusively used of him.[60] Combining *majesty* and *glory* demonstrates Peter's "predilection for grandiose terms."[61] If his vocabulary is grandiose, it is so for a reason. The event now recalled vividly remained in Peter's mind. The combination of descriptors attempts to capture the splendor and brilliance of God himself. Of course, Peter did not see God directly. He saw the majesty given to Jesus (1:16). Clearly, however, Jesus and God share the same character, and seeing Jesus' majesty brought Peter into the realm of God's majestic glory.

Once again the theme of shared glory occurs. Here the rationale is the filial relationship between Jesus and God: "This is my beloved Son." The Son shares and participates in the glory of the Father. Seeing the Son meant seeing the Father. Thus Peter used the term *majesty* of both God and Jesus. He saw "his [Jesus'] majesty" and heard from "the Majestic Glory [God]." He combined the terms *majesty* and *glory*, emphasizing further the amazing character they have. In this account of the transfiguration, God's glory is seen in his Son who shares it. Thus, to see the Son, Jesus, is to see the Father, God.[62]

Summary of 1 and 2 Peter

Peter attributes glory to God in three primary ways. First, he speaks of God directly. He calls God the "Majestic Glory" and indicates that God's glory is the basis of his calling persons to Christ. Thus God's glory is both an attribute and an activity. Peter can speak of glory in conjunction with God's character and his will.

Peter also speaks of Jesus' glory. Jesus brings glory to God in his suffering, death, and resurrection, and in his providing for the exercise of spiritual gifts in the church. Yet, like the other writers, Peter affirms that Jesus possesses an independent glory—the shared glory of God.

Finally, Peter speaks of the church as manifesting and contributing to the glory of God. She does so by living appropriately in the face of persecution

---

[60] "This term, though not used exclusively of God (LXX Jer. 40:9; Dan. 7:27; *1 Esdr.* 1:4; 4:40), was most commonly used of divine grandeur and majesty (Josephus, *Ant.* 1.24; 8.111; *C. Ap.* 2.168; Luke 9:43; Acts 19:27 [of Artemis]; *1 Clem.* 24:5; Ign. *Rom.* inscr. [of God and Christ]; *Diogn.* 10:5; cf. τὸ μεγαλεῖον, *1 Clem.* 49:3), sometimes in the first century of the divine majesty of the Emperor (Spicq, Lexicographie, 544)." Bauckham, *2 Peter, Jude,* 217.

[61] Ibid., 218.

[62] There are many studies of parallels between the transfiguration and Moses, most particularly the visible glory (*shekinah*) and the Mountain (Sinai). Interestingly, Peter does not build on this imagery. Perhaps it was irrelevant to his readers. The point is the glory of Jesus at the second coming and the power that glory brings with it. There was no need to demonstrate the superiority of Jesus over Moses.

and suffering, as Jesus did. She also brings glory to God by the exercise of spiritual gifts that, in the power of Christ, magnify God's grace.

Peter's primary emphasis is glorifying God in an evil world. Jesus became the model and the enabler. Unbelievers, even persecutors, will see God through the way Christians live their calling individually and collectively. Nothing can interfere with this manifestation of God's glory except the failure of the church. No circumstance keeps one from living God's will, and, similarly, nothing can keep the church from glorifying God. Amazingly, God has delegated his reputation to the church, allowing Christians to display his glory to the watching world.

Jude

Three times *glory* occurs in Jude. Once it echoes the use of 2 Peter 2:10, where the immoral ridicule the "glorious ones." Twice it occurs in a benedictory doxology.

The benediction includes a prayer for the believers' well-being and a doxology directed to God. The prayer asks that God "make you stand in the presence of His glory blameless with great joy" (v. 24 NASB). The phrase "His glory" probably speaks of the presence of God himself. Rather than address his person directly, Jude chose to identify him by his remarkable character.

This approach serves a didactic purpose, however. Believers are to stand "blameless" (v. 24). The term *blameless* is found frequently in Scripture, often the focus of a petition. For example, Christians are to be "blameless in holiness" (1 Thess. 3:13) and "holy and blameless" (Col. 1:22; Eph. 1:4). In order to achieve this, they are to present their bodies "holy and acceptable to God" (Rom. 12:1). Thus there is a morality expected of those who see God. The ambition of every believer is to be blameless now, in this life, and forever, in eternity.

When Jude combines the words *glory* and *blameless*, he brings together these ideas. To stand before God, before "his glory," requires that one share blamelessness, one aspect of God's glory. In sharing blamelessness, believers share glory.

The second occurrence of *glory* is in the doxology. Concluding his epistle, Jude pens the hope that God would have glory forever—that the true brilliance of God's character should last. Jude contributed to God's glory in the very expressing of this desire. He recognized God's ultimate and beautiful glory and prayed that it would be eternal. Most human character traits are tainted. They must be either eradicated or transformed by grace. Thus a prayer for permanent human glory is quite unexpected and out of character. Recognizing God's glory, however, acknowledges the splendor of his perfection. In such a doxology, the petitioner also hopes to contribute to enhancing God's glory. This he does by speaking of God's character and furthering his good reputation.

Conclusions

These portions of the New Testament display a remarkable unity in describing God's glory, even though the various writers speak of it in ways that serve their individual purposes. Some writers emphasize one aspect while others emphasize another. Having surveyed such diverse materials, we offer some general conclusions.

1) These portions of the New Testament do not define God's glory. The closest any writer comes to a definition is when the writer of Hebrews associates glory with "radiance" and "nature." But these are attributes of Christ as he relates to God's glory. A proper definition, therefore, must come from the manifestations of glory and its functions in the realm of human perception.

2) Glory is manifested. It is, then, revealed rather than achieved. God chooses to reveal his glory and, in so doing, reveals himself. His glory is the evidencing of his nature to his creation. As noted above, the particular characteristics manifested on any occasion are suited to the purposes of the writer and thus are never complete. The writers use the term *glory* in a comprehensible, though not comprehensive, way.

3) Glory is attributed to God. Normally using the verb rather than the noun, people may attribute glory to God. The doxologies fall into this category, although other passages also are included. Generally speaking, attributing glory to God is an acknowledgment that his nature surpasses expectations and that he should be appreciated eternally. In speaking of God's glory people contribute to the spreading of God's good reputation in the world. Humans cannot increase his glory but may increase awareness of and sensitivity to it.

4) God's glory is uniquely shared with Christ. God and Christ possess the divine glory. They share Deity's perfect nature, yet each has individual glory as well. The texts speak of God's glory and Christ's glory. The two work in perfect harmony. Christ glorifies God by his words and actions, and God is pleased to have Christ represent him so effectively. The shared glory demonstrates the deity of Christ.

5) God's glory is sometimes manifested in other ways. *Miracles* cause people to praise God for his working. Both Jesus' and the apostles' miracles show the glory of God entering this world. They display God's glory in a

twofold way: first by their unusual power (evident in the immediate reaction of people who observed them); second by their restoring wrong to proper order. They manifest God's kingdom, a perfect order entering a broken world.

Genuinely good works evidence God's glory. Illustrations are both positive and negative. Positively, conversion, Christian living, and the proper exercise of spiritual gifts demonstrate God's presence and are occasions for glorifying God. Negatively, abusing religious activities for one's own glory (hypocrites), claiming personal glory for God-given abilities (Herod), and persecuting "glorious ones" without regard for God put self above God. These latter examples stand as warnings for those who would fail to submit to the glory of God.

The *angels* manifest God's glory. Quite apart from the presence of God, the glory of the Lord accompanied the angels' visit to earth and their announcement of Jesus' incarnation.

Events reveal the glory of God. God's glory is seen in the resurrection of Jesus and will be further manifest in the parousia. The glory revealed is personal—that of Jesus and God the Father—but the event itself is glorious and manifests the glory of God.

6) God's glory is active. It is a way God works in the world. Those who see the glory of God feel its presence and are called to respond. The glory of God is the basis of the Christian's call to salvation, as God rights in individuals the wrongs done by sin. Like his moral power, his glory is an active attribute. It is his nature manifested.

7) God's glory is redemptive. Each of the writers surveyed speaks of God's glory in relation to salvation. While the purposes of God surpass the concerns of earth, people need redemption. This is God's primary focus in the human realm. From the glory surrounding the birth of Jesus to the glory of his parousia, God's work is salvation. And—as noted above—salvation results in attributing greater glory to God. It is by his glory and for his glory. God's glory is, then, related to his grace as well as his power.

Defining God's glory goes beyond the use of mere synonyms. The biblical writers assumed that their readers would understand this. God's glory must also be defined in terms of its manifestations and functions in a sinful world. The words and actions attributed directly to God the Father and Christ are the primary manifestations of their glory. They are the clearest evidences of God's magnificent person. Yet the words and actions of those who respond to his glory, Christian people, somehow also reveal the glory of God. They are the secondary manifestations. And both primary and secondary manifestations of God's glory call us to worship his majesty.

4

. . . .

The Glory of God in John's Gospel and Revelation

ANDREAS J. KÖSTENBERGER

. . . .

The great Reformer Martin Luther distinguished between the "theology of glory" and the "theology of the cross."[1] The "theology of glory," for Luther, embodied the essence of religion focused on works-righteousness and a preoccupation with external trappings of piety. The "theology of the cross," on the other hand, was the gospel message of salvation in Christ alone, by grace alone, and through faith alone. While not used in the same sense as Luther, John in his Gospel, strikingly and emphatically presents his own *theologia gloriae* ("theology of glory") and *theologia crucis* ("theology of the cross").

As I will attempt to develop in the remainder of this essay, the identification of the theology of glory with the theology of the cross is at the very heart of John's Gospel. What is more, while the Gospel reveals Jesus' *crucified* glory, the Apocalypse portrays the glory of the *risen* and *returning* Lord. While "glory" terminology is abundant in John's Gospel and Revelation, it is absent from John's letters. As will be seen, not only is Jesus' glory manifest

---

[1] See his 1518 Heidelberg Disputation and his sermon, "Two Kinds of Righteousness."

both in his signs and at the cross, but also the Johannine "glory" theme has an important Trinitarian dimension and sustains a link with references to God's presence, especially in the temple, in the Old Testament.

Fig. 4.1: "Glory" Terminology in the Johannine Writings

Johannine Writing	glory (*doxa*)	I glorify (*doxazō*)	Total
John's Gospel	19	23	42
John's Letters	0	0	0
The Apocalypse	17	2	19
Total	36	25	61

Glory in John's Gospel

Conventionally, it is held that John's Gospel is made up of two equal halves, the "Book of Signs" spanning chapters 1 through 12 and the "Book of Glory" ranging from chapters 13 through 21.[2] However, this terminology has some serious problems and in fact misrepresents John's theology of glory. The reason for this is that *both* halves of John's Gospel, not only the second one, feature glory terminology. Specifically, the noun *glory* (*doxa*) occurs sixteen times in John 1 through 12 and only three times in John 13 through 21. The verb *glorify*, for its part, occurs nine times in John 1 through 12 and fourteen times in John 13 through 21. A close study of glory terminology in John's Gospel, therefore, reveals that both "books" are saturated with glory language and thus are "Books of Glory," properly understood.[3]

Fig. 4.2: Distribution of "Glory" Terminology in John 1–12 and 13–21

John's Gospel	References to *doxa*	References to *doxazō*	Total
1–12	16	9	25
13–21	3	14	17
Total	19	23	42

In John 1 through 12, Jesus' glory is shown to be revealed in his messianic "signs" (2:11; 11:4; cf. 11:40, a possible inclusion). In John 13 through 21, Jesus' glory is shown at the cross (anticipated in 7:39; 12:16, 23; see 13:31; 17:1, 4, 5). John's message is that both in Jesus' "signs" and at the

---

[2] See, e.g., Raymond E. Brown, *The Gospel of John*, 2 vols., Anchor Bible 29–29A (New York: Doubleday, 1966, 1970); Francis J. Moloney, *The Gospel of John*, Sacra Pagina (Collegeville, MN: Liturgical Press, 1998). I, too, adopted this terminology in my commentary *John*, BECNT (Grand Rapids, MI: Baker, 2004).

[3] I now prefer to call John 1–12 the "Book of Signs" and John 13–21 the "Book of Exaltation." See my *The Theology of John's Gospel and Letters: The Word, the Christ, the Son of God*, Biblical Theology of the New Testament (Grand Rapids, MI: Zondervan, 2008).

cross Jesus' glory was revealed, and God's glory in and through him (cf. 1:14; see also 20:30–31). It is the mission of the obedient Son sent by the Father to manifest God's glory. What is more, for John there is emphatically no other glory than the Messiah's *crucified* glory, for it was God's good pleasure to redeem humanity by way of crucifixion, or, in Johannine parlance, by the "lifting up" of the "Son of Man" (3:14; 8:28; 12:32). It remains to survey the major aspects of John's "theology of glory" developed in his Gospel.[4]

Jesus' Glory as the One and Only Son
At the very outset, John makes clear that Jesus' glory is that "of the only Son [*monogenēs*] from the Father, full of grace and truth" (1:14). Building on this startling pronouncement, John asserts at the end of his introduction that "no one has ever seen God; the only God, who is at the Father's side, he has made him known" (1:18). While Isaiah emphatically declared that God will not share his glory with another (Isa. 42:8; 48:11), John announces that God *did* in fact share his glory with another, that is, Jesus. The reason for this, as the striking terminology of 1:18 makes clear, is that Jesus is God.[5] As Jesus says later in the Gospel, "I and the Father are one" (10:30); and "Whoever has seen me has seen the Father" (14:9).

Thus John declares to readers of his Gospel from its inception that Jesus shared God's glory because he himself was God and that his glory was that of "the only Son from the Father." As the Gospel unfolds, John uses "only Son" terminology in one other pericope where he explains that that Son was "lifted up" in demonstration of God's love for sinful humanity so "that whoever believes in him should not perish but have eternal life" (3:16; cf. 3:18). Thus "only Son" terminology ties Jesus' glory specifically and concretely to Jesus' crucifixion.[6] It is likely, in turn, that John's theological source here is Isaiah, who uses "lifted up" language with regard to the suffering servant who "shall be high and lifted up, and shall be exalted" (Isa. 52:13).

---

[4] For helpful studies of the glory motif in John, see G. B. Caird, "The Glory of God in the Fourth Gospel: An Exercise in Biblical Semantics," *NTS* 15 (1968–69): 265–77; and W. Robert Cook, "The 'Glory' Motif in the Johannine Corpus," *JETS* 27 (1984): 291–97.

[5] See also 1:1 with which 1:18 likely forms an inclusion; and 20:28, another possible inclusion with 1:1. On Jesus' deity in John's Gospel, see esp. Andreas J. Köstenberger and Scott R. Swain, *Father, Son and Spirit: The Trinity and John's Gospel*, New Studies in Biblical Theology 24 (Downers Grove, IL: InterVarsity, 2008), esp. chap. 1; and Murray J. Harris, *Jesus as God: The New Testament Use of Theos in Reference to Jesus* (Grand Rapids, MI: Baker, 1992).

[6] As shown below, this pattern continues in the book of Revelation.

Fig. 4.3: "Glory" Terminology

In the "Book of Signs"	In the "Book of Exaltation"
1:14	13:31, 32
2:11	14:13
5:41, 44	15:8
7:39	16:14
8:50, 54	17:1, 4, 5, 10, 22, 24
9:24	21:19
11:4, 40	
12:16, 23, 28, 41, 43	

Jesus' Glory in His Signs

In 1:14, John wrote that "the Word became flesh and dwelt among us, and we have seen his glory." This opening reference is picked up in the next instance of glory terminology in the Gospel at 2:11 where John writes that "this, the first of his signs, Jesus did at Cana in Galilee, and manifested his glory. And his disciples believed in him." Thus it is part of John's portrait of Jesus to show that the Messiah, in keeping with Old Testament expectations, furnished many remarkable demonstrations of his identity (cf. 7:31). The turning of water into wine at the wedding at Cana was one such instance, evoking Old Testament images of the Messiah as bridegroom ushering in an age of messianic joy and celebration.[7]

The corresponding reference to glory being brought to Jesus, and God, is found at the outset of Jesus' final and climactic sign narrated in John's Gospel—the raising of Lazarus. There, upon hearing of Lazarus's condition, Jesus said, "This illness does not lead to death. It is for the glory of God, so that the Son of God may be glorified through it" (11:4).[8] Thus, contrary to simplistic Jewish notions of the nature of suffering (cf. 9:2), Jesus affirmed that suffering may be a God-willed vehicle of, and path to, glory. While many would hold that glory consists in the *absence* of suffering, John's message is that glory comes *through* suffering. This understanding is part and parcel of John's theology of sin and redemption.

These two framing references to glory being brought to Jesus, and to God through Jesus by way of his messianic signs in 2:11 and 11:4, extending to his first and final signs, effectively envelop John's presentation of all of Jesus' signs in the first half of his Gospel, the "Book of Signs." This is underscored

---

[7] See Köstenberger, *John*, 99, who notes that "the messianic age commonly was thought to be the period when God would reveal his glory"; citing Pss. 97:6; 102:16; Isa. 60:1–2; *Pss. Sol.* 17:30–32; *1 En.* 49:2.

[8] Cf. 11:40; see also the similar terminology in 9:3–4.

especially when John quotes Isaiah twice at the end of the "Book of Signs" in order to draw a specific connection between the signs, their rejection by the Jewish people setting the stage for Jesus' crucifixion (narrated in John 13–21), and Isaiah's rendering his prophetic pronouncements because he saw Jesus' "glory" (12:37–41, esp. v. 41).[9] Importantly, this revelation of God's glory during the period of Jesus' earthly ministry to the Jewish people was provided by the same Jesus who would subsequently be crucified.

There is thus an identity of the Glorious and the Crucified. What is more, rather than presenting the crucifixion as an accident at the end of an otherwise glorious career, John makes clear that the cross represents the culmination of the mission of the glorious Messiah. In fact, it is at the cross that the glory accrued to the Son is the greatest, because it is here that Jesus revealed the full extent of God's love for the world, including and in particular for his own (13:1; cf. 3:16), and it is here that the well-pleasing mission of the obedient, sent Son of the Father found its climax (see esp. 17:1, 4, 5; see also vv. 22, 24). Glory and suffering are thus two sides of the same coin, as Peter and many other followers of Jesus would learn in due course (21:19).

The Father as the Source of the Son's Glory

John's account of Jesus' ministry to the Jews in chapters 1 through 12 features several references to the Father as the source of the Son's glory in polemical contrast to Jesus' opponents having each other as the (illegitimate) source of their "glory." At the end of the paternity dispute in chapter 5, Jesus explains, "I do not receive glory from people. But I know that you do not have the love of God within you. I have come in my Father's name, and you do not receive me. If another comes in his own name, you will receive him. How can you believe, when you receive glory from one another and do not seek the glory that comes from the only God?" (vv. 41–44). Thus the Pharisees' refusal to recognize the revelation of God's glory in Jesus, particularly in his signs, is shown to be at the heart of their rejection of Jesus' messianic claims. Their orientation is shown to be on a human, horizontal plane, and they are insufficiently sensitive and receptive to the evidence of God's power and glory furnished abundantly in the ministry of Jesus.

This, in turn, serves the purpose of theodicy, the demonstration of the righteousness and justice of God in condemning people for rejecting his revelation in Jesus and the redemption he provided. The series of ever more startling manifestations of Jesus' glory through his signs in the "Book of Signs" puts the burden squarely on the Jews and renders their unbelief

---

[9] See also the reference to the "arm of the Lord" in v. 38; and 20:30–31.

without excuse (see, e.g., 15:22). It is not that God has failed to provide sufficient proof of Jesus' true identity; culpability and guilt rest entirely on those who would reject Jesus despite ample evidence for those with spiritual eyes to see and spiritual ears to hear (12:37–41, citing Isa. 53:1; 6:10).

Consequently, Jesus declares, "My teaching is not mine, but his who sent me. If anyone's will is to do God's will, he will know whether the teaching is from God or whether I am speaking on my own authority. The one who speaks on his own authority seeks his own glory; but the one who seeks the glory of him who sent him is true, and in him there is no falsehood" (7:16–18). Thus it is not only Jesus' works (particularly his signs) but also his words (his teaching) that reveal God's glory, and rejection of Jesus' works *and* words reveals lack of a true desire to discern whether the source of Jesus' mission is God.

Jesus' emphatic claim that it is God who is the source of his glory provides a defense against the charge that his mission was self-appointed. In sharp conflict with his Jewish opponents, Jesus noted, "Yet I do not seek my own glory; there is One who seeks it, and he is the judge. . . . If I glorify myself, my glory is nothing. It is my Father who glorifies me . . . ." (8:50, 54). This assertion is part of the larger "witness" theme in John's Gospel, which parades a series of witnesses to Jesus' truthfulness, ranging from John the Baptist (1:7–8, 15, 19, 32–34; 3:26; 5:33–36) all the way to the evangelist (19:35; 21:24), including also God the Father (5:32, 36–37; 8:18), Moses and the Scriptures (5:39, 46), the Spirit (chaps. 14–16, esp. 15:26), the disciples (e.g., 15:27), and Jesus' own works (3:11, 32; 5:36; 8:14, 18; 10:25, 32, 37–38; 15:24; 18:37).[10] By contrast, Jesus' opponents "loved the glory that comes from man more than the glory that comes from God" (12:43).[11]

Jesus' Glory at the Cross
The references to Jesus' glory at the cross are for the most part conveyed by instances of the verb *doxazō* ("glorify") in the second half of John's Gospel, though there are two references in the "Book of Signs" that anticipate Jesus' glorification.[12] Thus John notes in 7:39 that "as yet the Spirit had not been given, because Jesus was not yet glorified." A similar reference is 12:16, where John writes that Jesus' "disciples did not understand these things at first, but when Jesus was glorified, then they remembered that these things had been written about him and had been done to him." Remarkably, in both

---

[10] See Köstenberger, *Theology of John's Gospel and Letters*, chap. 11; Andrew T. Lincoln, *Truth on Trial: The Lawsuit Motif in the Fourth Gospel* (Peabody, MA: Hendrickson, 2000).
[11] See also the instance of Johannine irony in 9:24 where the Pharisees adjure the blind man healed by Jesus to give glory to God.
[12] See fig. 4.2 above.

instances, the word *glorified* is used as a simple and broad cipher referring to the cross, a euphemism deliberately choosing to focus, not on the pain, shame, and suffering endured by Jesus at the cross, but on the glory brought to him in and through his sacrifice and the salvation he provided.

Jesus' startling pronouncement at 12:23 that "the hour has come for the Son of Man to be glorified" follows a series of previous references to Jesus' hour having *not yet* come (2:4; 7:30; 8:20). Jesus' self-reference to the Son of Man invokes the mention of this figure in Daniel 7:13, which in turn has been the subject of multiple Johannine references involving descent and ascent earlier in the Gospel (cf. John 1:51; 3:13–14). The reference to the glorification of the Son of Man in 12:23 is followed by Jesus' prayer in 12:28, "Father, glorify your name," immediately drawing a response by a voice from heaven saying, "I have glorified it, and I will glorify it again" (cf. 17:1). This pronouncement, then, provides a sort of pivot in the glory theology of John's Gospel in that it makes reference to both a past and a future glorification of Jesus. In light of the narrative development of this motif, it is possible that this brackets and encompasses both the manifestation of Jesus' glory in his signs (John 1–12) and the glorification of Jesus at the cross (John 13–21).

Even more startling is Jesus' pronouncement at the outset of the Farewell Discourse at 13:31 that "now" that Judas the betrayer had left the upper room, "the Son of Man" was "glorified, and God . . . glorified in him," adding, "God will also glorify him in himself, and glorify him at once" (13:32). This statement, in turn, is set within the context of a string of references affirming Jesus' foreknowledge of the events that would ensue throughout the Gospel, particularly in the second half of the Gospel (13:1–3; 18:4; cf. 6:70–71; 17:12). In this the reader is assured that the events surrounding the crucifixion do not take place by accident but are part of a divinely orchestrated plan in fulfillment of scriptural prediction and typology.

**Fig. 4.4: Agents of Glory
in John's Gospel**

The Father	8:54; 17:1, 5
The Son	17:4
The Spirit	16:14
Jesus' Followers	14:13; 15:8; 17:10; 21:19

Glory Brought to Jesus through His Followers
Anticipating the period subsequent to Jesus' glorification, the Farewell Discourse then turns to address the ways in which Jesus, once exalted, will receive glory through his followers. This is a striking turn of events indeed,

for until 14:13 all the references to Jesus receiving glory had God the Father as the source. In 14:13, however, it is said, "Whatever you ask in my name, this I will do, that the Father may be glorified in the Son." This relates to the dynamic of believing prayer addressed to the Father in and through Jesus once Jesus has died on the cross and been exalted with the Father. On the basis of his finished cross work, Jesus, from his exalted position with the Father, will be able to grant believing prayer offered in his name, with the result that the Father is glorified in the Son.

In the following chapter, Jesus addresses the vital question of how believers subsequent to his departure will be able to sustain a vital spiritual relationship with him. The answer is that they must remain in Jesus and in his word (15:1–7). On this basis, believers will bring glory to the Father by what they do: "By this my Father is glorified, that you bear much fruit and so prove to be my disciples" (15:8).[13] Earlier, Jesus had said, "Truly, truly, I say to you, unless a grain of wheat falls into the earth and dies, it remains alone; but if it dies, it bears much fruit" (12:24). His followers must "hate" their lives in this world and follow and serve him, and the Father will honor them (12:25–26). As they follow in the path of the cross, which is a path of glory through suffering (15:18–16:4), they will bear much fruit as they, through faith, are identified with the "lifted-up" Son of Man.

The next programmatic reference to Jesus' being glorified in and through his followers is found in 17:10 where Jesus states, "I am glorified in them." This is said of believers who are in but not of the world (17:6–16), whom Jesus prays would be sanctified in the truth of God's Word (17:17), and who are sent into the world as Jesus was (17:18; 20:21). Jesus prays, then, in anticipation of his disciples' mission, also "for those who will believe in me through their word" (17:20). The disciples' proclamation and extension of forgiveness in Jesus' name (20:22) will bring Jesus glory because it will reap a harvest for which the disciples have not labored (4:34–38), will bring "other sheep that are not of this fold" into Jesus' flock (10:16), and will "gather into one the children of God who are scattered abroad" (11:52). In keeping with Jesus' promise—"And I, when I am lifted up from the earth, will draw all people to myself" (12:32)—the mission of his followers, undergirded by the mission of the Spirit (15:26–27; 20:21–22), will result in "greater works" on the part of the disciples "because I am going to the Father" (14:12). Believers' works will be "greater" in large part because

---

[13] See the discussion in Köstenberger, *John*, 455.

they are "later," that is, predicated salvation-historically on the finished cross work of Christ (17:4; 19:30).[14]

Finally, the risen Jesus predicts that Peter will give his life in martyrdom, explicated by the fourth evangelist as a reference to "by what kind of death he was to glorify God" (21:19). Peter, the one who had once denied Jesus three times (18:16–18, 25–27), but who had, subsequent to the crucifixion and resurrection, been recommissioned three times (21:15–19), would make the ultimate sacrifice for his faith by dying a martyr's death, bringing glory to God.

**Fig. 4.5: The Father and the Son
as Recipients of Glory**

The Father	The Son
	1:14
	2:11
	7:39
	8:54
11:4, 40	11:4
	12:16
	12:23
12:28	12:41
13:31–32	13:31–32
14:13	14:13
	15:8
	16:14
17:1, 4	17:1, 5, 10, 22, 24

The Trinitarian Dimension of Glory in John's Gospel
The opening reference to the Word's glory already makes clear that his glory—the glory that John and the other apostles have perceived—is "glory as of the only Son from the Father" (1:14). This from the very outset establishes the Trinitarian framework of glory for the remainder of the gospel.[15] In 7:39, the giving of the Spirit is said to be predicated upon the glorification of Jesus, which shows the salvation-historical underpinnings of the glory motif in John's Gospel. Later on, Jesus makes clear that he does not derive glory from himself but that it is the Father who glorifies him (8:54). In 11:4, "the glory of God" and the glorification of the Son of God are mentioned in parallel fashion.

---

[14] See ibid., 432–33.
[15] See the discussion in ibid., 42.

The glory motif comes to a major climax at the end of the first half of John's Gospel, revealing both a Christocentric and a cross-centered orientation (cf. 12:23, 28, 41). When John affirms that Isaiah saw Jesus' glory and spoke of him (12:41), his point most likely is that the prophet foresaw that God was pleased with a *suffering* servant who would be "high and lifted up, and . . . exalted" (Isa. 52:13) yet who was "wounded for our transgressions" and "bore the sin of many" (Isa. 53:5, 12).[16] Thus Isaiah was aware that God's glory would be revealed through a suffering messiah, in contrast to the crowds (John 12:34). In the Father-Son (and Spirit) relationship, glory is centered on Jesus' redemptive suffering on the cross. Indeed:

> Jesus' own mission to the Jews, as narrated in the first twelve chapters in John's Gospel, although appearing to end on a note of rejection and failure, in fact accomplishes God's purpose: God's glory has been revealed in and through Christ, in keeping with the Baptist's vision . . . both as a result of the Son's perfect submission and complete obedience to the Father . . . and through Jesus' messianic "signs" and fulfillment of the symbolism inherent in various Jewish festivals and institutions. Both Jesus and the evangelist perceive in the Jews' rejection the world's opposition and Satan's antagonism but look to God to glorify himself in and through, rather than apart from or in spite of, the cross.[17]

The reciprocity of Father glorifying Son and Son glorifying Father is restated at the outset of the Farewell Discourse (13:31–32) and reiterated in Jesus' reference to the Father being glorified in the Son in 14:13. Remarkably, in 15:8 the Father is said to be glorified through Jesus' followers.

The exalted Jesus will receive glory not only through the Father and his followers but also through the ministry of the Holy Spirit:

> I still have many things to say to you, but you cannot bear them now. When the Spirit of truth comes, he will guide you into all the truth, for he will not speak on his own authority, but whatever he hears he will speak, and he will declare to you the things that are to come. He will glorify me, for he will take what is mine and declare it to you. (16:12–14)

---

[16] See Craig A. Evans, "Obduracy and the Lord's Servant: Some Observations on the Use of the Old Testament in the Fourth Gospel," in *Early Jewish and Christian Exegesis: Studies in Memory of William Hugh Brownlee,* ed. Craig A. Evans and William F. Stinespring, Homage 10 (Atlanta: Scholars Press, 1987), 221–36.

[17] Andreas J. Köstenberger, "John," in *Commentary on the New Testament Use of the Old Testament,* ed. G. K. Beale and D. A. Carson (Grand Rapids, MI: Baker, 2007), 482; see the entire discussion on pp. 476–83, including the treatment of the reference to Isaiah seeing "his glory" in John 12:41 on p. 483.

Just as Jesus brought glory to the Father through his teaching (7:18), the Spirit will bring glory to Jesus through his teaching ministry, which is vitally connected to Jesus' teaching while on earth. Spiritual illumination and a post-crucifixion vantage point are needed for Jesus' followers to understand the significance of his teaching, and it is the Spirit's role to continue Jesus' teaching ministry subsequent to his glorification and exaltation.

On the whole, one is struck by the mutuality and reciprocity entailed by many of the references to glory in John's Gospel. As mentioned, both the Father and Jesus are frequently said to be the recipients of glory. Most commonly, it is the Father receiving glory *through* Jesus and acting, in turn, to bring glory *to* Jesus. This dynamic finds its culminating expression in Jesus' final prayer: "Father, the hour has come; glorify your Son that the Son may glorify you. . . . I glorified you on earth, having accomplished the work that you gave me to do. And now, Father, glorify me in your own presence with the glory that I had with you before the world existed" (17:1, 4–5). As with the opening reference to Jesus' glory at 1:14, Jesus' glory is here rooted in his preexistent glory with the Father before the world came into being. This marks out Jesus' glory to be a pre-creation, supernatural glory that entirely transcends the realm of this world, in keeping with Johannine cosmology and John's overall worldview.[18]

The Manifestation and Withdrawal of God's Presence in Jesus

Another dimension of John's "theology of glory" relates to the manifestation and withdrawal of God's presence in Jesus. In 1:14, John's readers are told that "the Word became flesh and *dwelt* [literally, "pitched his tent," *skenoō*] among us, and we have seen his glory." This invokes previous manifestations of God's presence among his people in the tabernacle and later in the temple where, according to the Hebrew Scriptures, God's glory was revealed to Israel (Ex. 40:34–35; 1 Kings 8:10–11; 2 Chron. 5:13–14; 7:1–2; Ezek. 10:4; 43:5; 44:4; Hag. 2:7).[19] Now, the fourth evangelist tells his readers, this glory has come to dwell in Jesus, and while "no one has ever seen God; the only God, who is at the Father's side, he has made him known" (1:18). In light of this programmatic statement, placed strategically at the end of the

---

[18] See especially the references to the world "above" and the realm "below." See also Köstenberger, *Theology of John's Gospel and Letters*, chap. 6; Edward W. Klink III, "Light of the World: Cosmology and the Johannine Literature," in *Cosmology and New Testament Theology*, ed. Jonathan T. Pennington and Sean M. McDonough, Library of New Testament Studies (London: T & T Clark, 2008), 74–89.

[19] See the discussion in Andreas J. Köstenberger, "What Does It Mean to Be Filled with the Spirit? A Biblical Investigation," *JETS* 40 (1997): 230, who notes that "all the earth is, or one day will be, full of his glory"; citing Num. 14:21; Ps. 72:19; Isa. 6:3; 11:9; and Hab. 2:14.

introduction, John's message is that God's glory was revealed through Jesus' entire ministry, and that *all* his words and deeds revealed God's glory. This glory, in turn, was "glory as of the only Son from the Father, full of grace and truth" (1:14b); that is, it revealed God's loving-kindness and covenant faithfulness at this climactic juncture in salvation history.[20]

In the body of John's Gospel, the temple theme receives further development. At the inception of his ministry, Jesus clears the Jerusalem sanctuary and predicts its destruction, which, in customary Johannine double entendre, refers both to its literal destruction (which most likely had already taken place at the time of writing of John's Gospel) and Jesus' crucifixion (i.e., the "destruction" of his body, 2:21). By adding the narrative aside, "But he was speaking about the temple of his body" (2:21), the fourth evangelist makes clear that Jesus' body, which would be crucified and raised up in three days (2:19), was the fulfillment and replacement of the literal, physical temple, which would be destroyed and not be rebuilt. This constituted an invitation to Jews, proselytes, and God-fearers living in John's day to worship *Jesus* and recognize *him* as the replacement of the temple in the life of the community.[21]

A similar point is made by Jesus in his conversation with the Samaritan woman: "Woman, believe me, the hour is coming when neither on this mountain nor in Jerusalem will you worship the Father. . . . But the hour is coming, *and is now here*, when the true worshipers will worship the Father in spirit and truth, for the Father is seeking such people to worship him. God is spirit, and those who worship him must worship in spirit and truth" (4:21–24). Again, one notes the Trinitarian dimension of such worship, which is offered to the Father through the Son in the Spirit (though in the just-quoted passage, the reference to "spirit" is most likely generic—"spiritual" worship as opposed to worship focused on particular physical locations).[22]

Chapters 5 through 10 further intensify the portrayal of Jesus as the fulfillment of the symbolism inherent in various Jewish festivals, most notably symbolism related to Passover and Tabernacles.[23] Also pregnant with meaning are references to Jesus' withdrawals from the Jews, especially with reference to the temple. Thus, at the culmination of a major contro-

---

[20] See Köstenberger, *John*, 44–45.
[21] See my essay "The Destruction of the Second Temple and the Composition of the Fourth Gospel," in *Challenging Perspectives on the Gospel of John*, ed. John Lierman, WUNT 2:219 (Tübingen: Mohr Siebeck, 2006), 69–108.
[22] See Köstenberger, *John*, 156–57.
[23] See Köstenberger, *Theology of John's Gospel and Letters*, chap. 10.

versy with the Jews, Jesus asserts his preexistence: "Truly, truly, I say to you, before Abraham was, I am" (8:58). At this, the Jews pick up stones to throw at him, while John informs his readers that "Jesus hid himself and went out of the temple" (8:59). This withdrawal of Jesus' presence from the temple grounds ominously signifies divine judgment.

Subsequent to the raising of Lazarus, John observes that "from that day on they [the Jewish leaders] made plans to put him to death" and that "Jesus therefore no longer walked openly among the Jews, but went from there to the region near the wilderness" (11:53–54). Finally, at the conclusion of chapter 12, the fourth evangelist writes, "When Jesus had said these things, he departed and hid himself from them" (12:36). This is followed by a reference to God's judicial hardening of the Jews, with explicit mention of Isaiah 53 and 6, and the concluding explanation that "Isaiah said these things because he saw his glory and spoke of him" (12:41). This draws a stark contrast between Isaiah's glorious throne room vision and the hiding of Jesus' presence from the Jews.

Summary

John's theology of glory is at the same time a theology of the cross. Jesus' glory is rooted in his preexistence with God. As the Word made flesh, Jesus manifested God's glory through his messianic signs. Yet the ultimate manifestation of God's glory took place at the cross, where the Son gave his life as a sacrifice for the sins of the world. Space does not permit a full presentation of John's *theologia crucis*.[24] It must suffice to conclude that the cross is at the heart of John's glory theology and that the cross, in turn, is the most notable instance where the persons of the divine Godhead collaborate in bringing glory to one another. The entire Godhead—Father, Son, and Spirit—is glorious, and it is the manifestation of this glory in and through Jesus that forms the focus of John's Gospel.

Glory in the Apocalypse

Most likely, the Apocalypse consists of four visions, marked by the phrase "in the Spirit" (1:10; 4:2; 17:3; 21:10), depicting, respectively, Jesus' message to the seven churches (chaps. 1–3); God's judgment on the unbelieving world (chaps. 4–16); the events surrounding Jesus' return (chaps. 17–20); and the eternal state (chaps. 21–22). Throughout the book, God is the recipient of glory.[25] In two instances, the recipient of glory is Jesus Christ, the Lamb

---

[24] Though see ibid., chap. 14.

[25] For a survey of "glory" references in the Apocalypse, with special attention on 21:11, see Stephen S. Smalley, *The Revelation to John: A Commentary on the Greek Text of the Apocalypse* (Downers Grove, IL: InterVarsity, 2005), 557–58.

who was slain and who has freed believers from their sins by his blood (1:6; 5:12–13). Once it is said of an angel that "the earth was made bright with his glory" (18:1). It will be helpful to survey the references to glory in the Apocalypse in chronological order of occurrence within each vision.

Fig. 4.6: Referents and References to "Glory" in the Apocalypse

Vision 1		Vision 2		Vision 3		Vision 4
Jesus	God	Jesus	God	Angel	God	God
1:6	4:9, 11	5:12–13	7:12; 11:13; 14:7; 15:4, 8; 16:9	18:1	19:1, 7	21:11

The First Vision (chapters 1–3): The Glory of the One Who Was Pierced
The sole reference to glory in John's first vision has Jesus Christ as its referent. At the outset of the vision, John refers to Jesus Christ as "the faithful witness, the firstborn of the dead, and the ruler of kings on earth" (1:5), and he writes, "To him who loves us and has freed us from our sins by his blood and made us a kingdom, priests to his God and Father, to him be glory and dominion forever and ever. Amen" (1:5–6). He continues, "Behold, he is coming with the clouds, and every eye will see him, even those who pierced him" (1:7). The image of Jesus "coming with the clouds" invokes the imagery of Daniel 7:13; the reference to "those who pierced him" represents a quotation of Zechariah 12:10, which is also cited in John 19:37.

In John 19:37, Zechariah 12:10 is quoted alongside Psalm 34:20, concluding a series of Old Testament references said to have been fulfilled at Jesus' crucifixion. In the original context in Zechariah, the one on whom people look is none other than Yahweh himself. "Aided by the spirit of grace poured out on them, the people responsible for piercing the individual mentioned in 12:10 mourn and presumably ask God for forgiveness for what they have done."[26] The notion of the "piercing of Yahweh" is then fulfilled in the piercing of Jesus, the messianic shepherd, at the cross. At the second coming, John says in the Apocalypse, *every eye* will see Jesus, *even those who pierced him*, and Jesus' coming will be accompanied with wailing by all tribes of the earth (1:7).[27]

---

[26] Köstenberger, "John," in *Commentary*, 504.

[27] See G. K. Beale, *The Book of Revelation*, New International Greek Testament Commentary (Grand Rapids, MI: Eerdmans, 1999), 197, who notes that the Zechariah text has been altered in two significant ways: "every eye" and "of the earth" have been added "to universalize its original meaning": "The rejection of God's messenger and the consequent repentant mourning are not limited to Israelites but affirmed of all nations."

The notion of the Pierced One's glory is then given eloquent expression in the vision of "one like a son of man" in a long robe with a golden sash around his chest, his hairs white like wool, as white as snow, his eyes like a flame of fire, his feet like burnished bronze, his voice like the roar of many waters, his right hand holding seven stars, his mouth emanating a sharp two-edged sword, and his face like the sun shining in full strength (1:12–16). It is this glorious "Son of Man" who then reassures John the seer that he is the first and the last, the living one, who died and is alive forevermore, who has the keys of death (1:17–18), and who delivers his message to the seven churches.

Importantly, the adoration of Jesus with regard to his glory and power is profoundly countercultural, reminding the reader that only Jesus, not the Roman Emperor or any other earthly potentate, is worthy of worship, because Jesus alone is the Lamb who was slain for the sins of humanity and who effected redemption.[28] Both terms, *power* and *glory*, stand in "decided contrast to the imperial cult—only God and Christ, not Caesar, has dominion and is worthy of 'glory.'"[29] What is more, Jesus' glory and power are eternal, unlike the temporary glory and power of the emperor. In their present afflictions, the readers are assured that there is a sovereign Ruler who transcends their current circumstances and whose glory and power are unfading.

The Second Vision (chapters 4–16): The Glory of God on His Throne and of the Lamb

John's second vision, depicting God's judgment of the unbelieving world, is by far the longest in the entire book. The first scene translates the seer "in the Spirit" in God's throne room in heaven where the twenty-four elders (most likely believers of all ages) and four living creatures (most likely angels) are shown to unite in worship of the Lord God Almighty, ascribing to him glory and honor and thanks and power (4:9, 11). God is shown to be sovereign and seated on his throne at the outset of the terrible judgments sent on the unbelieving world (chaps. 6–16). As the Eternal One (the one "who was and is and is to come," 4:8), God is said to be perfectly holy ("holy, holy, holy," 4:8) and "worthy . . . to receive glory and honor and power," for he is the Creator, and by his will all things were created (4:11).

---

[28] Grant R. Osborne, *Revelation*, BECNT (Grand Rapids, MI: Baker, 2002), 67, observes that glory "celebrates the superior work and worth of God and Christ in defeating the powers of evil and effecting salvation," connoting the splendor or glory of "the King of kings, the sovereign Lord of the universe."

[29] Ibid.

Next in the sequence of the throne room vision is a depiction of the Lamb who receives a scroll from the one seated on the throne. In a virtual repeat of the previous scene, the twenty-four elders and the four living creatures fall down, now not in worship of God but of the Lamb who was slain, singing, "Worthy are you to take the scroll and to open its seals, for you were slain, and by your blood you ransomed people for God from every tribe and language and people and nation, and you have made them a kingdom and priests to our God, and they shall reign on the earth" (5:9–10; cf. 1:6). Again, countless angels sing, "Worthy is the Lamb who was slain, to receive power and wealth and wisdom and might and honor and glory and blessing" (5:12). Their worship is echoed by every creature in heaven and on earth (5:13).

It is noteworthy that in both instances where glory is ascribed to the Lamb who was slain, specific reference is made to the crucifixion and to the blood of the Lamb. This draws attention to the fact that the cross is the center of John's glory theology, not only in the Gospel, but also in the Apocalypse. It is the salvific mission of the Lamb of God as the one who took away the sin of the world (John 1:29, 36) that is the source of glory and honor and blessing, in a direct reversal of the world's judgment. What the world rejected, God highly esteemed and exalted: the atoning sacrifice of the obedient Son, in fulfillment of Passover symbolism and other Old Testament prediction and typology. As John's Gospel makes clear, Jesus was the "lifted up" Son of Man, the "Good Shepherd," and the suffering Servant who gave his life for the world.

Another scene of worship occurs at the occasion of the sealing of a great multitude from every nation who stand before God's throne and before the Lamb and acknowledge that salvation belongs to God and to the Lamb. Together with the elders and the four living creatures, they fall on their faces and worship God, saying, "Blessing and glory and wisdom and thanksgiving and honor and power and might be to our God forever and ever" (7:12). In what follows it is made clear that these are believers "coming out of the great tribulation" who "have washed their robes and made them white in the blood of the Lamb" (7:14). Glory is ascribed to God because he has provided salvation and deliverance through the blood of the Lamb and because he has preserved believers in and through the great tribulation.

The next reference to glory is found in 11:13, where seven thousand people are killed in an earthquake while the survivors are terrified and give glory to "the God of heaven." The 144,000 who had been sealed previously (in chapter 7) are shown in chapter 14 to sing a new song before God's throne and the elders and the living creatures. An angel is shown flying overhead, proclaiming an eternal gospel to those on the earth, crying with a loud voice, "Fear God and give him glory, because the hour of his judgment has come, and worship him who made heaven and earth" (14:7). The fact that this remarkable invitation is issued at this juncture makes clear that God's purpose is salvation and that judgment is executed only on those who refuse to respond in the face of repeated exhortations to believe in God's saving message.[30]

Toward the end of the second vision, those who had conquered the Beast are depicted as standing beside the sea of glass with harps of God in their hands, singing the song of Moses and the song of the Lamb, extolling the Lord God Almighty for his great and amazing deeds and his just and true ways, asking, "Who will not fear, O Lord, and glorify your name? For you alone are holy. All nations will come and worship you, for your righteous acts have been revealed" (15:4). Invoking exodus imagery, the scene extols God as glorious on account of his greatness, justice, and holiness. Clearly, it is God's glory, not the world's sin, that is at the center of the vision. In a memorable, moving image, the seer describes a scene where "the sanctuary was filled with smoke from the glory of God and from his power" (15:8).[31]

The final reference to God's glory in this portion of the Apocalypse is negative, underscoring the tragic nature of the world's rejection of its Creator and his salvation. As the seven bowls of God's wrath are poured out on the unbelieving world, those who resist God are shown to be scorched by the fierce heat, yet they continue to curse the name of God and fail to "repent and give him glory" (16:9; cf. v. 11).[32] Nothing, it appears, will bring unbelievers who are hardened in their sin to their knees, and rather than worship, they emit curses and adopt a defiant posture to the bitter end. Yet in a strange way their defiance further magnifies the justice and greatness

---

[30] See Richard Bauckham, "The Conversion of the Nations," in *The Climax of Prophecy: Studies on the Book of Revelation* (Edinburgh: T & T Clark, 1993), 238–337; and Andreas J. Köstenberger, "The Contribution of the General Epistles and Revelation to a Biblical Theology of Religions," in *Christianity and the Religions: A Biblical Theology of World Religions*, Evangelical Missiological Society Series 2 (Pasadena, CA: William Carey Library, 1995), 128–36, esp. 134–35.

[31] Osborne, *Revelation*, 571, draws attention to the following OT antecedent passages: (1) Ex. 40:34–35, referring to the tabernacle during the time of the exodus; (2) 1 Kings 8:10–12, where a "dark cloud" fills the temple with God's glory; (3) Isa. 6:1–4, with its reference to the temple being "filled with smoke" and the earth being "full of his [God's] glory"; and (4) Ezek. 10:2–4, where the judgment of Israel is signified by the departure of God's glory from the temple.

[32] Osborne, *Revelation*, 569, notes the contrast with 11:13 where some among the nations "gave glory to the God of heaven."

of God, who is shown as sovereign, glorious, and holy while executing his judgment on those who refuse to acknowledge his majesty.

The Third Vision (chapters 17–20): The Angel's Brilliance and Glory to God in Heaven

The first two of four references to glory in the third vision are not to God but to an angel and Babylon, respectively. At the depiction of the fall of Babylon, symbolizing the unbelieving world, an angel is portrayed as coming down from heaven, "having great authority, and the earth was made bright with his glory" (18:1). In this instance, "glory" denotes the brilliance and luminescence that is characteristic of heaven, the place where the glorious God dwells, a brilliance reflected by the angelic creatures.[33] By contrast, Babylon is shown as one who "glorified herself and lived in luxury" (18:7) and who is now subject to divine judgment. This, in turn, evokes rejoicing by a great multitude in heaven who along with the twenty-four elders and the four living creatures worship and praise God for his just judgment at the outset of Christ's return (19:1, 7).

The Fourth Vision (chapters 21–22): The Glory of God and the New Jerusalem

Once more the seer is transported to heaven "in the Spirit" (21:10). He is shown the New Jerusalem "coming down out of heaven from God, having the glory of God, its radiance like a most rare jewel, like a jasper, clear as crystal" (21:10–11; cf. 4:3). Throughout the entire book, it is made clear that heaven is a place of resplendent glory, in contrast to the earth, which is the scene of terrifying judgments visited upon the unbelieving world. Intermittent scenes of worship oscillate with depictions of unbelievers' refusal to acknowledge the glorious God, ensuing in an escalating series of divine retributions. The radiance of the New Jerusalem provides a fitting conclusion to a book that is full of depictions of God's glory in the midst of his vindication of believers and judgment of unbelievers.

Unlike the temporary manifestation of God's presence in the temple, in the new creation God's presence is not confined to a limited structure.[34]

---

[33] As Osborne, *Revelation*, 634, observes, "The members of the false trinity do not possess 'glory' in the Apocalypse. In fact, no celestial being possesses 'glory' in the book except here. Therefore, it is likely that the angel reflects the glory of God, implying he has come directly from the divine presence."

[34] Beale, *Book of Revelation*, 1066, notes multiple allusions to Isa. 40–66 in 21:1–22:5, with the reference to "the glory of God" most likely harking back to Isa. 58:8 and 60:1–2, 19. Beale also detects an allusion to Ezekiel 43, esp. vv. 2 and 4–5. See also Dan. 12:3 lxx and Phil. 2:15, which depicts God's children as shining "as lights in the world" "in the midst of a crooked and twisted generation."

Most importantly, in this final vision it is made clear that God shares his glory with his people in fulfillment of Jesus' vision and desire that his followers be allowed to see his preexistent glory (John 17:24; cf. 17:5). Thus, at long last, believers' suffering and afflictions have come to an end, and they are granted eternal rest and bliss in the presence of the Almighty and the Lamb. As they engage in eternal, grateful worship, they bask in God's glory in and through Christ, and the covenant formula will have come true: "Behold, the dwelling place of God is with man. He will dwell with them, and they will be his people, and God himself will be with them as their God" (21:3).

Summary

The primary glory in the Apocalypse is God's, the one who is seated on the throne. God shares his glory with the Lamb who was slain. His glory is also radiated by the angels, the inhabitants of heaven, and extended to believers who are welcomed into the heavenly Jerusalem. This, in turn, is part of John's Trinitarian theology. What is more, God's resplendent glory makes illumination from any heavenly bodies unnecessary. Also, there is no more need for a temple. Remarkably, glory is attached in Revelation to God's judgment of those who fail to give him glory, judgment that is delegated to the glorious "Son of Man," the Lord Jesus Christ. Ironically and tragically, while unbelievers worship the Beast (i.e., the Antichrist), they refuse to give glory to God, the one who alone is worthy to receive all glory, honor, and praise.

Conclusion

John's theology of glory is first and foremost a theology of the cross. In both the Gospel and the Apocalypse, glory accrues to Jesus on account of his atoning sacrifice for sinful humanity. At the same time, Jesus' glory is not acquired; it was his from eternity past as the preexistent Word. During his earthly ministry, Jesus revealed God's glory through his messianic signs. These signs, in turn, were rejected by their primary recipients, the Jewish people. For this reason John's theology of glory is shown to be by divine necessity a theology of the cross. It is through the suffering of the divinely appointed Lamb that God's glory is revealed. In John's Gospel, Jesus is the Lamb who gives his life for the sin of the world; in the Apocalypse, he is the risen Lamb who was slain, the one to whom all judgment is entrusted and who returns as the conquering warrior at the end of time. Thus John's theology of glory is for the most part Christocentric in orientation, especially in the Gospel.

At the same time, John's theology of glory has as its grand backdrop the glory of the eternal God. As the sender of Jesus, it is God, whom no one has ever seen, who is revealed by the Word made flesh. Jesus makes clear that his mission is not self-appointed or self-aggrandizing but has as its ultimate purpose the glorification of God. The God-oriented nature of John's theology of glory is even more palpable in the Apocalypse, where the vast majority of references to "glory" have God as their referent. In most such cases, God is depicted as seated on his throne and as the object of worship of a great multitude of believers and angels. Particularly in the Gospel but also in the Apocalypse, glory is part of the evangelist's Trinitarian theology as the Father and the Son are shown to bring glory to each other, first and foremost at the moment of Jesus' ultimate glorification, the cross.

In presenting his theology of glory as a theology of suffering, John is significantly indebted to the theology of Isaiah. In the prophet's call vision, he catches a glimpse of "the Lord sitting upon a throne, high and lifted up," worshiped by angels who cry, "Holy, holy, holy is the Lord of hosts; the whole earth is full of his glory" (Isa. 6:1, 3). The same prophet depicts the suffering servant as one who is supremely exalted ("lifted up") while dying for the sins of transgressors (Isa. 52:13–53:12). Remarkably, John cites both passages at the end of part 1 of his Gospel (12:38–41). John's theology of glory also draws on the portrayal of people looking on the one "they have pierced" (Zech. 12:10)—Yahweh in the first instance and Jesus as a fulfillment of the Isaianic vision (John 19:37; Rev. 1:7). Emphatically, Jesus is glorious as the one who was pierced, according to the predetermined eternal plan of God.

In the end, however, all suffering is swallowed up in glory. Satan is doomed, sin is judged, and all unbelief vanquished. God's kingly rule is complete and his authority unchallenged. In the new creation, God "will wipe away every tear from their eyes, and death shall be no more, neither shall there be mourning, nor crying, nor pain anymore, for the former things have passed away" (21:4). As the one seated on the throne declares, "Behold, I am making all things new" (21:5). "It is done! I am the Alpha and the Omega, the beginning and the end. . . . The one who conquers will have this heritage, and I will be his God and he will be my son" (21:6–7). "The Spirit and the Bride say, 'Come.' And let the one who hears say, 'Come.' And let the one who is thirsty come; let the one who desires take the water of life without price" (22:17).

5

. . . .

The Glory of God in Paul's Epistles

RICHARD B. GAFFIN JR.

. . . .

The concept of glory—divine preeminently and human derivatively—is prominent in the letters of Paul. In fact, glory terminology provides a window on virtually the whole of his theology. Nowhere are its Old Testament roots more apparent. His gospel, as much as anything, is "the gospel of the glory of Christ" (2 Cor. 4:4) and as such may be viewed as the good news of forfeited human glory restored and consummated.

There are basically two ways of handling our theme in this chapter. We could work through Paul's letters one by one, in either canonical or chronological order, surveying all the references to glory in each and then drawing some conclusions. Alternatively, we might proceed by identifying and reflecting on those aspects that are most basic and determinative in shaping his understanding of glory. These approaches are not at odds with each other; the findings of the one ought to overlap and complement those of the other. However, in this chapter, on guard to avoid missing anything significant that would be brought to light by the former approach, I will follow the latter. It is more helpful, it seems to me, to highlight and explore the controlling elements in Paul's teaching on glory in order to provide an overall perspective on that teaching.

Our approach, in other words, will be to ask, what is the center of Paul's teaching on glory? This is akin to a larger question: what is the center of his theology as a whole? But does Paul's theology even have a center? Some readers will be aware that this is a question debated by New Testament scholars. In my view, without entering into that debate here and despite the reservations of some, it seems difficult to deny such a center, particularly if that notion is not maintained rigidly or too narrowly, as if there is a single key concept or "doctrine," such as election or salvation or even God, from which everything can be shown to be deduced.

That is not the case. By the metaphor of a "center" I mean rather that in Paul's letters an overall set of concerns is identifiable in which some matters are plainly more important for him than others. Certainly, Paul may be approached from a variety of perspectives, and there is undeniable value in doing so. At the same time, however, each of his various concerns is not equally important or controlling. This fact points to a circle of interests in which each is more or less central, with room for debate in some instances as to relative centrality.

Assuming a center to Paul's theology in this soft sense, then, the question before us concerns the center of his teaching on glory and, in turn, how that center relates to the central concerns of his teaching as a whole. As we will see, answering the first part of this question is in large part to be answering the second.

Before addressing that question, however, it will be worth mentioning briefly another matter by way of introduction. Studying Paul presents a perennial challenge. Whoever considers his letters with any care is bound to recognize in them an impressive, even profound thinker. His is "the genius of the greatest constructive mind ever at work on that data of Christianity."[1] Similarly, though from a radically different outlook, he has been dubbed "the patron saint of thought in Christianity."[2] Yet his writings are not theological treatises; they have a nonsystematic or, perhaps better, nontopical format. For instance, we obviously do not have a single place in Paul's epistles where we find a discussion developed under the heading "glory." Rather, his writings are "occasional," genuine letters directed to concrete conditions and problems in specific church situations. A notably "practical" or pastoral concern is always present, even in those sections of Romans where doctrinal reflection is most apparent.

---

[1] Geerhardus Vos, *The Pauline Eschatology* (1930; repr. Grand Rapids, MI: Baker, 1979), 149.
[2] Albert Schweitzer, *The Mysticism of Paul the Apostle* (English translation, New York: H. Holt, 1931), 377.

So, a real difficulty in interpreting Paul is that he is a theologian accessible only through his letters and records of his sermons. His letters are not theological treatises, yet in them we undeniably encounter Paul the theologian. In his writings we meet a thinker of reflective and constructive genius, with a decidedly doctrinal disposition, but only as he writes in a largely nonformalized theological, often doxological idiom, using a nonsystematic or nontopical format. A helpful analogy for this situation is to compare his letters to the visible portion of an iceberg. What is above the surface is but a small fraction of the total mass, which remains largely submerged, so that what is taken in, particularly at a first glance, may prove deceptive.[3]

A less pictorial way of putting this point is the principle, so important for sound interpretation, expressed in chapter 1, section 6, of the Westminster Confession of Faith: the teaching of Scripture is not only its express statements but also what follows "by good and necessary consequence." Particularly in the case of Paul, if we are going to make full sense of his letters as a whole, we must be prepared to wrestle with matters of "good and necessary consequence," of underlying structure, and with the sometimes nettlesome questions that emerge. This state of affairs, in large part, makes the extensive interpretation of Paul inherently arduous, even the precarious enterprise that 2 Peter 3:16 alerts us to. Pointing up this difficulty, however, needs to be balanced with the essential caveat that we not lose sight of the more basic and pervasive clarity of his teaching as God's Word (cf. esp. 1 Thess. 2:13). After all, Peter does not say that in Paul "all things" but "some things" are "hard to understand" (2 Pet. 3:16). With these preliminary matters in mind, we turn to examining his theology of glory.

The Gospel-glory of Christ

As good an entree point as any is the reference in 2 Corinthians 4:4, already noted at the outset, to "the gospel of the glory of Christ." In the immediate context Paul is concerned in a fundamental way with his ministry and message as focused on Christ, as the sweeping summary statement that follows directly in verse 5 shows: "For what we proclaim is not ourselves, but Jesus Christ as Lord, with ourselves as your servants for Jesus' sake." "The glory of Christ" is evidently a basic description of the gospel's content. Correlatively, that content is "the glory of God in the face of Jesus Christ" (v. 6).

Verse 5 sees this gospel-glory focused in who Christ is as Lord. Earlier in writing to the Corinthians, also in a context where he is concerned at

---

[3] Cf. Richard Gaffin Jr., *Resurrection and Redemption: A Study in Paul's Soteriology* (Phillipsburg, NJ: P&R, 1979; 1987), 28. James Dunn also makes a brief use of this analogy in his *The Theology of Paul the Apostle* (Grand Rapids, MI: Eerdmans, 1998), 15.

length in a fundamental way with his apostolic ministry of the gospel (1 Cor. 1:18–4:20), Paul calls Christ "the Lord of glory" (2:8), a description we will consider further below. So, divine glory manifested in Christ as Lord is, as much as anything, the substance of the gospel message Paul preaches.

Further, this glory-quality of the gospel invests it with an inherently light-bringing character; it is more fully described as "the light of the gospel of the glory of Christ." That glory-light is seen (v. 4) and known (v. 6) by believers. The same God who called light into existence at creation has in salvation brought believers to a shining awareness of Christ's new creation glory (v. 6; note the use of Gen. 1:3). As Paul will say a little later, those "in Christ" are of the "new creation" (5:17);[4] already they share in its glory, which is his. At the same time this glory is "veiled to those who are perishing"; as the "god of this age," Satan has "blinded the minds of unbelievers" to it (4:3–4 NIV).

This passage, with its explicit reference to Genesis 1:3, points up the Old Testament roots of Paul's understanding of glory.[5] In a brief overview, there *glory* and *honor*, including related verbs and adjectives, translate several words, primarily a group that stems from the Semitic root *kbd*. This word group, particularly the noun *kābôd*, has various senses—concrete ("abundance," "wealth," Gen. 31:1; Isa. 61:6; "splendor," whether of persons, e.g., Gen. 45:13 NASB; 1 Chron. 29:28, or of things, e.g., Isa. 22:18 NASB; Ezek. 31:18 MESSAGE; Hag. 2:3, 9 NLT) as well as abstract ("dignity," Ps. 112:9; Prov. 29:23; Jer. 48:18; "respect" or "reverence," 2 Chron. 32:33; Isa. 42:12; Mal. 1:6 NASB).

The often silent but plainly controlling presupposition of these different senses, with their varied applications, is that glory is preeminently a divine quality; ultimately considered, only God has glory. In view of his sovereignty as the creator of heaven and earth (Isa. 42:5; cf. 40:12–28), brought to bear for Israel's deliverance through his anointed servant (42:1–5), and excluding all idol worship, the Lord declares, "My glory I give to no other" (v. 8). Still, he grants glory. In a derivative fashion, glory exists on the creaturely plane. In the words of David's prayer, "Yours, O LORD, is . . . the glory and the victory and the majesty, for all that is in the heavens and in the earth

---

[4] Here *ktisis* is almost certainly cosmic ("creation"), not personal ("creature"); see Vos, *Pauline Eschatology*, 46-49; Herman Ridderbos, *Paul: An Outline of His Theology* (English translation, Grand Rapids, MI: Eerdmans, 1975), 45–46.

[5] This and the following four paragraphs adapt material from my article "Glory," in *New Dictionary of Biblical Theology*, ed. T. Alexander and B. Rosner (Downers Grove, IL: InterVarsity, 2000), 507–9; C. C. Newman, *Paul's Glory-Christology: Tradition and Rhetoric* (Leiden: Brill, 1992) provides a full exploration of the background and function of glory language in Paul.

is yours." At the same time, "riches and honor come from you" (1 Chron. 29:11–12).

Not surprisingly, then, the "glory of the LORD" (*k^ebôd y^ehôwāh*) is a fixed and widely occurring expression (e.g., Ex. 16:7; 1 Kings 8:11; Ps. 63:2). Specifically, God's glory is the signal manifestation of his visible and active presence. Divine glory fills the entire creation (Ps. 19:1; Isa. 6:3) and is apparent among the nations (Ps. 97:6). But, especially and most prominently, and closely associated with his name (Ex. 33:18–19; Ps. 115:1), God's glory is his presence in the midst of his covenant people Israel (Ex. 16:7 is the first such instance). Related to his grandeur and power as creator and redeemer, glory is often associated specifically with the phenomenon of light or fire, sometimes overwhelming, of such awe-inspiring and fear-evoking brilliance and unendurable intensity that it is shrouded in a cloud or otherwise veiled (Ex. 16:10; 24:17; cf. 33:22–23 and 34:29–35).

The Septuagint's decision to translate the Old Testament *kābôd* with *doxa* initiated a process of substantial semantic change in the latter (in secular Greek it meant "opinion," "reputation," "praise"). That change carries through into the New Testament usage of glory vocabulary, especially in John and Paul, with well over half of its occurrences in the latter.

In the Old Testament, then, glory is preeminently the manifestation-mode of who God is in the fullness of his self-revelation as creator and savior. Against that broad background and with reference to the creation of light in Genesis 1 and to God's glory that Paul finds implicit there, 2 Corinthians 4:4–6 affirms that divine glory has found its focused manifestation and, as we will see ever more clearly from the immediate and broader context of his teaching, its full and final manifestation in Jesus Christ as Lord. Further, the glory-manifestation that Christ is specifies the content of Paul's gospel.

How or in what sense, more specifically, is the substance of the gospel Paul preaches Christ in his glory or, as we will see it may be put in an important rephrasing, Christ as glorified? These verses provide a partial answer in the way they indicate the outcome of his preaching. Negatively, as already noted, Christ's gospel-glory is veiled to blinded unbelievers and so they perish (vv. 3–4a). Positively, believers are those enlightened by that glory and so are saved.

This antithetical outcome echoes the thought earlier in 2:14–16 where Paul compares the knowledge of Christ spread abroad by his gospel preaching to a fragrance: "the aroma of Christ" is a fragrance of death to those

who are perishing but a fragrance of life to those who are being saved.[6]
The gospel as Christ's glory-light also brings to mind what he later writes
to the Colossians (1:13), that believers in being "transferred" into Christ's
kingdom have been "delivered from the domain of darkness." Christ's glory
is gospel-glory because it is saving glory; his glory is his primarily because
he is Savior.

We note further that Paul surely intends that the 2 Corinthians 4 passage
be read in the light of what he wrote earlier about his gospel at the beginning of 1 Corinthians 15. In verses 3 and 4 perhaps, though not certainly,
he utilizes an already existing confessional fragment: "For I delivered to
you as of first importance what I also received: that Christ died for our sins
in accordance with the Scriptures, that he was buried, that he was raised
on the third day in accordance with the Scriptures." Within the immediate and overall context of Paul's teaching, this statement prompts several
observations pertinent to our interest.[7]

First, in the prepositional phrase, literally "among first things" (*en prōtois*),
"first" almost certainly has, as virtually all commentators take it, a qualita-
tive, not a temporal, sense. Most English translations properly render it "of
first importance." So, Paul speaks here of paramount concerns that have
their focus in Christ's death and resurrection.

Second, in light of verses 1 and 2 ("Now I would remind you, brothers, of
the gospel I preached to you . . . "), this focus or center is plainly the center
of his gospel. This, in turn, prompts an even broader observation. At verse
1, Paul is best read as reflecting on his ministry as a whole among the Corinthians. In view is not just a part of his proclamation, not just an aspect
of his teaching, but his message in its entirety. That disposes us to say that
Paul's theology is his gospel; his is a "gospel-theology." Or, viewed in terms
of expanding concentric circles, the center of Paul's theology is the gospel,
and at the center of that gospel are the death and resurrection. The focus
of the whole, its gospel-center, is Christ's death and resurrection.

Third, the death and resurrection are not in view as bare, isolated, unin-
terpreted facts. Two things are stipulated. First, their occurrence is "in
accordance with the Scriptures." That is, they have their meaning as they
fulfill the Jewish Scriptures, as they involve fulfillment of the Old Testa-

---

[6] These verses make the important point that while surely the proper purpose of proclaiming the
gospel for Paul is to save, an inevitable attendant consequence is that some who hear that preaching and reject it in unbelief perish. This echoes statements of Jesus such as in Luke 12:51 ("Do you
think that I have come to give peace on earth? No, I tell you, but rather division."). God's glory, as
we will see, also has this dividing effect; see esp. 2 Thess. 1:8–10.

[7] For a fuller discussion see Richard Gaffin Jr., *"By Faith, Not by Sight": Paul and the Order of
Salvation* (London: Paternoster, 2006), 22–30.

ment. Second, the death is said to be "for our sins." At the center of Paul's gospel-theology, then, Christ's death, together with his resurrection, as the fulfillment of Scripture, has its significance in relation to human ("our") sin and its consequences.

This brings us to the baseline conclusion, reinforced by a number of other passages (e.g., 1 Cor. 2:2; Gal. 6:14; 2 Tim. 2:8), that at the center of Paul's theology, constituting that center as much as anything, are Christ's death and resurrection, or, more broadly, messianic suffering and subsequent glory, his humiliation and consequent exaltation or glorification.

Relating this conclusion to what we have seen in 2 Corinthians 4, we may draw a further conclusion: glory has a central place in Paul's theology as a whole, specifically as the glory of Christ, crucified and resurrected, who saves from sin. Further consideration of his teaching on glory may be appropriately oriented, as a controlling point of reference, to this gospel-glory of Christ.

Christ: The Glory-image of God

Readers may have already noted in 2 Corinthians 4:4 that the glory-light of the gospel is not simply Christ but "Christ, who is the image of God." This addition points to the close association in Paul between glory and the divine image, an association that is most important for his overall teaching on glory. This can be seen in several passages.

1 Corinthians 11:7

This connection is most explicit, even pronounced, in 1 Corinthians 11:7: man is "the image and glory of God" and woman is "the glory of man." As made in God's image, man possesses and reflects, derivatively and in a creaturely fashion, the glory inherent in that divine image. Without entering into the details of this passage, which has been at the center among those in the ongoing debate in recent decades over women's role in marriage and the church, verse 7 hardly intends to deny that a woman is God's image or somehow less so than a man. Paul's teaching here is not in conflict with Genesis 1:27, namely, that man considered generically and differentiated as male and female is God's image. Rather, with Genesis 1 and 2 in the background here, that image-bearing equality underlies the mutual dependence he affirms of man and woman particularly as husband and wife (vv. 11–12).

At the same time this interdependent relationship is an irreversibly structured one. In it man is not "from woman" but woman "from man," nor is man created "for woman" but woman "for man" (vv. 8–9). That irreversible structure, entailing headship, is expressed in verse 7 by saying that "woman is the glory of man." But the eliding of "image" and the replacing of "God" with "man" in this description of woman's glory to highlight the relative headship of man is not to deny that on other grounds she, too, is "the image and glory of God."[8] To speak of the divine image as Paul does here and elsewhere, as we will see, carries with it implicitly the notion of glory, so closely does he associate the two.

1 Corinthians 15:42–49

The link between glory and divine image-bearing, for Christ specifically in 2 Corinthians 4:4 and generically for man (male and female) in 1 Corinthians 11:7, may be explored further in 1 Corinthians 15:42–49. In fact, this passage warrants extended examination, for the comprehensive outlook that it provides carries far-reaching ramifications for Paul's overall understanding of glory.

Verse 35 raises two questions: "How are the dead raised? With what kind of body do they come?" Though these questions were apparently put to Paul in a derisive fashion by the opponents he has to deal with in Corinth,[9] he nonetheless takes them seriously, for they trigger in large part his argument to the end of the chapter. This argument, which begins at verse 12, is concerned with elaborating and defending the resurrection-hope of the church.[10]

Verses 42 through 49 are remarkable both for the comprehensive outlook they provide and for the way they do so. Asked important and fairly specific questions about the mode of the resurrection and the nature of the resurrection body, Paul's response may at first glance seem like theological "overkill." That is because his response provides a perspective that is cosmic in its scope and encompasses the whole of history from its beginning to its consummation. It is fair to say that nowhere in Paul (or the rest of Scripture)

---

[8] I say "relative headship" because more is in view regarding headship than the relationship of man and woman (husband and wife); cf. v. 3, ". . . the head of every man is Christ, the head of a wife is her husband, and the head of Christ is God." "Paul does not hereby deny that woman was created in God's image, or that she, too, is God's glory." Gordon Fee, *The First Epistle to the Corinthians* (Grand Rapids, MI: Eerdmans, 1987), 516.

[9] Note the sharpness of Paul's immediate response, "Fool!" (v. 36, softened in most English translations). This opposition comes into view already at v. 12 and is clearly centered in denying the resurrection of the body. Without entering here into the considerable scholarly discussion concerning the specific background of that denial, it appears safe to say that controlling was an outlook stemming from the prevalent pagan Hellenistic mind-set of the day with its depreciation of things material, including the body; see, e.g., the discussions of Fee, *First Epistle to the Corinthians*, 715–17, and Anthony Thiselton, *The First Epistle to the Corinthians* (Grand Rapids, MI: Eerdmans, 2000), 1172–76.

[10] The resurrection of unbelievers, though affirmed by Paul elsewhere (Acts 24:15), is outside his purview in this chapter (as is also the case in 1 Thess. 4:13–18).

do we get a more all-encompassing outlook on the work of Christ than in verses 44b through 49.[11] In fact, considerations fundamental not only to the apostle's eschatology and Christology but also to his anthropology, soteriology, and pneumatology are present in this passage, considerations that together have an important bearing on his understanding of glory.

This comprehensive outlook happens by means of the developed parallelism that structures this passage. It opens (vv. 42–44) by contrasting the pre-resurrection body, the body as it bears the consequences of the fall and human sin (see esp. vv. 21–22 and Rom. 5:12–19), and the resurrection body, both marked by their respectively antithetical qualities. The one is perishable,[12] marked by dishonor and weakness; the other is imperishable, invested with glory and power. In one word, the pre-resurrection body is "natural" (literally, "soulish"[13]), the resurrection body is "spiritual." Glory in verse 43, then, is a function of the resurrection body as "spiritual." Clarifying this association of glory with the resurrection will be of primary interest as our discussion of the passage unfolds.

Adam and Christ as the "Last Adam"

A notable feature is the broadening that takes place beginning with verse 45. Now the contrast is no longer between bodies but whole persons, Adam on the one side, Christ as the "last Adam" on the other. This broadening has two dimensions. First, as the verses that follow show, especially 48 and 49, both are plainly in view not merely as isolated individuals but as principal representatives or heads. Further, as such they bring into view contrasting

---

[11] John Murray (*The Imputation of Adam's Sin* [Grand Rapids, MI: Eerdmans, 1959], 39) does not overstate, "In I Corinthians 15:22, 45–49 Paul provides us with what is one of the most striking and significant rubrics in all of Scripture."

[12] This quality (*phthora*) is not merely the capacity or liability for corruption that can result in mortality but actual mortality (cf. the word's use elsewhere in Paul, v. 50; Rom. 8:21; Gal. 6:8; Col. 2:22). After all, this body is "sown," a graphic reference to burial. Since for Paul human death is the result of sin (see esp. Rom. 5:12ff. with its closely related antithetical parallelism), the pre-resurrection body in vv. 42–44a is the post-fall, sin-cursed body. In v. 44b the pre-fall body comes into view. In this regard note the paragraph break at v. 44b in the NIV, appropriate in my judgment, to mark this shift.

[13] A satisfactory English translation of the adjective *psychikon* is notoriously difficult here. An apparently insurmountable challenge is how to bring out the tie in the Greek text with its cognate noun *psychē* in v. 45 ("soul," referring, as it does in Gen. 2:7 cited here, not to a constituent part but Adam as a whole, so "being," "person"). Both "natural," the most frequent proposal, and "physical" (RSV, NRSV) are deficient. The latter is thoroughly misleading because paired here antithetically with "spiritual," it leaves the seriously erroneous impression that the resurrection body, in contrast, is nonphysical or immaterial. "Natural" is ambiguous. From the normative vantage point of the original creation, brought into view as we will presently note in v. 45, the actually sin-ravaged and mortal pre-resurrection body is decidedly abnormal, "unnatural"; only in terms of creation as now under the effects of the fall is it all too "natural" (so Paul's only other use of the adjective in 2:14).

orders of life; each represents an environment or order of existence, the earthly order and the heavenly order, respectively. Adam is preeminently "the earthly one" and so has associated with him all human beings as "the earthly ones"; Christ, the last Adam and second man, is preeminently "the heavenly one" and has associated with him believers as "the heavenly ones." This environmental scope of the broadening is clear from the way the contrast is framed in explicitly cosmological language ("earth," "earthly"— "heaven," "heavenly") in verses 47 through 49.[14]

Second, the broadening to whole persons beginning with verse 45 is not only corporate and cosmic but also temporal. On the one side of the contrast Adam is introduced with an appeal to Genesis 2:7 and the creation narrative. Adam, in other words, is in view as he is by virtue of creation, not as fallen but as he was before the fall.[15] This expansion has the effect of providing, *in nuce*, a "philosophy" of history, Paul's outlook on history from its beginning up to and including its consummation.

The comprehensive sweep of that outlook is notable from the way Adam and Christ are identified and function in the argument. Adam is "first" (*prōtos*, v. 45); there is no one *before* him. Christ in his adamic identity is "second" (*deuteros*, v. 47); there is no one *between* Adam and Christ.[16] Christ as "second" is also "last" (*eschatos*, v. 45); there is none *after* him; he is, literally, *the* eschatological man. The order of Adam is first and has become subject to corruption and death through human sin (vv. 21–22; Rom. 5:12–19). The order of Christ is second and last; it is incorruptible and eschatological (see as well vv. 52–54). All told, then, in view are creation and its consummation, creation and new creation. In terms of the two-aeon construct taken over from Second Temple Judaism and rooted in the Old

---

[14] In v. 46 the neuter singular substantive expressions, *to psychikon* and *to pneumatikon* ("the natural," "the spiritual"), are most likely to be taken as generalizing expressions, after which an implied "body" (*soma*) ought not to be read, as do some translations and commentaries. To do so misses the environmental broadening that Paul has already clearly intimated in v. 45 and works out in vv. 47–49. *To psychikon* is the "natural" order, *to pneumatikon*, the "spiritual" order.

[15] The pre-fall situation is already in view on the one side in v. 44b ("If there is a natural body, there is also a spiritual body"), which the appeal to Gen. 2:7 in v. 45 functions to support. As Vos has observed (*Pauline Eschatology*, 169 n. 19), "From the abnormal body of sin no inference could be drawn to that effect [the resurrection body]. The abnormal and the eschatological are not so logically correlated that the one can be postulated from the other."

[16] As Paul is viewing things here, no one else in covenant history comes into consideration. No one else "counts" but Adam and Christ—not Noah, not Abraham and the promise, not Moses the lawgiver, not David as the Lord's anointed. Israel's unfolding "story," as important and integral as that undoubtedly is elsewhere in Paul's theology and for his reflections on redemptive history, is below the storyline or, better, below the narrative line of covenant history. Israel's history, though certainly included implicitly, is eclipsed and remains below the horizon encompassing the whole of history, as Paul sketches that horizon here.

Testament, in view are this present and provisional world-age and the com-ing eschatological world-age, each beginning with its own Adam.

Why does Paul proceed as he does in this passage? He broadens the sweep of the Adam-Christ contrast in two ways. First, he introduces Adam, as he was created, before the fall. Second, with that Paul broadens the con-trast to include the normal, pre-fall creation, before, in Adam, it became abnormal, subject to the corrupting and death-dealing effects of sin noted in verses 42 and 43. Why? The answer appears to be that Paul is intent here on showing that already at creation, prior to and apart from the fall, God's purpose anticipates and provides for a higher kind of bodily and personal existence, including the environment for that existence.[17]

This divine purpose, with the other considerations in the passage already noted that point to it, leads to the culminating statement of verse 49: "Just as we have borne the image of the man of dust, we shall also bear the image of the man of heaven." The *imago Dei* in which Adam was created, what Adam and those in him are by virtue of creation, is eschatologically ori-ented. That image comes to its intended and full realization not in Adam but instead now, because of his fall, in the last Adam, Christ, and in those in union with him.[18]

So, we may conclude, that the gospel-glory of "Christ, who is the image of God" (2 Cor. 4:4) is specifically the glory he possesses as the "heavenly" image-bearer seen within the comprehensive dimensions of the Adam-Christ parallelism that Paul utilizes in comparing the pre-resurrection and resurrection bodies. The glory predicated of the resurrection body in verse 43, then, belongs to this eschatological image-bearing. But what, more spe-cifically, does that glory aspect include and entail? Answering that question requires taking account of a facet of the passage not yet considered, one that is also of paramount importance not only for its overall sense but for Paul's understanding of glory.

Christ "Became a Life-giving Spirit"

As the last Adam, verse 45 states, Christ "became a life-giving spirit" (*pneuma zōopioun*). What is the sense of this assertion? First, it should be noted, "life-giving spirit" is not a timeless description of Christ but who he "*became*" (*egeneto*). When did that happen? What is the time point of this

---

[17] So Vos, *Pauline Eschatology*, 169, n. 19.

[18] Put in more formal theological idiom, this passage shows that for Paul protology (first things), apart from soteriology (matters pertaining to salvation), anticipates an eschatology (last things); there is an eschatology in view for the creation even before the fall. Correlatively, given human sin and the fall, the soteriology made necessary by that sin and secured in Christ is the means for realizing that eschatological goal.

"becoming"? There is little, if any, room for doubt that the answer is at his resurrection or, more broadly, together with the ascension, his exaltation. The flow of reasoning in chapter 15 makes that virtually certain.

The controlling thesis of the entire argumentation beginning at verse 12 to the end of the chapter is the use of the term "firstfruits" (*aparchē*) applied to Christ as resurrected, in verses 20 and 23. This agricultural image captures the unity, the unbreakable bond, that there is between his resurrection and the future bodily resurrection of believers. To extend the metaphor as Paul surely intends, Christ's resurrection is the "firstfruits"—the beginning of the resurrection—"harvest" that will include theirs at his return.[19] His resurrection is not merely an event, however stupendous, isolated in the past. In its past historicity it initiates and makes visible the harvest of resurrection belonging at the end of history as it has already entered history.

This "firstfruits" bond or solidarity is implicit in the hypothetical pattern of argument in the immediately preceding section (vv. 12–19). The two resurrections, Christ's and the future bodily resurrection of believers, are in view not as two separate events but as two episodes of one event. So much are the two of one piece that Paul can argue in both directions, not only from the resurrection of Christ to the resurrection of believers (v. 12), but also, conversely, to deny their resurrection is to deny his (vv. 13, 15, 16).

It would make no sense for Paul to argue for the resurrection of believers in this way, staking everything on the inseparable harvest-bond between Christ's resurrection and theirs, if Christ were "life giving" by virtue, say, of his preexistence or incarnation, or any consideration other than his resurrection. This is not to suggest that his preexistence and incarnation are unimportant or nonessential for Paul, but they lie outside his purview here. Expressed in key terms of the chapter, as "firstfruits" of the resurrection-harvest, Christ is "a life-giving spirit"; conversely, as "a life-giving spirit" he is "the firstfruits."

Further, according to verse 47, the last Adam, as "the second man," is now, by virtue of his ascension, "from heaven."[20] In this sense, as resurrected and ascended, he is, preeminently, "the man of heaven" (v. 48). So, as he has become "a life-giving spirit" in his resurrection, the last Adam is the primary, "firstfruits" instance of the heavenly image (v. 49) with its glory

---

[19] As noted earlier, it should be kept in mind that the resurrection of unbelievers is not within Paul's purview in this chapter; see above, n. 10.

[20] In view of the immediate context, this prepositional phrase is almost certainly an exaltation predicate ("heaven" is where Christ now belongs), not a description of origin, say, out of preexistence at the incarnation.

(v. 43). Christ's glory, as he has become life-giving Spirit, is climactically manifested as he is the bearer of the heavenly glory-image.

Second, if "a life-giving spirit" is who Christ became in his resurrection and who he now is as exalted, what is the meaning in this description of "spirit" (*pneuma*)? This question is disputed, and a satisfactorily detailed treatment is beyond the scope of this chapter, so I will merely state my view with a brief indication of supporting grounds.[21]

The reference is to the person of the Holy Spirit. In support of that understanding is the link between *pneuma* ("spirit") in verse 45 and *pneumatikon* ("spiritual") in verses 44 and 46. Each has its sense as they are plainly related as cognate noun and adjective. Elsewhere in Paul the adjective, which occurs repeatedly, regularly refers, with only one clear exception (Eph. 6:12), to various matters associated with the activity of the Holy Spirit (e.g., Rom. 7:14; Gal. 6:1; Eph. 1:3; Col. 1:9). As the adjective has that reference, so the noun in verse 45 refers, correlatively, to the person of the Spirit, as it does frequently and almost always elsewhere in Paul. This consideration is reinforced by the only other occurrence in Paul (or the New Testament) of the *psychikon/pneumatikon* contrast earlier in 1 Corinthians (2:14), where in the immediate context (vv. 10ff.) the adjective refers to the believer (*ho pneumatikos*) as enlightened and led by the Spirit.[22]

A consideration reinforcing this conclusion is that the last Adam did not simply become "spirit" but "life-giving" (*zōopoioun*) spirit. This participial modifier is an instance of a verb that Paul most often uses with the Holy Spirit as its subject (Rom. 8:11; 1 Cor. 15:22; 2 Cor. 3:6; by implication, Gal. 3:21). So, in verses 44 through 46 as the adjective *pneumatikon* refers to what is marked by the activity of the Spirit, the noun *pneuma* refers to his person (and its English translation ought to be capitalized, "Spirit").

The last half of verse 45 states, then, that in being raised from the dead, Christ, as the last Adam, became life-giving Spirit in the sense of the Holy Spirit. The terms of this equating or identifying of the resurrected Christ with the Spirit need to be noted. It is not ontological as if Paul is here expressing a purely functional Christology that is indifferent to or denies the personal distinction between Christ and the Spirit. Eternal, inner-Trinitarian

---

[21] For a full argumentation see Richard Gaffin Jr., "The Last Adam, the Life-giving Spirit," in S. Clark, ed., *The Forgotten Christ* (Nottingham: Apollos; Inter-Varsity, 2007), 211–25 and the literature, pro and con, cited there.

[22] Note also Jude 19, "worldly people (*psychikoi*), devoid of the Spirit." I take it that the long-standing effort to enlist 1 Cor. 2:14–15 in its immediate context in support of an anthropological trichotomy (with *pneumatikos* here referring to the human *pneuma* come to its revived ascendancy) is not successful and ought to be abandoned; see, e.g., J. Murray, *Collected Writings of John Murray*, vol. 2 (Edinburgh: Banner of Truth, 1977) 23–33, esp. 23–29.

relationships and distinctions are outside his purview. Rather, Paul has in view what has happened in *history* and as Christ is the last *Adam*, the second *man*. He has in view what is true in terms of his genuine humanity, not his essential deity.[23] With these qualifications maintained uncompromised, the equation affirmed in verse 45 may be termed "functional" or "eschatological" or, in older theological idiom, "economic" (in distinction from "ontological"). Verse 45 affirms that the resurrected Christ and the Spirit are one in the specific respect of giving life—eschatological, resurrection life with its inherent glory (v. 43).

Subsequently in writing to the Corinthians Paul will say, "Now the Lord is the Spirit, and where the Spirit of the Lord is, there is freedom" (2 Cor. 3:17). We will consider this statement in its context below but on the understanding noted here that, though commentators are divided, the more plausible case to be made is that "Lord" refers to the exalted Christ and the statement is closely related to 1 Corinthians 15:45.[24] The "is" of 2 Corinthians 3:17, we may say, rests on the "became" of 1 Corinthians 15:45. Also, the "freedom" in view is eschatological, the close concomitant of Spirit-worked resurrection life with its glory (e.g., in Rom. 8:2, 21: "For the law of the Spirit of life has set you free in Christ Jesus"; "the freedom of the glory of the children of God").

Third, within 1 Corinthians 15 and the contrast of the immediate context (vv. 42–49) two closely related considerations appear to coalesce in the affirmation of verse 45c. At his resurrection the incarnate Christ (a) was thoroughly transformed *by* the Spirit and (b) came into complete and permanent possession *of* the Spirit. The resulting relationship between the incarnate Christ and the Spirit is so unprecedented and climactic that it is properly and appropriately captured by saying that Christ became the life-giving Spirit.

So far as the relationship between the resurrected Christ and believers is concerned, the preceding paragraph accents (a) the continuity between them and (b) his uniqueness and the difference between them. Regarding (a), as the life-giving Spirit Christ is the first instance of the resurrection body, the "firstfruits" (v. 20) manifestation of the same body that believers will possess at his return (cf. 1 Thess. 4:13–17). What, through the Spirit,

---

[23] A recent and convincing demonstration of Paul's clearly Trinitarian understanding of God is in Gordon Fee, *God's Empowering Presence: The Holy Spirit in the Letters of Paul* (Peabody, MA: Hendrickson, 1994), 825–45, esp. 839–42. The personal, parallel distinction between God (the Father), Christ as Lord, and the (Holy) Spirit—underlying subsequent doctrinal formulation—is clear enough in, e.g., 1 Cor. 12:4–6; 2 Cor. 13:13; Eph. 4:4–6.

[24] See Gaffin, "The Last Adam, the Life-giving Spirit," 222–24 for argumentation as well as literature, pro and con, cited there.

God has done in raising Jesus from the dead he will also do for believers (the most likely meaning of Rom. 8:11). As the life-giving Spirit and by virtue of the transformation he has experienced in his resurrection, he now bears the heavenly image with its glory that believers, too, will one day bear bodily (v. 49).

It continues to be necessary to point out in the face of widespread and persistent misunderstanding that "spiritual" does not refer to the makeup of the resurrection body, to the immaterial substance of which it is composed. Rather, that adjective is Paul's single label of choice for the resurrection body with its glory because it most adequately and appropriately describes the body that has been perfected with the effects of sin entirely eradicated by the activity of the Holy Spirit. In view is the transmuted but genuinely physical character of the believer's resurrection body, the eschatologically transformed physicality of the believer's person by the Spirit.[25] The work of the Spirit with and in the individual believer reaches its culmination in the resurrection of the body. As we will see in more detail below, God's "good work" begun in believers finds its "completion at the day of Jesus Christ" in the change that will take place in their bodily resurrection with its manifest glory (Phil. 1:6 with 3:21).

Glory, then, is one of the three characteristics, together with imperishability and power, that Paul predicates of the Spirit-renovated and perfected resurrection body, the Spirit-consummated heavenly image. These characteristics are not merely mentioned as several from a larger list; they are essential. Because of what has transpired in Christ's resurrection and ascension and who he now is as exalted, there is the closest association throughout Paul between the Spirit, eschatological life, glory, and power. Within this conceptual complex the Spirit clearly has priority in the sense that life, glory, and power are related to the Spirit as "products to the Producer."[26]

So, from the vantage point of glory the body of the resurrected Christ, the "life-giving Spirit," is "the body of His glory" (Phil. 3:21 NASB). And in the parallelism of 1 Timothy 3:16 Christ's justification "in the Spirit" correlates with his ascension "in glory" (NASB). The tie between glory and eschatological life is also seen in Romans 2:7 ("glory and honor and immortality . . . eternal life"; cf. v. 10) and Colossians 3:4 ("When Christ who is your life

---

[25] With an eye to this transformation the resurrection body is also aptly labeled "transphysical," as N. T. Wright, coining a term, has recently proposed—"the 'trans' is intended as a shortening of 'transformed.'" *The Resurrection of the Son of God* (Minneapolis: Fortress, 2003), 477; see also 606–7, 612, 661.

[26] Vos, *Pauline Eschatology*, 302.

appears, then you also will appear with him in glory"), as well as, correlatively, the link between glory and power in Ephesians 1:18–19 ("the riches of the glory of His inheritance" [NASB] of the ascended Christ among the saints is on the order of "the immeasurable greatness of his power" toward them) and elsewhere (Eph. 3:16; Col. 1:11; 2 Thess. 1:9).

The close linking of the Spirit, life, glory, and power also appears in the indications of agency in Christ's resurrection. While that agency is attributed to the Spirit (Rom. 1:4; 8:11; 1 Tim. 3:16) and to God's power (1 Cor. 6:14), according to Romans 6:4, he "was raised from the dead by the glory of the Father." All told, we may say that life and power are related to the inner, hidden side and glory to the outer, visible side of the eschatological transformation wrought by the Spirit.[27]

The resurrection body with its qualities that Christ has by becoming the life-giving Spirit is the first instance of the resurrection body each believer will have. Only he, however, is the life-giving Spirit. That cannot be said of "the heavenly ones," only of "the heavenly one." Believers do not themselves become givers of the Spirit. They have the Spirit only as they have received the Spirit. Christ, not the church together with Christ, is the source of the Spirit. The pattern of expression in Romans 8:9–10 is instructive on this point. Because Christ has become the life-giving Spirit, the Spirit is now "the Spirit of Christ." Consequently, only as Christ by the Spirit is "in" those who "belong to him" (who are "in him," as Paul frequently says elsewhere) is the Spirit "in" them and are they "in the Spirit."[28] Christians, then, are not themselves sources of glory. Their glory is theirs only as it is derivative of Christ's in his role as the life-giving Spirit.

Conclusion

We have given considerable attention to 1 Corinthians 15:42–49 with its single reference to glory for the perspective it provides, more comprehensive than any other single passage in Paul, on glory. That is so particularly as his gospel is at the center of his theology as a whole and concerns, as much as anything, the glory of Christ as the image of God. Drawing together the threads of our discussion of the passage, glory is preeminently the glory of the exalted Christ, the consummate glory he both possesses and, as we will consider further, shares with believers, as he has been constituted

---

[27] This is the conclusion of ibid., 314. See his penetrating discussion of this relationship (302–15).

[28] 1 Cor. 15:45c may be seen as a one-sentence commentary on Pentecost and its significance. What Peter delineates in Acts 2:32–33 (resurrection—ascension and heavenly session—reception of the Spirit—outpouring of the Spirit), Paul telescopes by saying, "The last Adam became a life-giving spirit."

the life-giving Spirit by being resurrected bodily and, as ascended, is the heavenly image-bearer. The glory-image of the last Adam in its finality and permanence answers to and is the realization of God's purposes in the beginning in the creation of Adam as his image-bearer. In passing here, but not unimportantly, this eschatological divine image-bearing of Christ by virtue of his resurrection is reinforced in Colossians 1:15–20. This passage has a sweeping outlook spanning his role in creation and redemption: as "the firstborn from the dead" (v. 18) he is "the image of the invisible God, the firstborn of all creation" (v. 15).[29]

For Paul, glory is associated primarily with the Spirit and his power in giving resurrection life and effecting eschatological transformation, first in Christ himself, "the man of heaven" (v. 48), and then in "those who belong to Christ" (v. 23), "those who are of heaven" (v. 48). Virtually everything that Paul teaches about glory traces back in one way or another to the resurrection-based matrix of the Spirit, life, power, and glory present in this passage.

This basic conclusion, that, for Paul, Christ's gospel-glory is a predicate rooted in his exaltation, may seem unduly limiting. In particular, it may appear to fail to account adequately for his statement that if "the rulers of this age" had grasped the hidden mystery of "God's wisdom" revealed in the cross, "they would not have crucified the Lord of glory" (1 Cor. 2:7–8 NASB). Does not Paul here attribute glory to Christ prior to his resurrection? Certainly, but in what sense?

In 1 Corinthians 1:18–29 Paul is emphatic: "the word of the cross" (v. 18) and "Christ crucified" (v. 23), deemed foolish, weak, and despicable by the "world" of unbelief (v. 20), are "the power of God and the wisdom of God" (v. 24). So, though not explicitly stated, by extension, particularly in view of the reference to power,[30] Christ's cross also exhibits the glory of God. This, however, does not mean that Paul invests the cross with an isolated glory of its own as if, in dialectical fashion, the suffering and ignominy of the cross are in themselves a matter of glory.[31]

Without his subsequent resurrection from the dead, Christ's cross lacks any efficacy and is completely devoid of power and glory, and the unbelieving world's assessment of the cross would be irrefutable. Paul could hardly

---

[29] I must dispense with a detailed discussion of this passage, including questions concerning its literary structure and possibly pre-Pauline origin.

[30] Cf. the link between glory and power in 1 Cor. 15:43, already discussed.

[31] There is surely, however, "the divine irony" noted by Fee (*First Epistle to the Corinthians*, 106). Just those who in "the wisdom of this age" (1 Cor. 2:6) crucify Christ bring about the eternally purposed "wisdom of God" (v. 7) revealed in Christ (1:24, 30).

make that clearer than he does later in chapter 15:14, 17–19. So, when in 2:2 he says, "For I decided to know nothing among you except Jesus Christ and him crucified," this fundamental epistemic commitment is not made to the exclusion of the resurrection. Worth noting at this point, because it is particularly applicable to Paul, is the observation, made at least as early as Calvin,[32] that in Scripture, references to Christ's death alone or to his resurrection alone are a synecdoche. To speak of the one always has in view the other in its significance. They are unintelligible apart from each other; each conditions the meaning of the other. The glory of Christ secured and revealed in his resurrection casts an anticipatory aura on his cross.

An important key to what Paul intends by "the Lord of glory" in 1 Corinthians 2:8 is present just prior in verse 7: the cross concerns the wisdom that "God decreed before the ages for our glory." As we have seen Paul makes clear later in chapter 15, this eternal divine purpose is realized in the glory associated with the resurrection body. So, commensurately, Christ is "the Lord of glory" with a view to the glory that he would and now does possess as resurrected.

In Galatians 6:14 Paul declares, "But far be it from me to boast except in the cross of our Lord Jesus Christ." Here "boasting" (*kauchasthai*), semantically related to glory, is associated with the cross in an exclusive manner reminiscent of 1 Corinthians 2:2. Yet the qualification immediately follows that for him (and, representatively, for every believer) the cross effects a mutual crucifixion to "the world" that results, in turn, in belonging to a "new creation" (cf. 2 Cor. 5:17), the consummate eschatological order that dawns with Christ's firstfruits resurrection with its attendant glory (1 Cor. 15:20, 23).

2 Corinthians 3:6–11
This passage has the highest concentration of glory language in Paul, a total of ten occurrences of the noun and related verb (*doxazō*) in verses 7 through 11. At verse 6, in the course of defending and reflecting on his apostolic ministry (2:14–4:6), Paul contrasts the old (cf. 3:14) and new covenants in terms of a fundamental, life-and-death antithesis: "the letter kills" marks the former,[33] "the Spirit gives life," the latter. Interestingly here, glory is

---

[32] John Calvin, *Institutes of the Christian Religion*, trans. F. L. Battles, ed. J. T. McNeill, The Library of Christian Classics, 20 (Philadelphia: Westminster Press, 1960), 1:521 [2:16:13].

[33] This is true by metonymy. Strictly speaking, Paul is clear elsewhere (e.g., esp. Rom. 7:7–13) that it is not the letter or the law but sin that kills (cf. vv. 14–15). The law with its imperatives but without the antecedent indicative of grace confirms and intensifies death as the consequence of sin (Rom. 6:23). 2 Cor. 3:6 should be read in the light of Gal. 3:21, the law is not able to make alive from sin and death; only the Spirit has that capability.

the common denominator of this antithesis. The old covenant was by no means lacking in glory; it had its own glory (v. 7). However, even with the unbearable intensity of the light phenomenon associated with the glory of the old (v. 7), the glory of the new covenant is greater (vv. 8, 9). In fact, the surpassing glory of the new is so transcending that it is as if the old had none by comparison (v. 10). All told (v. 11), the essential difference is the "fading" (cf. v. 7 NASB) and transient glory of the old in relation to the "permanent" and abiding glory of the new. Since this consummate new covenant glory is preeminently "of the Spirit" (v. 6), verses 6 through 11 reinforce the link between glory and the Spirit, in particular his eschatological life-giving activity, prominent in 1 Corinthians 15:42–49.

A noteworthy feature in this passage is that the new covenant with its glory is "the ministry of righteousness" (v. 9). Since this characterization is in antithesis to the old covenant as "the ministry of condemnation," it is best taken as referring specifically to the righteousness that justifies. This brings into view a wide and important terrain in Paul's teaching that we will not explore but make only the following observation. The justifying righteousness established in Christ's "becoming obedient to the point of death" (Phil. 2:8) and his resurrection (e.g., Rom. 4:25; 2 Cor. 5:21) is invested with eschatological glory. Accordingly, the justification of "the ungodly" (Rom. 4:5) in their being united to Christ by faith (e.g., Gal. 2:16–17; Phil. 3:9) and based exclusively on that righteousness likewise shares in that final glory.

In verses 7 through 11 Moses stands for the old covenant, the Spirit for the new. In verses 12 through 15, however, a shift in persons occurs on the one side. Moses continues to represent the old covenant but, instead of the Spirit, Christ (v. 14) represents the new. This has the effect of raising the question of the relationship between Christ and the Spirit under the new covenant. As if in answer, verse 16 relates the unveiling of Moses in the glory-presence of the Lord in Exodus 34:34 to Christ as Lord, and verse 17a states, "Now the Lord is the Spirit" ("the Lord who is the Spirit," v. 18).[34]

This affirmation is related to what Paul wrote earlier: "the last Adam became a life-giving spirit" (1 Cor. 15:45); the "is" of the one statement flows from the "became" of the other. The equation or unity expressed in both is not ontological but economic or functional. By his exaltation the incarnate Christ and the Spirit are one; in 2 Corinthians 3:17 they are one in granting eschatological freedom, and the Lord-Christ is now the eschatological glory-image (v. 18, cf. "the image of the man of heaven," invested by the Spirit with resurrection and ascension glory, 1 Cor. 15:49).

---

[34] See above, n. 21.

Conformity to the Glory-image of Christ

The focus of this chapter so far has been on Christ and his glory. The glory of Christians, however, has also come into view in a number of ways because his glory and theirs are not really susceptible to separate treatment in Paul. By the nature of the case Christ's glorification is not only for himself but also for them. His glory, as we have seen, is preeminently his gospel-glory, that is, his glory as the savior of sinners. The glory he has as "the heavenly one" is not an isolated glory or for himself alone. Rather, it is the glory that he shares together with believers, "the heavenly ones," who are destined with him to bear that exalted glory-image. It remains for us to detail some further aspects of this sharing in Christ's glory.

Romans 3:23 provides the most appropriate point of departure: "for all have sinned and fall short of the glory of God." The variation in tense here is instructive. The reference to sin is in the aorist tense (*hēmarton*) and speaks to the settled reality that all human beings are sinners. Most likely in view are both having actually sinned, just described so unsparingly in verses 10 through 18, as well as original sin, addressed subsequently in 5:12–19. The reference to falling short or lacking glory is in the present tense (*hysterountai*), to the ongoing consequence of sin.[35]

How is this persisting universal human lack of divine glory to be understood? The answer lies in the close connection, prominent in Paul, between glory and divine image-bearing, not only for Christ but also for human beings generally.[36]

Romans 3:23 is, in effect, a pointed summary of the preceding lengthy indictment of human sin as universal in 1:18–3:20. The passage opens (1:18–20) condemning the inexcusable suppression of the truth about God, specifically the truth of "his eternal power and divine nature," as creation itself clearly reveals these "invisible attributes." These characteristics, as openly manifested, are primarily in view in 1:23 as "the glory of the immortal God." There the point is made that this glory has been "exchanged . . . for an *image* in the form of corruptible *man* and of birds and four-footed animals and crawling creatures" (NASB). This exchange stems from the "futile" and "foolish" thinking that did not "honor (*endoxasan*) him as God," that is, thinking that did not glorify him or acknowledge his revealed glory as God

---

[35] "The sinning is represented as past; the present and abiding consequence of sin is the want of the *glory of God.*" Charles Hodge, *Commentary on the Epistle to the Romans* (Grand Rapids, MI: Eerdmans, 1955), 90.

[36] See the comments above (pp. 133–34) on 1 Cor. 11:7. Some commentators (e.g., Hodge) take "glory" in Rom. 3:23 in the sense of "praise" and as referring to the divine approbation that sinners are lacking or, in other words, their guilt. The guilt that sin incurs is certainly a prominent consideration in the immediate context (e.g., v. 19) but is not likely the point here.

(1:21). Climactically, all that is involved in this suppression of the truth is summed up as having sinfully "exchanged the truth about God for a lie," an exchange that ultimately consists in having "worshiped and served the creature rather than the Creator" (1:25).

For Paul the essence of human sin is the rebellion of the creature against the Creator in whose image he has been made, a renouncing of the truth of the creaturely dependence that divine image-bearing entails, for the lie of human self-sufficiency and independence from God. This deeply rooted revolt is such that human beings refuse to acknowledge God's glory evident in the entire creation and evident particularly in and to themselves because they, uniquely as creatures, are God's image. The creaturely capacities given with being that image, capacities to be for God, for doing his will and obeying his law, are instead directed against him in devoting to self or some other creature the worship and service due to him alone. The result of sin is not the loss of the divine image but its defacement or distortion, the loss of image-bearing integrity. In this sense all human beings are sinners who "fall short of the glory of God" (3:23).

This forfeited privilege of reflecting God's glory, however, is not Paul's final word about that glory for sinful image-bearers. Rather, at work is the operative principle, "where sin increased, grace abounded all the more" (Rom. 5:20). The glory-image, universally defaced and perverted in Adam, is restored and perfected first in Christ and then in those in union with him. As we have seen, 1 Corinthians 15:44b–49 especially shows that (cf. vv. 21–22; Rom. 5:12–19). In response to human sinfulness and the loss of image-bearing glory, God displays his glory specifically in his saving grace. His evident glory as creator is now enhanced by the revelation of his glory as redeemer, by his gospel-glory, preeminently and especially "the glory of God in the face of Jesus Christ" (2 Cor. 4:6).

To that end God has predestined salvation through the cross "before the ages for our glory" (1 Cor. 2:7; cf. 1:18, 23). In Ephesians 1 his more ultimate purpose for those "he chose . . . in [Christ] before the foundation of the world, that we should be holy and blameless before him," correlatively, for those "he predestined . . . for adoption as sons through Jesus Christ," is "the praise of the glory of His grace" (vv. 4–6 NKJV). The glory of his grace (vv. 12, 14) is such that he is, as "the God of our Lord Jesus Christ, the Father of glory," who provides for the saints in all of its richness "his glorious inheritance" (or "the glory of his inheritance," *tēs doxēs tēs klēronomias autou*, Eph. 1:17–18).

This linking of glory with saving grace in Ephesians 1 and specifically with adoption (God as Father, inheritance) and holiness, is present as well, with the additional inclusion of image-bearing, in the overall perspective on God's predestinating purposes in Romans 8:29–30. Verse 29 states, in a telescoping fashion, the ultimate goal, the omega-point, of God's effective and discriminating foreknowledge issuing in the predestination of its objects: it is for them to be "conformed to the image of his Son, in order that he might be the firstborn among many brothers." This image is specifically the Son's as he has been glorified; he is "the firstborn among many brothers" because he is "the firstborn from the dead" (Col. 1:18). As verse 30 then delineates, this brotherly or familial image-conformity, with Christ as preeminent ("that in everything he might be preeminent," Col. 1:18), is, in a word, their being "glorified."[37] To that ultimate end they have been called and justified. Their justification is the essential precondition for their glorification. Because they "have been justified by faith" they "have peace with God" and so in this settled state of "grace," they "rejoice in hope of the glory of God" (Rom. 5:1–2). Their confident justification-based expectation is that because of the way God's glory has been manifested in Christ, they will share in that glory in their own glorification.

This future glorification, as 1 Corinthians 15:49 in its immediate context (vv. 42ff.) makes clear, will be realized in their bodily resurrection at Christ's return. Then and only then will they bear bodily "the image of the man of heaven" and experience the psycho-physical change that resurrection will entail (cf. v. 51). Only then will their bodily image-bearing be rid of perishability, dishonor, and weakness and invested instead with glory along with its close correlatives, imperishability and power (vv. 42–43). Then, by his power as resurrected Christ, he "will transform our lowly body" (literally, "the body of our humiliation") "to be like his glorious body" ("the body of his glory," Phil. 3:21). Then, in their possession of this "spiritual" body, with their bodily existence now transformed by the Spirit, the conformity to Christ's image in view in Romans 8:29 will be complete. In this sense, "when Christ who is your life appears, then you also will appear with him in glory" (Col. 3:4).

This appearance in resurrection-glory at Christ's return will not happen in a vacuum but involves an "ecology." As we have already noted in 1 Corinthians 15:45–49, the bodily resurrection of believers has a cosmic setting. That cosmic scope comes out even more clearly and remarkably in Romans 8:18–23. There Paul writes of the incomparable "glory that is

---

[37] This past tense almost certainly does not describe glorification as already completed since in view from v. 18 on is "the glory that is to be revealed" at the time of the resurrection of the body (v. 23). The aorist tense (*edoxasen*) is best taken as proleptic, "intimating the certainty of its accomplishment." John Murray, *The Epistle to the Romans* (Grand Rapids, MI: Eerdmans, 1959), 1:321.

to be revealed to us" (v. 18). That future glory has in view "the redemption of our bodies," that is, the bodily resurrection that believers eagerly await as their "adoption" (v. 23).[38]

At the same time, the creation as a whole has a stake in this adoptive bodily resurrection-redemption of believers.[39] Presently it exists in a state of "eager longing" for their "revealing [as] the sons of God" (v. 19). This longing is, more specifically, an expectant, even hope-filled groaning, "a grand symphony of sighs,"[40] itself to be unburdened, along with believers, from the "futility" that now permeates it because of the curse on human sin. It will be freed with them from this "bondage to corruption" so that it shares in their coming into full possession of "the freedom of the glory of the children of God" (vv. 20–21). With sin and all its consequences removed, the adoptive glory revealed in the resurrection of the body will be coincident with the "glorification" of creation, a transformation so resplendent that the entire creation will radiate eschatological glory.[41]

The glorification of believers is not only future, in the change that will be effected in the resurrection of the body, but is also present in a renewal already initiated and underway. Specifically, in terms of a basic anthropological distinction for Paul, "though our outer self is wasting away, our inner self is being renewed day by day" (2 Cor. 4:16).[42] In the deepest recesses of who they now are, at the core of their being—what Paul elsewhere and more frequently calls the "heart" (e.g., Rom. 1:24; 2:29; 8:27; 1 Cor. 4:5; 2 Cor. 3:2–3)—believers are no longer turned away from God's glory but are drawn toward it and even into it in a transforming way.

As "Christ was raised from the dead by the glory of the Father," he is the source of "newness of life," life that finds its expression in their "walk," their ongoing, daily conduct (Rom. 6:4). This new life is specifically his resurrection life, the life he possesses as the "life-giving Spirit" and even now, with its inherent glory, shares with believers in union with them. In that vital sense, not only a representative sense, they are already "raised with Christ" (e.g., Eph. 2:5–6; Col. 2:12–13; 3:1). All told, though still "in [the]

---

[38] Clearly they are already God's adopted children and have received "the Spirit of adoption" (vv. 14–16). In v. 23 (cf. v. 21) their bodily resurrection openly reveals that adoption. For a fuller discussion see my *By Faith, Not by Sight*, 92–94.

[39] In view is the entire non-image-bearing creation, inanimate as well as animate, with the evident exclusion of Satan and all who serve him, unrepentant human, and angelic beings (cf. Eph. 6:12).

[40] Murray, *Romans*, 1:305 (quoting Philippi).

[41] Vv. 20–22 are fairly seen as Paul's commentary, in effect, on the account of the fall in Genesis 3.

[42] Cf. Gaffin, *By Faith, Not by Sight*, 53–58; Ridderbos, *Paul*, 115–21.

mortal body" they are nonetheless "alive from the dead" (Rom. 6:12–13 NASB). Along with this present sharing in resurrection-glory believers are given a new identity. No longer are they slaves of sin but of God and righteousness, which they are now free to serve (vv. 13, 16–22).

The sanctifying of the church for which Christ has cleansed it by lovingly giving himself is already underway, with the end in view that at his return (cf. Phil. 1:6), "without spot or wrinkle or any such thing . . . holy and without blemish," it, too, like him, might be "in splendor" or "glorious" (*endoxon*, Eph. 5:25–27). So, all they now do, down to the details of their everyday living, is to be "to the glory of God" (1 Cor. 10:31). As an important instance, in their sexual conduct they are to know that their "body is a temple of the Holy Spirit within you" (cf. 1 Thess. 4:8), so that in view of the glory inherent in that indwelling of the Spirit, as God's own bought possession they are to "glorify God in [their] body" (6:19–20).

Paul's most pointed assertion of present glorification, also explicitly associated with image-bearing, is 2 Corinthians 3:18: "And we all, with unveiled face, beholding the glory of the Lord, are being transformed into the same image from one degree of glory to another." At verse 6 Paul begins contrasting old- and new-covenant glory in order to highlight the surpassing glory of the new (v. 11) as "the ministry of the Spirit" (v. 8).[43] The Spirit-efficacy of new-covenant glory is seen in particular as the veil of unbelief is removed when one turns to Christ as Lord (vv. 14, 16). In fact, "the Lord is the Spirit" (v. 17a) and Christ, glorified as Lord, and the Spirit are one in their activity of granting eschatological "freedom" (v. 17b; cf. the resurrected Christ as "a life-giving spirit," 1 Cor. 15:45).

That freedom is such that "with unveiled face," that is, by faith in Christ and the gospel (cf. "the gospel of the glory of Christ," 4:4), Christians "behold" (or less likely, "reflect") his glory as Lord or, as Paul says a few verses later, "the glory of God in the face of Jesus Christ" (4:6). This faith beholding (cf. 5:7) is such that they are presently being transformed into "the same image," the glory-image of the exalted Christ. Already, in their "inner self" (4:16; cf. "Christ . . . formed in you," Gal. 4:19) they are undergoing the transformation for which, as we have seen, they have been predestined (Rom. 8:29) and which will be completed in their "outer self," by bodily resurrection (1 Cor. 15:49; Phil. 3:21). This transformation into his image, as it comes "from" Christ, "the Lord who is the Spirit," is already underway "from glory to glory" (NASB; *apo doxēs eis doxan*). This is true whether this means a process "from one degree of glory to another" or, as seems more

---

[43] See the discussion of this passage above, 144–45.

likely, the glory-transformation from its already realized initiation to its still future consummation.[44]

This present glorification of the church parallels the experience of its "Lord of glory" prior to his resurrection (1 Cor. 2:8). In an important aspect of Paul's teaching that we can touch on only briefly here, the Spirit-worked, open-faced transformation brought about by faith in the gospel is for now veiled by suffering and adversity.[45] A fundamental condition of the Christian life is that "we suffer with him in order that we may also be glorified with him" (Rom. 8:17b; cf. 2 Cor. 1:5). In fact, until our future bodily resurrection, conformity to Christ's glory-image takes place as much as in any other way, just as his resurrection power finds expression—in "becoming like him in his death" and as we "share his sufferings" (Phil. 3:10–11; cf. 2 Cor. 4:10–11).[46] Accordingly, for Paul, too, as Peter puts it, believers are to rejoice as they share in Christ's suffering not only as they look for the future revelation of his glory but also because in the midst of that suffering "the Spirit of glory and of God rests upon [them]" (1 Pet. 4:13–14). In his resurrection glory Christ, the life-giving Spirit, is ever with the church in its present trials and suffering.

In view of this pervasive duress Paul's prayer is that believers might be powerfully strengthened by God "according to his glorious might (*to kratos tēs doxēs autou*), for all endurance and patience with joy" (Col. 1:11). And he assures them that the "light momentary affliction" associated with their present "outer self" existence is producing "an eternal weight of glory beyond all comparison" (2 Cor. 4:17; cf. v. 16). Taking everything into consideration, "the sufferings of this present time are not worth comparing with the glory that is to be revealed to us" (Rom. 8:18). On that "day," at Christ's return as Lord, not only will those who have rejected the gospel be punished with "eternal destruction," consisting of separation from his presence and from "the glory of his might," but he, climactically, will "be glorified in his saints" (2 Thess. 1:8–10). To that end Paul prays for the church that until then in every way, "the name of our Lord Jesus may be glorified in you, and you in him" (v. 12).

---

[44] Cf. Paul Barnett, *The Second Epistle to the Corinthians* (Grand Rapids, MI: Eerdmans, 1997), 208.

[45] For a discussion of relevant passages, primarily in Paul, see my "The Usefulness of the Cross," *WTJ* 41 (1978–1979): 228–46.

[46] In my view the two uses of "and " in v. 10 are best taken not as coordinating but explanatory: to "know Christ" is to know "the power of his resurrection" which, in turn, is to know "the fellowship of His suffering," an experiential knowing that, all told, is glossed as "being conformed to His death" (NASB).

Conclusion

We have considered God's glory as a central theme in Paul's gospel because that gospel is at the center of his theology as a whole. In Colossians 1:23, in a context where at a later point in his gospel ministry he is reflecting on that ministry in its entirety, he speaks of "the hope of the gospel." Unsurprisingly but impressively, this gospel-hope is focused on who Christ is and what he has achieved, particularly in his death and resurrection. Through Christ's death on the cross God has reconciled all things to himself (vv. 20, 22) and Christ is now "the firstborn from the dead" (v. 18). As crucified and resurrected, he is "the firstborn of all creation" (v. 15) and "in him all the fullness of God was pleased to dwell" (v. 19; cf. 2:9).

As such, Christ further is "the mystery hidden for ages and generations but now revealed" (v. 26)[47]—the realization, at last, of the salvation purposed by God from eternity for all nations, not just one, for Gentiles as well as Jews. The magnitude of this universal salvation in its full dimensions is such that it prompts Paul to speak of it in terms of its glory, in fact "the riches of the glory of this mystery." And then, as if to bring to a focus again all that he has been saying about Christ in the preceding verses, he adds that the mystery revealed is "Christ in you, the hope of glory" (v. 27; cf. 2:2–3). For Paul this as much as anything centers the hope of the gospel—the exalted Christ present with the church and indwelling every believer. "Christ in you, the hope of glory"—it would be difficult to find a more appropriate note on which to end a study of the glory of God in Paul.

---

[47] On the use of "mystery" here and elsewhere in Paul, see especially Ridderbos, *Paul*, 46–49.

6

. . . .

Toward a Theology of the Glory of God

CHRISTOPHER W. MORGAN

. . . .

The design of the ensuing discourse is to declare some part of that glory of our Lord Jesus Christ which is revealed in the Scripture, and proposed as the principal object of our faith, love, delight, and admiration. But, alas! After our utmost and most diligent inquiries, we must say, How little a portion is it of him that we can understand! His glory is incomprehensible, and his praises unutterable.

—John Owen

As clowns yearn to play Hamlet, so I have wanted to write a treatise on God.

—J. I. Packer

Such are the opening lines of two classic works: John Owen's *The Glory of Christ* (1684) and J. I. Packer's *Knowing God* (1973).[1] Both writers exude an appropriate spirit of humility, something critical for all of us as we grapple with these wonderful truths about our triune God. This humility does not,

---

[1] John Owen, *The Glory of Christ: His Office and Grace* (1684; reprint, Fearn, Ross–shire, UK: Christian Heritage/Christian Focus Publications, 2004), 23; J. I. Packer, *Knowing God* (Downers Grove, IL: InterVarsity, 1993), 11. Packer later reminds, "The more complex the object, the more complex the knowing of it" (35).

however, keep Owen or Packer from writing the best books they can about God. For while they feel the burden of their finitude, both authors also know that God has spoken—and they bear the conviction that they must strive to understand as much as possible about what God has spoken.

As we have seen thus far in this volume, we can study nothing as monumental or overwhelming as our glorious God. Yet through creation, humanity, the person of Jesus Christ, and his Scripture, God has graciously revealed himself—and truth about himself—to us. To be sure, his revelation is not exhaustive but partial, as is inherent for communication from an infinite God to his finite creatures. But though God has not spoken exhaustively, he has spoken truly and sufficiently. This means that while the depths and particularities of these truths about God and his glory will remain out of our reach, by God's grace and through his revelation, we can and do know in part.

Up to this point, we have been studying particular portions of the Bible to see what they teach about God's glory, arguably "the foundational theme of New Testament theology,"[2] biblical theology in general,[3] and the very purpose of all creation and history. Now it is time to try to see how these truths cohere. Attempting to formulate a systematic theology of the glory of God seems more than a bit foolish for finite persons. It is like wading in a vast ocean: we may have some experience and knowledge of the sea, but we can make no pretense of plumbing its immense depths. Thus, instead, we will take on the much more manageable task of working *toward* a theology of the glory of God. To do so we will seek to uncover how the Bible defines God's glory, how it links this holistically to God, and how it displays varied expressions of God's glory.

The challenge is enormous. In a way that is consistent but by no means uniform,[4] every major section of Scripture addresses the subject of the glory of God: Law, Prophets, Writings, Gospels, Acts, Pauline Epistles, General Epistles, and Revelation. Every major doctrine is also significantly related to it: revelation, God, humanity, sin, Christ, salvation, the church, and eschatology. Further, many key turning points in the biblical story stress God's glory and attest to its varied manifestations:[5]

---

[2] Thomas R. Schreiner, *New Testament Theology: Magnifying God in Christ* (Grand Rapids, MI: Baker, 2008), 135.

[3] James M. Hamilton Jr., "The Glory of God in Salvation through Judgment: The Centre of Biblical Theology," *TynBul* 57.1 (2006): 57–84.

[4] Note the distinctions and subtleties to the presentations of God's glory in comparing, e.g., Exodus to Isaiah, Psalms to Ezekiel, Luke to John, or any of the above to Paul.

[5] Several of these manifestations were highlighted well in Everett F. Harrison, "Glory," in *ISBE* 2:477–83.

1. God's glory is revealed through creation (Genesis 1; Ps. 19:1–2; Rom. 1:18–25).

2. God's glory is identified with humans' being created in the image of God, crowned with glory (Genesis 1–2; Ps. 8:3–5; 1 Cor. 11:7).

3. God's glory is linked to the exodus (Exodus 3; 13:31; 16:10; 24:9–18; 34:29).

4. God's glory is linked to fire/bright light/shining (Exodus 3; 13:31; 16:10; 24:9–18; 34:29; Lev. 9:23; Isa. 60:1–3; 60:19; Ezek. 1:28; 10:4; 43:2; Luke 2:9; 2 Cor. 3:7; 4:4–6; Heb. 1:3; Rev. 18:1; 21:11, 23).

5. God's glory is linked to a cloud (Ex. 16:7, 10; 24:16; 40:34; Lev. 9:6, 23; Num. 14:21; 16:19, 42; 20:6; Deut. 5:22–24; 1 Kings 8:10; 2 Chron. 5:14; Luke 9:26–36; Acts 1:8–11).

6. God's glory is linked to the Sabbath (Exodus 19, 24).[6]

7. God's glory was manifested to Moses (Ex. 33:18–23), when Moses described his experience of God's glory in something resembling physical form.

8. God's glory fills the tabernacle (Ex. 40:34; cf. Lev. 9:6, 23; Num. 14:21; 16:19, 42; 20:6).

9. God's glory fills the earth (Num. 14:20–23; Ps. 19:1–2; Isa. 6:3).

10. God's glory fills the temple (1 Kings 8:11).

11. God's glory is above the heavens (Ps. 8:1; 113:4: "The LORD is high above all nations, and his glory above the heavens!").

12. God's glory is revealed in a vision to Isaiah (Isa. 6:1–5).

13. God's glory is revealed in a vision to Ezekiel (Ezek. 1:28; 3:12, 23; 8:4; 9:3; 10:4, 18; 11:22).

14. God's glory is identified with his people, Israel (Isa. 40:5; 43:6–7; 60:1).

15. God's glory is identified with Christ, including his incarnation (John 1:1–18; notice also the light theme; Mark 9:2; Heb. 1:3); birth narratives (Luke 2:9, 14, 32); miracles (John 2:11; 11:38–44); transfiguration (Matt. 17:1–13; Mark 9:2–13; Luke 9:28–36; 2 Pet. 1:16–21); suffering and crucifixion (John 7:39; 12:16, 23–28; 13:31–32; 17:1–5; 21:19; Luke 24:26; Rom. 3:25–26; 1 Pet. 1:10–11); resurrection/exaltation (Acts 3:13–15; Rom. 6:4; Phil. 2:5–11; Heb. 2:5–9; 1 Pet. 1:21; Rev. 5:12–13; cf. Acts 2:32–33; 3:13; 1 Tim. 3:16); ascension (Acts 1; 1 Tim.

---

[6] Meredith G. Kline, *Images of the Spirit* (1980; repr. S. Hamilton, MA: self-published, 1986). Cf. Michael S. Horton, *People and Place: A Covenant Ecclesiology* (Louisville, KY: Westminster, 2008), 14: "Creation and new creation are interdependent themes, especially with the unifying theme of the procession of creation into the 'seventh–day' consummation led by the creature bearing the Creator's image and likeness."

3:16); session/reign (Stephen's vision in Acts 7:55–56; Mark 10:37); and coming/victory/judgment (Matt. 16:27; 19:28; 24:30; 25:31; Mark 8:38; 10:37; 13:26; Luke 9:26; 21:27; Rom. 8:21; 2 Thess. 1:6–9; Titus 2:13).

16. God's glory is identified with the Holy Spirit (1 Pet. 4:14; cf. John 16:14; Eph. 1:13–14).

17. God's glory is identified with the church (Eph. 1:22–23; 3:20–21; 5:22–29).

18. God's glory is manifested in the new creation (Isaiah 66; Rom. 8:18–27; Rev. 21–22).[7]

Glory and Glories

As we might expect concerning a truth so interwoven into the fabric of the biblical story, we find that the Bible speaks of the glory of God in different senses. This is partly why God's glory is, as John Frame acknowledges, one of the hardest Christian terms to define.[8] Because of this, we need to use care as we construct definitions that faithfully represent the Bible's own usage.

At a basic level, it is helpful to notice that the "glory of God" is sometimes used in the Bible as an adjective, sometimes a noun, and sometimes a verb: *God is glorious* (adjective), *reveals his glory* (noun), *and is to be glorified* (verb).

More particularly, "glory" translates the Hebrew term *kabod* and the Greek term *doxa*.[9] *Kabod* stems from a root that means "weight" or "heaviness." Depending on its form, it could have the sense of honorable, dignified, exalted, or revered. C. John Collins explains that it became "a technical term for God's manifest presence." It is similar in many respects to the concept of God's name in the Old Testament.[10]

According to Sverre Aalen, *doxa* in secular Greek refers to an opinion, conjecture, repute, praise, or fame. He maintains that the concepts were transformed by the Septuagint. Aalen also maintains that *doxa* translated

---

[7] Many of these themes are in Revelation 21–22: Eden, temple, ark, light, creation, Israel, church, Christ, etc.

[8] John Frame, *The Doctrine of God, A Theology of Lordship* (Phillipsburg, NJ: P&R, 2002), 592.

[9] See chapter 2 in this volume by Tremper Longman III, "The Glory of God in the Old Testament." Although it receives attention in sermons, *shekinah* occurs primarily in the inter-testamental period. See Gerhard Kittel, ed., *Theological Dictionary of the New Testament*, trans. Geoffrey W. Bromiley (1964; repr. Grand Rapids, MI: Eerdmans, 2006), 2:232–55.

[10] C. John Collins, "*kabod*," in *New International Dictionary of Old Testament Theology and Exegesis*, ed. Willem A. VanGemeren (Grand Rapids, MI: Zondervan, 1997), 2:577–87; cf. Gerhard von Rad, *Old Testament Theology*, trans. D. M. G. Stalker (1962; repr. Peabody, MA: Hendrickson/Prince, 2005), 1:238–41.

kabod and took on the same meaning, referring to God's manifestation of his person, presence, and/or works, especially his power, judgment, and salvation.[11]

Using these terms, the Bible speaks of the glory of God in several distinct senses. First, *glory is used as a designation for God himself.* For example, Peter refers to God the Father as the "Majestic Glory" (2 Pet. 1:17). This rare phrase is apparently a Hebrew way of referring to God without stating his name.

Second, *glory sometimes refers to an internal characteristic, an attribute, or a summary of attributes of God.* This is similar to saying that glory is occasionally used as an adjective. God is intrinsically glorious in the sense of fullness, sufficiency, majesty, beauty, and splendor. Examples of this usage abound. Psalms refer to God as "the King of glory" (24:7–10) and "God of glory" (29:3). Stephen speaks of "the God of glory" (Acts 7:2), and the apostle Paul prays to "the Father of glory" (Eph. 1:17). Displaying a remarkably high Christology, James refers to Jesus as the "Lord of glory" or the "glorious Lord," depending on how one translates it (2:1).[12] Either way, the point is the same: like the Father, Jesus is characterized by glory. The Spirit, too, is identified with glory (1 Pet. 4:14; cf. John 16:14; Eph. 1:13–14), especially through the language of presence, indwelling, and temple (John 14–16; Rom. 8:9–11; 1 Cor. 3:16; 6:19–20; 14:24–25; 2 Cor. 6:16; Eph. 2:11–22; 5:18; 1 Thess. 4:8).

Third, the Bible speaks of *glory as God's presence.* As we noted, Collins and Aalen both underscore this in their explanations of the Hebrew and Greek terms for glory. This understanding of glory is emphatic in the events surrounding the exodus. The glory cloud (Exodus 13–14; 16:7, 10; 20; 24; cf. Rev. 15:8), the manifestations to Moses (Exodus 3–4; 32–34), and God's presence in the tabernacle (Ex. 29:43; 40:34–38) all highlight God's covenant presence.[13] Walter Kaiser puts it simply, "Glory, then, is a special term that depicts God's visible and active presence."[14] This connotation of God's glory also emerges in passages related to the ark of the covenant (1 Samuel 4–5), the temple (1 Kings 8:10–11; 2 Chronicles 5–7), the eschatological temple in Ezekiel (43:1–5), the person of Christ (John 1:1–18; Colossians

---

[11] Sverre Aalen, "*doxa*," in *NIDNTT*, 2:44–48; cf. Kittel, 2:232–55.

[12] See Christopher W. Morgan, *A Theology of James*, Explorations in Biblical Theology, ed. Robert A. Peterson (Phillipsburg, NJ: P&R, 2010).

[13] See Longman, "The Glory of God in the Old Testament," in this volume.

[14] Walter C. Kaiser Jr., *The Majesty of God in the Old Testament: A Guide for Preaching and Teaching* (Grand Rapids, MI: Baker, 2007), 120.

1–2; Hebrews 1), the Holy Spirit (John 14–16), and indeed heaven itself (Revelation 21–22).

Fourth, the Bible often depicts *glory as the display of God's attributes, perfections, or person.* John's Gospel speaks of glory in this way, as Jesus performs "signs" that manifest his glory (2:11). The Bible uses various terms for this concept but the idea is clear: God glorifies himself in displaying himself. As he puts his works on display he glorifies himself. His mercy, grace, justice, and wrath are all displayed in salvation and judgment (cf. Rom. 9:20–23; Eph. 2:4–10).

A fifth connotation of *glory is as the ultimate goal of the display of God's attributes, perfections, or person.* Exodus and Ezekiel are replete with passages that unfold God's actions for the sake of his name, or in order that people will know he is the Lord.[15] Jesus instructs that Lazarus's death and subsequent resurrection had an ultimate purpose: it was for the glory of God (John 11:4; cf. 14:13). Peter's death also shared this purpose (John 21:19). Paul points out that God chooses, adopts, redeems, and seals us "to the praise of the glory of His grace" (Eph. 1:6, 12, 14 NASB). That is, in saving us, God displays his grace; and in displaying his grace, he brings glory to himself. Further, the whole Trinitarian plan of redemption displays this goal, as seen in the mutual glorification of each person of the Trinity. The glorious Father sends the glorious Son, who voluntarily humbles himself and glorifies the Father through his incarnation, obedient life, and substitutionary death (Phil. 2:5–11; cf. John 6, 10, 17). In response the Father glorifies the Son, resurrecting him from the dead and exalting him to the highest place (Acts 3:13–15; Rom. 6:4; Phil. 2:9–11). The Father sends the glorious Spirit who glorifies the Son (John 16:14). And this all redounds to the glory of the Father (Phil. 2:11).[16]

Sixth, *glory sometimes connotes heaven, the heavenly, or the eschatological consummation of the full experience of the presence of God.* Hebrews 2:10 speaks of "bringing many sons to glory"; Philippians 4:19 offers the covenant promise "and my God will supply every need of yours according to

---

[15] See Jonathan Edwards, "The End for Which God Created the World," in *God's Passion for His Glory*, ed. John Piper (Wheaton, IL: Crossway, 1998), 237–39; cf. Hamilton, "The Glory of God in Salvation through Judgment," 64, who lists: "For texts that declare that people or other things will *know that I am Yahweh* (and related expressions), see Exod. 6:7; 7:5, 17; 8:18 (ET 22); 10:2; 14:4, 18; 16:12; 29:46; 31:13; Deut. 29:5; 1 Ki. 20:13, 28; Isa. 45:3; 49:23, 26; 60:16; Jer. 9:23 (ET 24); 24:7; Ezek. 5:13; 6:7, 10, 13, 14; 7:4, 9, 27; 11:10, 12; 12:15, 16, 20; 13:14, 21, 23; 14:8; 15:7; 16:62; 17:21, 24; 20:12, 20, 38, 42, 44; 21:4, 10 (ET 5); 22:16, 22; 24:27; 25:5, 7, 11, 17; 26:6, 14; 28:22, 23, 26; 29:6, 9, 21; 30:8, 19, 25, 26; 32:15; 33:29; 34:27, 30; 35:4, 9, 12, 15; 36:11, 23, 36, 38; 37:6, 13, 14, 28; 38:23; 39:6, 7, 22, 28; Joel 4:17 (ET 3:17)."

[16] See "The Glory of God in John's Gospel and Revelation" by Andreas Köstenberger, in this volume.

his riches in glory in Christ Jesus" (cf. Eph. 3:16, "according to the riches of his glory"). The people of God will ultimately receive glory, honor, immortality, and eternal life, which are used somewhat synonymously (Rom. 2:7). Such glory was prepared for them in eternity (Rom. 9:23). Jesus is also said to be "taken up in glory" (1 Tim. 3:16), which could be understood as in heaven or gloriously or a combination of the two. The bodies of believers, too, will be raised "in glory" (1 Cor. 15:43), and faithful elders will receive an unfading crown of glory (1 Pet. 5:4).

Seventh, *giving glory to God may also refer to appropriate response to God in the form of worship, exaltation, or exultation.*[17] Psalm 29:2 urges, "Ascribe to the LORD the glory due his name." At Jesus' birth, after God's glory shines (Luke 2:9), the heavenly host resounds with "glory to God in the highest" (Luke 2:14) and the shepherds are "glorifying and praising God" (Luke 2:20). Further, the Bible is filled with doxologies, such as Romans 16:27, that accentuate our need to give glory to God: "To the only wise God be glory forevermore through Jesus Christ" (cf. Rom. 11:36; Gal. 1:5; Eph. 3:20–21; Phil. 4:20; 2 Tim. 4:18; Jude 24–25; Rev. 1:5–6). Some doxologies are directed toward Christ (2 Pet. 3:18; cf. Heb. 13:21). Similarly, other passages instruct God's people to glory in Christ (2 Cor. 10:17), in his cross (Gal. 6:14), and in our suffering by virtue of our union with Christ (2 Corinthians 11–12). Glorifying God is an expected and appropriate response of God's people (Matt. 5:13–16; 15:31; Mark 2:12; Luke 4:15; John 15:8). We are even commanded to glorify God in our bodies (1 Cor. 6:20), in our food and drink choices along with their corresponding relationships (1 Cor. 10:31), and in the proper exercise of spiritual gifts (1 Pet. 4:11). Romans 14 and 15 underline the importance of the church glorifying God with a unified voice; as the church displays unity to the glory of God (15:6–7), the Gentiles will glorify God (15:8–9; cf. Rev. 4–5).

It is important to notice that these multiple meanings are distinct but related. We might think of it this way: *the triune God who is glorious displays his glory, largely through his creation, image-bearers, providence, and redemptive acts. God's people respond by glorifying him. God receives glory and, through uniting his people to Christ, shares his glory with them—all to his glory.* The divinely initiated and sovereignly guided interaction spirals forward to the consummation and throughout eternity. Though a chart can by no means capture these ideas, it might be helpful.

---

[17] For a more detailed list of passages, see C. C. Newman, "Glory," *DLNT*, 395–96.

Figure 6.1: Glory to Glory

God's Internal Glory		God's External Glory		Creatures' Response to Glory		God Receives Glory		God Shares Glory		All unto God's Glory
(glory possessed)	→	(glory displayed and shared)	→	(glory ascribed)	→	(glory received)	→	(glory displayed and shared)	→	(glory purposed)

So the Bible speaks of various nuances of God's glory, all central in the biblical story:

- glory possessed
- glory purposed
- glory displayed
- glory ascribed
- glory received
- glory shared

To restate, the God who is intrinsically glorious (*glory possessed*) graciously and joyfully displays his glory (*glory displayed*), largely through his creation, image-bearers, providence, and redemptive acts. God's people respond by glorifying him (*glory ascribed*). God receives glory (*glory received*) and, through uniting them to the glorious Christ, shares his glory with them (*glory shared*)—all to his glory (*glory purposed, displayed, ascribed, received, and graciously shared throughout eternity*). It could be argued that the entire biblical plotline of creation, fall, redemption, and consummation is the story of God's glory.[18]

At the ground of all this is the fact that the intrinsically glorious God extrinsically displays his glory. So to God's intrinsic and extrinsic glory we now turn.

God's Intrinsic and Extrinsic Glory

Fundamentally, the glory of the triune God is both intrinsic and extrinsic. God is intrinsically glorious, in the sense of fullness, sufficiency, majesty, honor, worth, beauty, weight, and splendor. God's glory is then extrinsically set forth, as John Calvin memorably put it: "The world was no doubt made,

---

[18] Glory possessed and glory displayed will be treated under "God's Intrinsic and Extrinsic Glory"; glory ascribed under "Divine Sovereignty and Human Responsibility"; glory received under "Full and Received"; glory shared under "Unique and Shared"; and glory purposed under "God's Ultimate End and Other Ends."

that it might be a theatre of the divine glory."[19] Because of God's gracious communication, his glory is something that may be seen, marveled at, and rejoiced in.

Jonathan Edwards saw this and referred to God's glory as internal and also as a communication of himself.[20] More recently, David Huttar observed that God's glory is intrinsic, "prior to any external manifestation of it" and "fundamentally independent of external manifestation." He added, "Yet it is also true that God's glory is also manifest."[21]

While most theologians grant that the glory of God is in some sense intrinsic and extrinsic, they vary on how they categorize it and especially how they understand what I call here "intrinsic." For example, in his *New Testament Theology* Donald Guthrie lists glory first in his discussion of God's attributes.[22] Walter Elwell references "God's glory as his being."[23] R. Albert Mohler Jr. asserts, "God's glory is best understood as the intrinsic beauty and external manifestation of God's being and character."[24] John Piper exults that "the glory of God is the infinite beauty and greatness of his manifold perfections."[25] J. I. Packer designates it as "fundamental to God" and refers to God's glory as the "excellence and praiseworthiness set forth in display."[26] In his *Systematic Theology*, Wayne Grudem addresses glory as the last summary attribute (after perfection, blessedness, and beauty) and focuses his definition on its extrinsic nature: "God's glory is the created brightness that surrounds God's revelation of himself." Later he clarifies:

This "attribute" of God is really not an attribute of God in the sense that the others were, for here we are speaking not of God's own character but of the

---

[19] John Calvin, *Commentaries on the Epistles of Paul the Apostle to the Hebrews* (repr. Grand Rapids, MI: Baker, 2003), 266. These are his comments on Hebrews 11:3.

[20] Edwards, "The End for Which God Created the World," 230–41.

[21] David K. Huttar, "Glory," in *Evangelical Dictionary of Biblical Theology*, ed. Walter A. Elwell (Grand Rapids, MI: Baker, 1996), 287–88.

[22] Donald Guthrie, *New Testament Theology* (Downers Grove, IL: InterVarsity, 1981), 90–94; cf. Timothy George, "The Nature of God: Being, Attributes, and Acts," in *A Theology for the Church*, ed. Daniel L. Akin (Nashville: Broadman, 2007), 222.

[23] Walter A. Elwell, *Topical Analysis of the Bible* (Grand Rapids, MI: Baker, 1991), 41.

[24] R. Albert Mohler Jr., "In the Beginning: The Glory of God from Eternity," a sermon preached at the Ligonier Ministries' 2003 National Conference. In this sermon, Mohler suggests that there is a tension between God's internal glory, which is unchanging, and its external manifestation, which varies.

[25] John Piper, "To Him Be Glory Forevermore (Romans 16:25–27)," a sermon delivered December 17, 2006.

[26] J. I. Packer, "The Glory of God," in *New Dictionary of Theology*, ed. Sinclair B. Ferguson and David F. Wright (Downers Grove, IL: InterVarsity, 1988), 271–72. Packer refers to this as "glory shown" and distinguishes it from his other category, "glory given," which is "honor and adoration expressed in response to this display."

created light or brilliance that surrounds God as he manifests himself in his creation. Thus, God's glory in this sense is not actually an attribute of God in himself. Nevertheless, God's glory is something that belongs to him alone and is the appropriate outward expression of his own excellence.[27]

In his treatment of the theology of Jonathan Edwards, John Gerstner places the treatment of God's glory at the end of the natural attributes of God and at the beginning of the moral attributes, because, according to Gerstner, Edwards viewed the glory of God as belonging to both and as expressing infinite knowledge, holiness, and happiness.[28] Gerstner explains:

> In the sermon on Psalm 89:6 Edwards had the glory of God consisting in God's greatness (natural attribute) and goodness (moral attribute). *So glory is another word used for the sum total of all divine excellencies. It refers to the internal as well as manifestative glory. The latter amounts to a setting forth of the attributes in their reality and fullness.*[29]

These helpful definitions and descriptions reveal the inherent challenge related to speaking of God's glory. Biblical and systematic theologians struggle to answer the question, "Is God's glory an attribute, a summary attribute, his being, or the outward expression of his being?"

Old Testament scholars tend to come at all this differently. Some, like John Collins, underscore God's glory as his manifest presence.[30] Raymond Ortlund speaks similarly, but also ties glory to God's nature and beauty: "What is the glory of the Lord? His glory is the fiery radiance of his very nature. It is his blazing beauty. . . . The glory of the Lord . . . is God himself becoming visible, God bringing his presence down to us, God displaying his beauty before us."[31] Others, like John Hartley, view God's glory as the manifestation of his essence, which is often linked to God's holiness.[32]

---

[27] Wayne Grudem, *Systematic Theology: An Introduction to Biblical Doctrine* (Grand Rapids, MI: Zondervan, 1994), 220–21.

[28] John H. Gerstner, *The Rational, Biblical Theology of Jonathan Edwards* (Powhatan, VA: Berean, 1993), 2:33–34.

[29] Ibid., 2:34 (italics added).

[30] Collins, "*kabod*," in *NIDOTTE*, 2:577–87.

[31] Raymond C. Ortlund Jr., *Isaiah: God Saves Sinners*, Preaching the Word, ed. R. Kent Hughes (Wheaton, IL: Crossway, 2005), 237.

[32] More work needs to be done on the relationship between God's holiness and glory. Hartley is helpful: "Holiness, being the quintessential character of God, is the center of divine motivation. It affects everything God does. Moreover, the adjectives attached to holiness, such as majestic, glorious, and awesome, inform us that the essence of beauty is holiness. . . . Holiness is powerfully manifested in God's revelations: God's commission of Moses at the burning bush (Ex. 3:1–4:17), God's deliverance of Israel at the sea (Ex. 15:2–18), the theophany at Sinai (Ex. 19:1–24:18) and Moses' special vision of God (Ex. 33:18–34:9). . . . The holy God often manifested his presence

Hartley follows C. Vriezen here, who defines *glory* as "the radiant power of [God's] Being, as it were the external manifestation of [God's] mysterious holiness."[33]

I suggest that the way forward is to perceive what lies behind both approaches. Despite the initial differences, there is a shared understanding of the glory of God as the extrinsic manifestation of the intrinsic. While some highlight God's presence,[34] others see the intrinsic glory as an attribute, or as some sort of summary of his attributes, or even more broadly as God's holiness, essence, or nature. *Some sort of holistic or macro approach to understanding the intrinsic nature of God's glory becomes necessary, however, because the Scripture plainly links the extrinsic display of God's glory to a variety of God's attributes and works, as well as to terms that stress his very person and nature.*

Further, it seems best to understand *God's extrinsic glory as the communication of God's intrinsic fullness and sufficiency.* In Romans 11:36, for example, Paul concludes: "For from him and through him and to him are all things. To him be glory forever." God's self-sufficiency and glory are intricately linked: God is the creator ("from him"), sustainer ("through him"), and goal ("to him") of all things. The self-sufficient and independent God creates out of fullness, guides out of fullness, and receives back according to his communicated fullness.[35]

Before we proceed, we should pause and recognize that if God's intrinsic glory were not displayed extrinsically, we would be unable to know any of this. All we know about God's intrinsic glory is through God's self-revelation, particularly Scripture, which records and interprets the extrinsic display of God's intrinsic glory. Further, since the infinite God does not exhaustively communicate himself to finite creatures, the extrinsic display is less than the intrinsic. As awe-inspiring as the extrinsic glory is, it never fully expresses

---

as a glowing brightness comparable to a fire. . . . This glory-holiness juxtaposition is very similar to that found in Isaiah 6:3. . . . [Ex 40:34–35] is the denouement of the book of Exodus. The glory that had led Israel out of Egypt and had appeared on Mount Sinai now came and occupied the newly built tabernacle. The holy God had come to dwell among the covenant people. This powerful manifestation of God's glory communicated to the Israelites the power, dignity, and splendor of God's holiness" (420–22). See John E. Hartley, "Holy and Holiness, Clean and Unclean," in *Dictionary of the Old Testament Pentateuch*, ed. T. Desmond Alexander and David W. Baker (Downers Grove, IL: InterVarsity, 2003), 420–31.

[33] C. Vriezen, *An Outline of Old Testament Theology* (Newton Center, MA: C. T. Branford, 1966), 150; cited in Hartley, "Holy and Holiness, Clean and Unclean," 422.

[34] In such discussions, it is important to remember God's unity/simplicity. See Louis Berkhof, *Systematic Theology* (Grand Rapids, MI: Eerdmans, 1941), 62; Grudem, *Systematic Theology*, 178–80.

[35] Frame, *The Doctrine of God*, 607; Edwards, "The End for Which God Created the World," 150–61. I thank Steve Wellum for his ideas related to this point.

the fullness of God's intrinsic glory that it communicates. That being so, even to begin to understand God's intrinsic glory, we must examine his extrinsic displays.

Note how Scripture adjoins the display of the glory of God to a variety of his attributes: holiness (Lev. 11:44; Isa. 6:1–8; Revelation 4–5; 21–22); uniqueness (Isa. 42:8); power (Ex. 13:21ff.; 16:10ff.; John 11:40; Rom. 6:4; 2 Thess. 1:8–9); beauty; majesty; and goodness.[36] God's glory is also tied to his works: creation (Genesis 1–2; Psalm 19); salvation (Ex. 13:21–22; Ephesians 1); providence (Ex. 16:10–12; 40:36–38); judgment (Num. 14:10–23; 16:41–45; Ezek. 39:21–29; Matt. 16:27–28; 2 Thess. 1:8–9); and victory (Ex. 16:7–12; Ps. 57:5–11; Isa. 2:10–21). Even more astounding is that Scripture links our triune God's glory with more holistic ideas that stress his very nature: God's presence (Ex. 33:13–18; 40:34; 1 Sam. 4:21–22; Ps. 84:11; 2 Thess. 1:8–10; Jude 24; Revelation 21–22);[37] name;[38] holiness, which many Old Testament scholars see as his essence (Lev. 11:44; Isa. 6:1–8; Revelation 4–5; 21–22); face; Spirit; fullness; and honor (1 Tim. 1:17; cf. 2 Pet. 1:17).

Since God's glory is the extrinsic display of so many attributes, of a panorama of God's works, and of holistic terms related to God's very nature, it is clear that God's intrinsic glory must be viewed holistically. Put differently, if the display of God's power is a display of his glory, if a display of God's holiness is a display of his glory, and if his presence is a central meaning of his glory, then glory must be something broad enough to cover such wide-ranging depictions.

This also makes sense of other biblical data, those that relate to the ultimate end of all things. The Bible repeatedly affirms that God's activities of creation, providence, salvation, and judgment are all for his glory. Yet the Bible offers various attributes that will be set forth in display to

---

[36] A. H. McNeile defines glory as "a spectacle of outward beauty as a visible sign of His moral perfection." *Book of Exodus*, WC (London: Methuen, 1908; repr. 1931), 215.

[37] Newman, "Glory," 396, suggests that along with wisdom, spirit, image, word, name, and power, glory "formed part of the semantic-filled words that could sign God's revealed presence."

[38] See Bruce K. Waltke with Charles Yu, *An Old Testament Theology: An Exegetical, Canonical, and Thematic Approach* (Grand Rapids, MI: Zondervan, 2007), 474. Waltke suggests that the glory and name theologies complement each other: "The glory of God is unapproachable and dangerous, but the name of God is something with which his worshippers are permitted to become familiar. God's glory is preferred when the context is that of the dramatic, exceptional manifestations of God, but 'name' is used in contexts where the kind of revelation and the people's response is more intimate." Waltke bases some of this on J. Gordon McConville, "God's Name and God's Glory," *TynBul* 30 (1979): 156–57. Cf. Edwards, "The End for Which God Created the World," 239; John Piper, *The Pleasures of God: Meditations on God's Delight in Being God* (Portland, OR: Multnomah, 1991).

be marveled at; and displays of those attributes are not subsumed under a primary attribute but are depicted as ultimate. For example, in Exodus God acts so that others will recognize his utter uniqueness and power. In Romans God's saving action is to display his righteousness, justice, wrath, power, mercy, and riches of his glory (Rom. 3:21–26; 9:20–23). In Ephesians God acts for the ultimate display of at least three attributes: grace (1:6, 12, 14), kindness (2:4–10), and wisdom (3:10–11).

Such biblical data suggests that God's intrinsic glory is broader than a single attribute. It corresponds with his very being and sometimes functions as a sort of summation of his attributes. Edwards is again helpful: "The thing signified by that name, the glory of God, when spoken of as the supreme and ultimate end of all God's works, is the emanation and true external expression of God's internal glory and fullness . . . or, in other words, God's internal glory, in a true and just exhibition, or external existence of it."[39]

We turn now to see how various truths related to God's intrinsic and extrinsic glory emerge. Each pair initially appears to be in tension but actually coheres.

Expressions of God's Intrinsic and Extrinsic Glory

- God's Glory Is Transcendent and Immanent
- God's Glory Is Full and Received
- God's Glory Is Unique and Shared

God's Glory Is Transcendent and Immanent

Since God's glory is both intrinsic and extrinsic, it makes sense that it would also be both transcendent and immanent, which we will consider in reverse order. God has chosen to display his glory among his people in various ways, and many of the more familiar ones are immanent. Such an instance is the familiar encounter of Moses with God and the glory-cloud on Mount Sinai, in which it is said, "The glory of the LORD dwelt on Mount Sinai" (Ex. 24:16; cf. Deut. 5:22–27). Such an immanent view of God's glory is also found in narratives concerning the ark of the covenant:

> There was nothing in the ark except the two tablets of stone that Moses put there at Horeb, where the LORD made a covenant with the people of Israel, when they came out of the land of Egypt. And when the priests came out of the Holy Place, a cloud filled the house of the LORD, so that the priests could not stand to minister because of the cloud, for the glory of the LORD filled the house of the LORD. Then Solomon said, "The

---

[39] Edwards, "The End for Which God Created the World," 243.

LORD has said that he would dwell in thick darkness. I have indeed built you an exalted house, a place for you to dwell in forever" (1 Kings 8:9–13; cf. 2 Chron. 5:13–6:2).

God's glory is said to fill the temple and the earth, as Psalm 19 and Isaiah 6 attest. This immanence is most clearly seen in the incarnation of Jesus, as the eternal Son of God dwells among us and displays his unique glory (John 1:1–18).

Yet in all these passages, the assumption is that God's glory is intrinsically transcendent. Paul House's comments on Exodus show how God graciously displays his transcendent glory immanently:

> At last Yahweh's intention to dwell among the nations is fulfilled. Moses erects the edifice as he has been commanded (40:1–33). The result is stunning. God's "glory," literally "God's heaviness," fills the tabernacle (40:34). Such is the heaviness of God's presence that not even Moses can enter (40:35). This glory eventually subsides, but not totally, since God does remain in the people's midst. Evidence of this ongoing presence leads Israel to break camp and travel when necessary (40:36–38). Thus, Yahweh not only dwells with the people; Yahweh also keeps the promise to go with Israel and eventually give them the promised land (cf. 33:14; 34:1–14).[40]

That God's glory is immanent and transcendent is also evident in the temple narratives of 1 Kings. We saw that 1 Kings 8:11 discloses this immanence: "The glory of the LORD filled the house of the LORD." And Solomon's prayer of dedication of the temple, recorded in 1 Kings 8:27, acknowledges the transcendence of God's glory: "But will God indeed dwell on the earth? Behold, heaven and the highest heaven cannot contain you; how much less this house that I have built?" Isaiah 6 also makes this clear. Geoffrey Grogan explains:

> The language of fullness . . . occurs three times in these verses (6:1, 3, 4), twice in application to the temple and once to the whole earth. So this passage, insisting as it does on the awesome transcendence of the sovereign God, also emphatically teaches his immanence. His transcendence is not remoteness or aloofness but is known through his presence in his created world and temple.[41]

---

[40] Paul R. House, *Old Testament Theology* (Downers Grove, IL: InterVarsity, 1998), 125.
[41] Geoffrey W. Grogan, *Isaiah*, Expositor's Bible Commentary (Grand Rapids, MI: Zondervan, 1986), 55–56.

Psalmists frequently express God's glory as transcendent. It is "above the heavens." For example, Psalm 8:1: "O Lord, our Lord, how majestic is your name in all the earth! You have set your glory above the heavens." Willem VanGemeren lauds how God's transcendent glory is also immanent:

> The Redeemer-King of Israel is the creator! His name (Yahweh) is glorious over all the earth, by virtue of his creative activities (cf. Gen 1:1–31). What is marvelous is the Great King's revelation of his glory in, and thereby his self–involvement with, his creation. He, the glorious One, has endowed the earth with glory! . . . The "majesty" of Yahweh's name radiates from his work on earth and heaven. . . . All creation reveals the power and glory of God's name.

Psalm 113:4 also resounds with exalted language to stress the transcendent glory of God: "The Lord is high above all nations, and his glory above the heavens!" (cf. 57:5, 11). This idea of God's glory being above the heavens underlines his transcendence and gives a rhetorical effect, making the reality of his immanence even more striking.[42] Observing the transcendent and immanent nature of God's glory, Walther Eichrodt concluded:

> The sense that Yahweh's majesty was exalted far above all created things . . . asserted itself. This came about in various ways; either by stressing the absolute transcendence of the *kabod*, so that mortal man had always to be kept apart from it, or by reducing it to a spatially and temporarily limited medium of Yahweh's self-manifestation, a means by which the transcendent God made his personal presence visible to his own.[43]

God's Glory Is Full and Received

Another expression of God's intrinsic and extrinsic glory is the dual reality of the fullness of his glory and genuine reception of glory. To be sure, God is self-sufficient, independent, lacks nothing, and does not need our faith, worship, and ascription of honor (Isaiah 42–66; Acts 17:16–34). Yet the God who is all-glorious displays his glory, his people respond by glorifying him, and in this God receives glory.

God's reception of glory does not imply that he does not already have intrinsic glory in all its fullness, as John Owen forcefully reminds:

---

[42] Willem A. VanGemeren, *Psalms*, Expositor's Bible Commentary (Grand Rapids, MI: Zondervan, 1991), 714.

[43] Walther Eichrodt, *Theology of the Old Testament*, trans. J. A. Baker, Old Testament Library (Philadelphia: Westminster, 1961, 1967), 2:31.

All things that are, make no addition to God, no change in his state. His blessedness, happiness, self-satisfaction, as well as all other his infinite perfections, were absolutely the same before the creation of anything, whilst there was nothing but himself, as they are since he has made all things: for the blessedness of God consists in the ineffable mutual in-being of the three holy persons in the same nature, with the immanent reciprocal actings of the Father and the Son in the eternal love and complacency of the Spirit.[44]

God creates and acts out of his fullness *and* is pleased to manifest his glory to his creatures. Completely sufficient, God is pleased to receive glory from them, but not in the sense that they add something to him. Rather they acknowledge, enjoy, love, and delight in God and his glory.[45] As the Westminster Shorter Catechism states, "Man's chief end is to glorify God, and to enjoy him for ever." We extol God, reflect God, and find ourselves satisfied in him, by having the manifestation of his fullness communicated to us and by our appropriate response of dependent faith and awe-inspired worship.[46] In this way, our faith acknowledges our insufficiency and depends on his sufficiency. This glorifies God as we recognize our creaturely dependence and his infinite independence. Similarly, our worship is triggered by our awareness of his infinite worthiness. All this glorifies him as it manifests his fullness, self-sufficiency, and glory as the beginning, middle, and end of this process (cf. Rom. 11:33–36).

That God's glory is both full and received is articulated marvelously in Revelation 4:8–11:

> And the four living creatures, each of them with six wings, are full of eyes all around and within, and day and night they never cease to say, "Holy, holy, holy, is the Lord God Almighty, who was and is and is to come!" And whenever the living creatures give glory and honor and thanks to him who is seated on the throne, who lives forever and ever, the twenty-four elders fall down before him who is seated on the throne and worship him who lives forever and ever. They cast their crowns before the throne, saying, "Worthy are you, our Lord and God, to receive glory and honor and power, for you created all things, and by your will they existed and were created."

In the form of a prayer, Owen also portrays our appropriate response to these truths: "Blessed Jesus! We can add nothing to you, nothing to your

---

[44] Owen, *The Glory of Christ*, 160.
[45] Cf. Ps. 29:1–3; Isa. 41:16; 42:1; 43:21; 46:13; Matt. 5:16; John 15:8; Rom. 15:6–9; 1 Cor. 6:20; 10:31.
[46] See Edwards, "The End for Which God Created the World," 154–68.

glory; but it is a joy of heart to us that you are what you are, that you are so gloriously exalted at the right hand of God; and we do long more fully and clearly to behold that glory, according to your prayer and promise."[47]

God's Glory Is Unique and Shared

Another expression of God's intrinsic and extrinsic glory is that his glory is both unique and shared. God alone is intrinsically glorious. He is uniquely and incomparably glorious. As Richard Gaffin points out in his previous chapter, glory is preeminently a divine quality; ultimately only God has glory.[48] And according to Isaiah 42:8, God jealously guards his glory: "I am the LORD; that is my name; my glory I give to no other, nor my praise to carved idols." In the intrinsic sense, God's glory is unique. No one and nothing else is glorious. All idols are unworthy of comparison.

Yet amazingly the glorious God extrinsically manifests his glory and communicates his fullness. In so doing, he remains ontologically unique and distinct from his creatures[49] and graciously shares his glory and makes glorious many things. For example, the Bible makes it clear that humans are created in God's image with glory, honor, and dominion. Psalm 8:4–8 is instructive: though humans are small in comparison to God or the heavens, God remembers and has special concern for them. Indeed God has even "crowned" humans "with glory and honor" (8:5), which connotes kingship (cf. 29:1; 104:1).[50]

Further, God shares his glory with Israel (cf. Rom. 9:4). In the same section of Isaiah appear statements like "my glory I will not give to another" (as we saw in 42:8; cf. 48:11; 62) and those that refer to God calling and putting his name on Israel (43:1–6; 44:1–5), glorying in Israel (46:13), and yes, even making Israel glorious. "My glory I will not give to another" in context refers to God's unique glory and his warnings to Israel that he allows no idols and has no rivals (cf. 48:11–12). Nevertheless, Isaiah declares to the people of God that the Lord "has glorified you" (55:5). Even more, Isaiah 60 shows that God's glory has risen upon them (60:1) and will be seen on them (60:2), and that other nations will see their radiance and glory for God has made them beautiful (60:3–9; 62:2). God says to them, "I will

---

[47] Owen, *The Glory of Christ*, 128.

[48] Richard B. Gaffin Jr., "The Glory of God in Paul's Epistles" (this volume); Richard B. Gaffin Jr., "Glory," in *New Dictionary of Biblical Theology*, ed. T. Desmond Alexander and Brian S. Rosner (Downers Grove, IL: InterVarsity, 2000), 508.

[49] Horton, *People and Place*, 62: "Even those rendered one in Christ by the gospel become brothers and sisters, not a fusion of persons."

[50] VanGemeren, *Psalms*, 112–14. Hebrews 2:7–8 (quoting Psalm 8) ascribes "glory/honor" and dominion to Adam and Eve before the fall. V. 8 says these were lost; v. 9 says Christ, the second Adam, recovered them; and v. 10 speaks of Christ's people being led to glory as a result.

make you majestic forever, a joy from age to age" (60:15), and in turn God himself will be glorified (60:21).

This hope of the glorious God not only manifesting his glory to Israel but also sharing it with them is echoed in Simeon's blessing of Jesus:

> Lord, now you are letting your servant depart in peace,
>   according to your word;
> for my eyes have seen your salvation
>   that you have prepared in the presence of all peoples,
> a light for revelation to the Gentiles,
>   and for glory to your people Israel. (Luke 2:29–32)

This idea of the uniquely glorious God sharing his glory with his people would appear bizarre, except for the fact that it is such a prominent theme. The breadth of the New Testament teaching on this is astounding.

In his High Priestly Prayer Jesus reveals, "The glory that you have given me I have given to them, that they may be one even as we are one" (John 17:22). Peter refers to himself as a partaker in the glory that will be revealed (1 Pet. 5:1) and encourages the suffering that "the God of all grace, who has called you to his eternal glory in Christ, will himself restore, confirm, strengthen, and establish you" (1 Pet. 5:10).

But it is the apostle Paul who most develops this idea that we share in God's glory. Because of our union with Christ, we, in some sense and to the extent it could belong to a creature, participate and share in his glory.[51] As Michael Horton ably puts it, "What happens for us is the basis for what happens to us and in us."[52] Paul instructs the Thessalonian believers that God calls us into his own kingdom and glory (1 Thess. 2:12). He also prays for their faith, "so that the name of our Lord Jesus may be glorified in you, and you in him" (2 Thess. 1:12). Paul encourages the Thessalonians to gratitude because God called them so that they "may obtain the glory of our Lord Jesus Christ" (2 Thess. 2:14; cf. Col. 1:27; 3:4).

To the Corinthians Paul also highlights the shared nature of this glory in conjunction with Jesus' identity as the new Adam and his saving work, particularly in the cross and resurrection: "But we impart a secret and hidden wisdom of God, which God decreed before the ages for our glory.

---

[51] See Sinclair Ferguson, *The Holy Spirit*, Contours of Christian Theology (Downers Grove, IL: InterVarsity, 1996), 91–189. Cf. Horton, *People and Place*, 27: "Only the Spirit can keep us aware simultaneously of the otherness of Jesus and our communion with and in him." Cf. Horton's helpful critique of Eastern Christendom's approach to deification in his *Covenant and Salvation: Union with Christ* (Louisville, KY: Westminster, 2007), 267–307.
[52] Horton, *People and Place*, 307.

None of the rulers of this age understood this, for if they had, they would not have crucified the Lord of glory" (1 Cor. 2:7–8). Because of our union with Christ and his resurrection, our bodies too will be raised in glory (15:42–58). Later, in one of the most penetrating Christological and soteriological statements in all of Scripture, Paul explains: "And we all, with unveiled face, beholding the glory of the Lord, are being transformed into the same image from one degree of glory to another" (2 Cor. 3:18).[53] He develops this more in chapter 4, where he culminates his argument by stating that "this light momentary affliction is preparing for us an eternal weight of glory beyond all comparison" (4:17). Related truths about sharing in glory appear throughout Paul's writings, especially Romans and Ephesians, which we will examine in more detail later.

God's Extrinsic Glory and Redemptive History

Thus far, we have studied God's intrinsic and extrinsic glory and their multiple expressions, including his glory as transcendent and immanent, full and received, and unique and shared. We still need to survey some important expressions of God's extrinsic glory. These redemptive-historical expressions of God's extrinsic glory are helpfully viewed from the following vantage points/tensions:

- Particularity and universality
- Already and not yet
- Divine sovereignty and human responsibility
- God's ultimate end and other ends

Particularity and Universality
God has extrinsically displayed his glory both particularly and universally. Note Exodus's portrayal of the particularity of God's glory:

- Pillar of cloud and fire (14–15)
- God's glory displayed in judgment of Israel (16:7–10)
- Glory in cloud (19:9)
- Cloud, thunder, lightning, mountain, trumpet blast, smoke, fire (19:16ff.; 20:18ff.)
- Sinai, cloud, mountain, fire (24:15ff.)
- Ark of the covenant, court of tabernacle, presence, power, and covenant (24–27; 29:43–46)

---

[53] See Gaffin, "The Glory of God in Paul's Epistles," in this volume.

- Moses' encounter with God (33–34)
- God withdraws his presence in the wilderness due to sin (33:3ff.)
- Glory filled the tabernacle, cloud covered tent of meeting (40:34)

The particularity of the revelation of God's glory is also found throughout Scripture as God manifests himself particularly in the temple (1 Kings 8:11), Israel, the church, heaven, and so forth. We recognize these covenantal and particular expressions and are inclined to focus on them—and rightly so.

We should not fail, however, to notice also that God's glory is universal. Interestingly, the familiar story of Isaiah's encounter with God in Isaiah 6 (cf. John 12:41 showing it is a Christophany) reveals that God's glory is both particular and universal. It is particular in that the vision is of God's glory filling the temple with all the accompanying shakes, sounds, and smoke. Yet God's glory is also depicted as universal: "The whole earth is full of his glory" (6:3). "YHWH's abundant glory presses . . . beyond the sphere of the heavenly-earthly temple and the royal palace into the world."[54] This particularity and universality is frequent in Isaiah, especially in chapters 40 through 66. For instance, Isaiah 66:18 states, "For I know their works and their thoughts, and the time is coming to gather all nations and tongues. And they shall come and shall see my glory."

The Psalms also convey God's glory as particular and universal. Psalm 26:8 stresses particularity, "O LORD, I love the habitation of your house and the place where your glory dwells" (cf. Ex. 40:34–35; 1 Kings 8:11). And Psalm 19 underlines universality, that the glory of God is communicated to all people at all times in all places (general revelation) through the witness of creation (cf. Psalm 8; 72:19). Indeed, creation witnesses universally of God's glory.

Already and Not Yet

Another redemptive-historical expression of God's extrinsic glory can be viewed from the vantage point of the already–not yet tension. God is glorious. His glory has been and is presently being displayed. That is clear from many of the texts and topics we have already referenced:

- Creation (Psalm 19)
- Humans being created as the image of God (Gen. 1:26–28; Psalm 8; James 3:9–12)
- Particular manifestations (cf. Isa. 6:3)

---

[54] Horst Dietrich Preuss, *Old Testament Theology* (Louisville, KY: Westminster, 1995), 167.

- Christ (John 1:14–18)
- Salvation (Ephesians 1–2)

Yet history still awaits God's ultimate display of himself.[55] Commenting on Isaiah, Ortlund puts it passionately: "His glory will be admired and delighted in and trembled at everywhere."[56] Later he adds: "God is moving toward the new heavens and the new earth. He has promised the full display of his glory."[57]

At the consummation, Jesus' return will be glorious (Matt. 16:27–28; 24:30; Mark 13:26; Luke 21:27; 2 Thess. 1:6–11; Titus 2:13). Further, his victory will be glorious, his judgment will be glorious, and his punishment of the wicked in hell will be glorious (Rom. 9:20–23; Rev. 20:11–15). Most of all, Jesus' revelation of himself in the new creation will be glorious (Revelation 21–22). And as we previously noted, through his saving work and our union with him, the church will be presented as glorious (Eph. 5:27; cf. Rom. 8:18–30; 2 Cor. 4:17–18).

Gregory Beale's insights into this are helpful. Beale sees the central theological theme of Revelation as follows: "The sovereignty of God and Christ in redeeming and judging brings them glory, which is intended to motivate saints to worship God and reflect his glorious attributes through obedience to his word."[58] Even more, "nothing from the old world will be able to hinder God's glorious presence from completely filling the new cosmos" nor "hinder the saints from unceasing access to that divine presence."[59]

Since the glory of God is extrinsic, it is closely related to the biblical story and thus tied to the already–not yet tension. As such the glory of God is now being displayed, and yet its ultimate display has not yet occurred (1 John 3:2).

Divine Sovereignty and Human Responsibility

Another vantage point by which to examine the redemptive-historical expressions of God's extrinsic glory is that of the truths of divine sovereignty

---

[55] See Isa. 4:2–6; 40:5; 48:5; 55:5; 59:19; 60:1, 19; 62; 66:12, 18–20, 21–24; Hab. 2:14; Luke 2:25–32; Rom. 5:2; 2 Cor. 4:17; Phil. 2:10–11; 1 Pet. 4:13; Revelation 4–5, 21–22; Edwards, "The End for Which God Created the World," 155; Gregory K. Beale, *The Temple and the Church's Mission*, New Studies in Biblical Theology (Downers Grove, IL: InterVarsity, 2004).

[56] Ortlund, *Isaiah*, 236.

[57] Ibid., 385.

[58] Gregory K. Beale, *The Book of Revelation*, New International Greek Testament Commentary (Grand Rapids, MI: Eerdmans, 1999), 174. Cf. ibid., 1174: "The whole community of the redeemed is considered priests serving in the temple and privileged to see God's face in the new holy of holies, which now encompasses the entire temple-city." Cf. 1119–20.

[59] Ibid., 1115.

and human responsibility. God is glorious, manifests his infinite glory, and will receive the glory he is due. As we have seen, the not yet is coming. Nothing can thwart it. It is the goal of God's cosmic redemptive history, and God will sovereignly bring it to pass (cf. Rom. 8:18–30; 9:20–23; 11:33–36; Eph. 1:3–14, esp. v. 11; Phil. 2:5–11).

But it is also clear that humans are responsible to glorify God as God and worship him.[60] Indeed, Isaiah chastises the people of Judah for their defiance of God's glory (3:8). Israel was often encouraged to obedience for the sake of God's name (Isa. 52:3–6; Rom. 2:24). The people also prayed to that end (Ps. 57:5, 11; 108:5).

Jesus similarly urges his followers, "Let your light shine before others, so that they may see your good works and give glory to your Father who is in heaven" (Matt. 5:16). He later reminds: "By this my Father is glorified, that you bear much fruit and so prove to be my disciples" (John 15:8).

In Romans Paul stresses that our refusal to glorify God as God and our subsequent foolish exchange of his glory for that of the creaturely is the basis of our guilt (1:18–32; cf. 5:12–21; Eph. 2:1–3). Paul later underlines human responsibility as he urges the church to be united for the glory of God,

> that together you may with one voice glorify the God and Father of our Lord Jesus Christ. Therefore welcome one another as Christ has welcomed you, for the glory of God. For I tell you that Christ became a servant to the circumcised to show God's truthfulness, in order to confirm the promises given to the patriarchs, and in order that the Gentiles might glorify God for his mercy. As it is written, "Therefore I will praise you among the Gentiles, and sing to your name." (Rom. 15:6–9)

Paul also reminds the Corinthians of their responsibility to glorify God in all their actions: "For you were bought with a price. So glorify God in your body" (1 Cor. 6:20). "So, whether you eat or drink, or whatever you do, do all to the glory of God" (1 Cor. 10:31). Our responsibility to glorify God is profound as it shapes our sex lives, food choices, and social relationships. Paul likewise encourages the Philippians: "so that you may approve what is excellent, and so be pure and blameless for the day of Christ, filled with the fruit of righteousness that comes through Jesus Christ, to the glory and praise of God" (1:10–11).

The apostle Peter too stresses our responsibility to glorify God, even adjoining it to the nature and mission of the church:

---

[60] See Edwards, "The End for Which God Created the World," 155–56.

But you are a chosen race, a royal priesthood, a holy nation, a people for his own possession, that you may proclaim the excellencies of him who called you out of darkness into his marvelous light. Once you were not a people, but now you are God's people; once you had not received mercy, but now you have received mercy. Beloved, I urge you as sojourners and exiles to abstain from the passions of the flesh, which wage war against your soul. Keep your conduct among the Gentiles honorable, so that when they speak against you as evildoers, they may see your good deeds and glorify God on the day of visitation. (1 Pet. 2:9–12)

Peter later instructs: "Whoever speaks, as one who speaks oracles of God; whoever serves, as one who serves by the strength that God supplies—in order that in everything God may be glorified through Jesus Christ. To him belong glory and dominion forever and ever" (1 Pet. 4:11).

Thus, God is already intrinsically glorious and he will sovereignly bring about the consummation and receive ultimate glory. At the same time, we are still responsible to glorify him.

God's Ultimate End and Other Ends

A fourth helpful way of viewing the redemptive-historical expressions of God's extrinsic glory is that of God's ultimate and multiple ends. That God's ultimate purpose is his glory is clear enough in Scripture and standard in Reformed theology.[61] It is the goal of creation; the exodus; Israel; Jesus' ministry, life, death, resurrection, and reign; our salvation; the church; the consummation; and all of salvation history. Paul often highlights this cosmic goal: "For those whom he foreknew he also predestined to be conformed to the image of his Son, in order that he might be the firstborn among many brothers" (Rom. 8:29); "all things were created through him and for him" (Col. 1:16; cf. Rom. 11:33–36; Heb. 2:10).[62]

While the Bible teaches that God's glory is his ultimate end, it also shows that God often acts with multiple ends in mind. Take the exodus, for instance. Why did God redeem his people from slavery in Egypt? One might quickly reply, "For his glory." Certainly God redeems his people from slavery to glorify himself. But many other things also play a part in this. The book of Exodus presents God's reasons for deliverance in a multifaceted way:

---

[61] See ibid., 125–36; William G. T. Shedd, *Dogmatic Theology*, 3rd ed., ed. Alan W. Gomes (Phillipsburg, NJ: P&R, 2003), 344, 364; Charles Hodge, *Systematic Theology* (repr., Peabody, MA: Hendrickson, 2003), 1:535–36, 566–67; Berkhof, *Systematic Theology*, 136.

[62] See Edwards, "The End for Which God Created the World," 210–20; Piper, *Desiring God*, 250–66, 306.

- His concern for his oppressed people (3–4)
- His faithfulness to the covenant promises made to Abraham, Isaac, and Jacob (3:15; 4:5; 6:8; 32:13; 34:6; cf. Deut. 7:6–10)
- That Israel would serve the Lord (4:23; 6:5)
- That you should know "I am the LORD" (6:7; 10:2; 13:1ff.)
- To give the Promised Land (6:8)
- That the Egyptians will know "I am the LORD" (7:5; 14:3–4; 14:15–18)[63]
- That Pharaoh will know the Lord as incomparable (7:17; 8:10–18)
- To display his power (9:16)
- That his name might be proclaimed in all the earth (9:16)
- To pass down a heritage to the children (10:1–2)
- That his wonders might be multiplied (11:9)
- To get glory over Pharaoh and his army (14:3–18)
- For Israel's sake (18:8)

So God delivered his people for a variety of reasons, not merely one. The account here makes this plain. The incomparable God acts out of love, covenant faithfulness, and jealousy (notice the *uniqueness* emphasis). He does so for his glory, for Israel's good, for judgment on Egypt, and for the continuance of his covenant people. Recognizing and stressing these multiple ends does not detract from an emphasis on God's glory but actually underlines it. Indeed, in the exodus, God displays his love, covenant faithfulness, jealousy, providence, and power through his wonders, salvation, and judgment, in which he manifests himself and thus glorifies himself.

Or we can consider the doctrine of salvation and ask, "Why does God save us?" One might hastily retort, "For his glory." Again, that is right and critical. But the Bible provides a wide range of reasons. That God's motive in saving us is his love is set forth powerfully and regularly. John 3:16 states, "For God so loved the world, that he gave . . ." (cf. 1 John 4:9–10). Ephesians 1:4–5 extols, "In love" God predestined us (cf. Deuteronomy 7), and Ephesians 2:4 ties our salvation to God's love, mercy, and grace (cf. Titus 3:4–5). John 17 records Jesus' High Priestly Prayer, interweaving God's glory and the good of his people, praying and acting in part, "for their sake" (17:19).

---

[63] Pharaoh arrogantly questions God in Ex. 5:2: "Who is the LORD, that I should obey his voice and let Israel go?" Hamilton observes that "the narrative recounts Yahweh's campaign to remedy Pharaoh's ignorance." Hamilton, "The Glory of God in Salvation through Judgment," 72; cf. House, *Old Testament Theology*, 87–125.

Romans 8:28 also makes it clear that redemptive history is, in large part, for the good of God's people.

So why does God save? For many reasons, as we noted above, but in and through all of them, God displays who he is and thus glorifies himself. God manifests his glory because in saving us he displays his wisdom (Rom. 11:33–36; 1 Cor. 1:18–31; Eph. 3:10–11), righteousness, justice (Rom. 3:25–26), love, mercy, kindness (Eph. 2:4–7; Rom. 9:20–23), freedom, wrath, and power (Rom. 9:20–23). Texts like Ephesians 2:4–10 set this forth with clarity and power:

> But God, being rich in mercy, because of the great love with which he loved us, even when we were dead in our trespasses, made us alive together with Christ—by grace you have been saved—and raised us up with him and seated us with him in the heavenly places in Christ Jesus, so that in the coming ages he might show the immeasurable riches of his grace in kindness toward us in Christ Jesus. For by grace you have been saved through faith. And this is not your own doing; it is the gift of God, not a result of works, so that no one may boast. For we are his workmanship, created in Christ Jesus for good works, which God prepared beforehand, that we should walk in them.

Understanding this is significant, as it helps us address a common question concerning God's glory: "If God seeks his own glory above all things, does this mean that he is selfish? After all, if we seek our own glory, we are deemed selfish." The standard answer to that line of questioning is that God is the ultimate being and the highest end, and we are not. Good behavior seeks the highest end, so God making himself his own ultimate end is appropriate. If we make ourselves the highest end, however, we are acting inappropriately because we treat ourselves as the highest end when we are not. That argument is surely correct and beneficial in many ways but fails to do justice to much of the biblical emphasis concerning God's goodness and love. The argument understates God's genuine desire for the good of his creatures, and it fails to show how God's love and his glory are united. Passages like the ones we just read underline how God saves us out of love, displays his kindness toward us for all eternity, and is glorified through the entire display. In this way, God is self-giving and self-exalting, saving us for our good and for his glory. He gives himself to us, which simultaneously meets our needs and demonstrates his sufficiency. Thus, his love and glory cohere.[64]

---

[64] Edwards, "The End for Which God Created the World," 248–49.

That God is simultaneously self-giving and self-exalting is also displayed in the mutual glorification of the persons of the Trinity. The glorious Father sends the glorious Son, who voluntarily humbles himself and glorifies the Father through his incarnation, obedient life, and substitutionary death (Phil. 2:5–11; cf. John 1:18; 6; 7:18; 10:1–30; 14:13; 17). In response the Father glorifies the Son, resurrecting him from the dead and exalting him to the highest place (Acts 3:13–15; Rom. 6:4; Phil. 2:9–11). The Father sends the glorious Spirit who glorifies the Son (John 16:14). And this all takes place to the glory of the Father (Phil. 2:11).

Each member of the Trinity gives to the others as a display of love and as a way of accomplishing cosmic redemption. The Son says to the Father, "I love you and the people you have given me, so I will undergo humiliation and suffering for you and them." And then the Father responds to the Son, "I love you and these people, so for your sake and theirs, I want to raise and exalt you to the highest place and reputation." Amazingly, through serving the Father, the Son is glorified, and through blessing the Son, the Father is glorified (Phil. 2:5–11). Further, the Father blesses the Son with people to save, depicted as love gifts from the Father. The Son, in turn, saves and keeps all of these love gifts, giving them back to the Father (John 6, 10, 17). The Father blesses the Son with gifts (us!), and the Son blesses the Father by giving the gifts in return. Plus, the Spirit communicates the gifts, disclosing what belongs to the Father and the Son to believers (John 16:14–15).

Jesus' High Priestly Prayer also reveals that the self-giving and self-exalting triune God draws his redeemed people into the circle of fellowship, mutual blessing, and shared glory. Jesus begins his prayer, "Father, the hour has come; glorify your Son that the Son may glorify you" (John 17:1). Notice that Jesus longs to be glorified not for his own benefit but for the glory of the Father and of his people (17:20–24). Owen underscores this: "It is evident that in this prayer the Lord Christ has respect to his own glory and the manifestation of it, which he had in the entrance asked of the Father (John 17:4–5). But in this place he has not so much respect to it as his own, as to the advantage, benefit, satisfaction, and blessedness of his disciples in the beholding of it."[65] Such is the peculiar nature of Christ; he is the loving Lord who gives and serves (Matt. 20:26–28; John 13:1–17; Phil. 2:5–11). From that same verse we also learn that the Father grants glory to the Son because of his eternal love for the Son (17:24). Does any of this sound selfish? Not at all! The Father is out to bless the Son, and the Son is out to bless the Father! The mutuality and reciprocating love of

---

[65] Owen, *The Glory of Christ*, 42.

God displayed within the Trinity flows outward even to bless us. By union with Christ, we are recipients of God's love and its corresponding blessings, including forgiveness of our sins, adoption into his family, and final glorification (17:22). And because it is God who accomplishes all of this, it is for our good *and* for his glory!

God's Glory and Our Salvation

Before the beginning of the biblical story, the eternal triune God already exists, self-sufficient, glorious in his perfections, content, and in need of nothing. He creates all that is out of nothing, not because he is lonely or needs us, but to display himself, as Louis Berkhof explains:

> The Church of Jesus Christ found the true end of creation, not in anything outside of God, but in God Himself, more particularly in the external manifestation of His inherent excellency. This does not mean that God's receiving glory from others is the final end. The receiving of glory through the praises of His moral creatures, is an end included in the supreme end, but is not itself that end. God did not create first of all to receive glory, but to make his glory extant and manifest. The glorious perfections of God are manifested in His entire creation; and this manifestation is not intended as an empty show, a mere exhibition to be admired by the creatures, but also aims at promoting their welfare and perfect happiness. Moreover, it seeks to attune their hearts to the praises of the Creator, and to elicit from their souls the expression of their gratefulness and love and adoration. The supreme end of God in creation, the manifestation of His glory, therefore, includes, as subordinate ends, the happiness and salvation of His creatures, and the reception of praise from grateful and adoring hearts.[66]

To this end, the eternal, independent, self-sufficient, good, and glorious God is personally involved in each detail of the creation, crafting it in a way that pleases him and benefits his creatures (Genesis 1–2). On the sixth day, he personally created man in his own image, breathing life into him (Gen. 1:26–28). The personal God has made us personal as well, with the ability to relate to him, live in community with each other, and have dominion over creation. By creating us in his image, God distinguishes us from the rest of creation and establishes that he is distinct from us—we are not gods, but creatures made in his image. Even more, being created in the image of God also means we have glory, honor, and dominion, as Psalm 8:4–8 makes clear. While all of creation testifies to the glory of God (Ps. 19:1–6; Rom. 1:18–25), humans are unique in their identity and role, as

---

[66] Berkhof, *Systematic Theology*, 136.

they have spirituality and bear God's image to the world, serving as stewards and kings over the land, plants, and animals. Genesis 1 and 2 depict this as good, as Adam and Eve are blessed with an unhindered relationship with God, intimate enjoyment of each other, and delegated authority over creation. Only one prohibition is set forth: they must not eat of the tree of the knowledge of good and evil.

But we know what happened: they rebelled against God's command. The story of the fall is described rapidly in Genesis 3:6: "she saw," "she took," "she ate," "she gave," culminating in "he ate." The forbidden fruit did not deliver what the tempter promised but brought that which was warned of by the good and truthful covenant Lord. The effects, though appropriate, are devastating. The couple immediately feels shame, realizing they are naked (3:7), estranged from God (3:8–10), and fearful (3:9–10). Their alienation from each other also emerges, as the woman blames the Serpent, and the man blames the woman and even God (3:10–13)! Pain, sorrow, and disruption of their relationship also ensue (3:15–19). Even worse, the couple is banished from Eden and God's glorious presence (3:22–24). In sum, sin disrupted their relationship to God, to themselves, to each other, and to creation.

Although sin originated in the garden, it did not stay there. It still brings forth spiritual death, further sin, and condemnation for all, who are described as "in Adam" (Rom. 5:12–21; Eph. 2:1–3). Sin is depicted as exchanging the glory of the incorruptible God for something less, like idols (Rom. 1:23; cf. Ps. 106:20; Jer. 2:11–12). Sin is falling short of the glory of God (Rom. 3:23) and brings disrepute on the name of God (Rom. 2:24). Richard Gaffin puts it cogently:

> Sin enters in the creation through Adam (Rom. 5:12–19). Consequently, "although they knew God," human beings "neither glorified him as God nor gave thanks" (Rom. 1:21); that is, they have withheld worship and adoration, their due response to the divine glory reflected in the creation around them and in themselves as God's image bearers. Instead, with futile minds and foolish, darkened hearts (cf. 1 Cor. 1:18–25), they have idolatrously exchanged God's glory for creaturely images, human and otherwise (Rom. 1:21–23). Having so drastically defaced the divine image, they have, without exception, forfeited the privilege of reflecting his glory (Rom. 3:23). This *doxa*-less condition, resulting in unrelieved futility, corruption and death, permeates the entire created order (Rom. 8:20–22).[67]

---

[67] Richard B. Gaffin Jr., "Glory, Glorification," in *DPL*, 348.

The irony of all this is striking: as humans we all refused to acknowledge God's glory and instead sought our own glory. In so doing, we forfeited the glory God intended for us as his image-bearers. Thankfully, God does not completely eradicate humanity for such cosmic treason, but graciously begins a restoration project. He begins the process of redeeming humanity and the cosmos, particularly restoring humans as full image-bearers, so that we can participate in and reflect the glory we longed for the whole time. Establishing a covenant with a people (Israel) whom he chooses and calls, God promises to bless those people so that they can in turn bless the nations, and then the nations in turn will worship and glorify him. When the covenant people are oppressed as slaves in Egypt, God hears their cries and redeems them, displaying his glory so that they, as well as the Egyptians, will know he is the incomparable God and worthy of worship. His name is linked to his people and his presence guides them. Along the way, he displays his glory through awe-inspiring theophanies, the giving of the Law, and prescriptions for appropriate worship. His glory is particularly made manifest through the tabernacle, the ark of the covenant, the temple, and the kingdom. He sends prophets at key points to redirect the sinful people away from empty and worthless idols and back to himself, the uniquely glorious God. These prophets also point to a time when Israel will become what it was intended to be—glorious (cf. Isaiah 60–66)—a time linked to the Messiah's arrival (cf. Luke 2:29–32).[68]

As the Messiah, Jesus was glorious but not in the way most Jews expected. They hoped for a political, military, and spiritual leader to restore Israel to its former glory as a kingdom. But Jesus' redemption was of a different sort and his glory not so nationalistic. But Jesus' glory is actually deeper than anyone could have anticipated, because he is the Lord of glory (1 Cor. 2:8; James 2:1), the radiance of God's glory (Heb. 1:3), even Yahweh himself (cf. John 12:41; Isa. 6:1; Dan. 7:13–14).[69] Jesus the Messiah is the eternal Son, intrinsically glorious, who humbles himself to become incarnate (John 1:1–18; Phil. 2:5–11). His birth is marked by ordinary shepherds yet also by angelic hosts and glory (Luke 2:1–20). His miracles/signs witness to his glorious identity and the presence of God and his kingdom (John 2:11; 11:38–44, esp. 40). At one point, Jesus' glory is manifested visibly to three

---

[68] See Tremper Longman, "The Glory of God in the Old Testament"; Jeff D. Griffin, "The Glory of God as the God of Glory: The Messiah as the Center of Old Testament Theology," a paper presented at the Southern Regional Meeting of the Evangelical Theological Society, New Orleans, LA, Spring 2005.

[69] For more on Jesus' identification with Yahweh, see Gordon D. Fee, *Pauline Christology: An Exegetical-Theological Study* (Peabody, MA: Hendrickson, 2007).

disciples (the transfiguration in Mark 9:2–13; Matt. 17:1–13; Luke 9:28–36; 2 Pet. 1:16–21).

Jesus' glory is also linked with his suffering and his saving death on the cross (John 7:39; 12:16, 23–28; 13:31–32; 17:1–5). Yet, in another sense, the cross was Jesus' path to glory, as Luke 24:26 points to it as necessary to "enter into his glory" (cf. 1 Pet. 1:10–11).[70] Further, the cross actually displays God's glory as it demonstrates his righteousness, justice, and love (Rom. 3:25–26). Three days later Jesus was raised by the glory of the Father (Rom. 6:4) unto glory, exalted to the highest status (Acts 2:32–33; 3:13; 1 Tim. 3:16; Phil. 2:9–11; Heb. 2:5–9; 1 Pet. 1:21; Rev. 5:12–13).[71] He then ascended gloriously (Acts 1; 1 Tim. 3:16) and reigns gloriously (Acts 7:55–56; Mark 10:37ff.). And at the grand finale of salvation history, Jesus' coming, victory, and final judgment will all be glorious (Matt. 16:27; 19:28; 24:30; 25:31; Mark 8:38; 10:37; 13:26; Luke 9:26; 21:27; Rom. 8:21; 2 Thess. 1:6–9; Titus 2:13).

In Gaffin's chapter of this volume, he captures how the glory of Christ is linked to the image of God. I quote here his insights concerning 1 Corinthians 15 and Jesus as the new Adam:

> Drawing together the threads of our discussion of the passage, glory is preeminently the glory of the exalted Christ, the consummate glory he both possesses and, as we will consider further, shares with believers, as he has been constituted the life-giving Spirit by being resurrected bodily and, as ascended, is the heavenly image-bearer. The glory-image of the last Adam in its finality and permanence answers to and is the realization of God's purposes in the beginning in the creation of Adam as his image-bearer. In passing here, but not unimportantly, this eschatological divine image-bearing of Christ by virtue of his resurrection is reinforced in Colossians 1:15–20. This passage has a sweeping outlook spanning his role in creation and redemption: as "the firstborn from the dead" (v. 18) he is "the image of the invisible God, the firstborn of all creation" (v. 15).
>
> For Paul, glory is associated primarily with the Spirit and his power in giving resurrection life and effecting eschatological transformation, first in Christ himself, "the man of heaven" (v. 48) and then in "those who belong to Christ" (v. 23), "those who are of heaven" (v. 48). Virtually everything that Paul

---

[70] Gaffin, "Glory, Glorification," *DPL*, 349: "This present glory of the church, paradoxically and parallel to the experience of its Lord prior to his resurrection, is veiled by afflictions and adversity. Sharing in 'the fellowship of his sufferings' is the way believers experience 'the power of his resurrection' (Phil. 3:10; cf. 2 Cor. 1:5); the condition for those who aspire to be glorified with Christ is that for now 'we suffer with him' (Rom. 8:17)."

[71] See Richard B. Gaffin Jr., *Resurrection and Redemption: A Study in Paul's Soteriology*, 2nd ed. (Phillipsburg, NJ: P&R, 1987), 126.

teaches about glory traces back in one way or another to the resurrection-based matrix of the Spirit, life, power, and glory present in this passage.[72]

How the glorious Christ saves and makes glorious his people is articulated in Romans and Ephesians. Romans stresses that God has graciously and gloriously displayed his justice by Christ's substitutionary death on the cross (3:21–26), and that we receive this by faith, which undercuts all human boasting and glorifies God because it "looks to God as the one who can provide and act on our behalf" (see 3:27–31; cf. 4:1–20).[73] Donald Guthrie pointed out:

> [In Pauline theology] the same pattern for measuring man's shortcomings is the 'glory of God' (Rom. 3:23), which implies that man's sin has made it impossible for him to be the reflector of God's glory as he should have been. Nevertheless, through . . . justification Paul sees the possibility of men again sharing in God's glory (Rom. 5:2). . . . He sees an interaction between the glory of God and the glory shared by Christians (2 Cor. 3:18).[74]

And because we have been justified by faith, we "rejoice in hope of the glory of God" (5:2). Even more, Christ was raised from the dead "by the glory of the Father" (6:4). Because we have been united to him, we too have new life, which Paul previously likened to the receiving of "glory and honor and immortality" (2:7; note here that Paul tells us to seek glory; cf. John 5:44). So though we may suffer now, God is sovereignly guiding history to his intended goals, which include "that we may also be glorified with him" [Christ] (8:17). He develops this by discussing "the glory that is to be revealed to us" (8:18), "the freedom of the glory of the children of God" (8:21), our ultimate conformity to the image of Christ (8:29), and our certain glorification (8:30). Indeed, God will manifest his mercy, power, and wrath "to make known the riches of his glory for vessels of mercy, which he has prepared beforehand for glory" (9:22–23).

Later in his letter to the church at Ephesus, Paul shows that our union with Christ is "to the praise of his glorious grace" (1:6), "to the praise of his glory" (1:12, 14), and results in personal and cosmic redemption (1:3–14), even our "glorious inheritance" from "the Father of glory" (1:17–18). And while recounting our union with Christ and our manifold resultant privi-

---

[72] Gaffin, "The Glory of God in Paul's Epistles," 142–43 in this volume; cf. Fee, *Pauline Christology*, 174–86, 251; Charles Sherlock, *The Doctrine of Humanity*, Contours of Christian Theology (Downers Grove, IL: InterVarsity, 1996), 65–72.
[73] Schreiner, *New Testament Theology*, 145.
[74] Guthrie, *New Testament Theology*, 91.

leges, Paul carefully shows that Christ possesses a unique identity and role
with glory, ultimate and universal authority, and as the head of the church
(1:20–23). As much as we are united to Christ, we are not Christ.[75] He is
still unique, but we are united to him and as such we share his glory, even
here called his fullness (1:22–23). Indeed we were dead in our sins but
God out of love united us to Christ, and as a result we have life in him and
reign with him.

Paul then prays that God would strengthen his people "according to the
riches of his glory" (3:16) that they might "be filled with all the fullness of
God" (3:19). So the glorious triune God manifests his glory, and through
union with Christ even shares his glory with his people. This leads Paul to
burst into doxology: "Now to him who is able to do far more abundantly than
all that we ask or think, according to the power at work within us, to him be
glory in the church and in Christ Jesus throughout all generations, forever
and ever" (3:20–21). We should not miss what he said: "glory in the church
and in Christ Jesus." This sharing of glory is thoroughly Christological and
ecclesiological. Paul describes the church in glory language, "the church,
which is his body, the fullness of him who fills all in all" (1:22–23). The
church is God's "holy temple" and "a dwelling place for God" (2:20–22).

By union with Christ and through the gracious gifts of Christ, the church
is to attain to "the measure of the stature of the fullness of Christ" (4:13).
Even more than creation in general, the church is the witness and theater
of God's glory (3:10–11). The church is now being sanctified so that one
day Christ will "present the church to himself in splendor, without spot
or wrinkle or any such thing, that she might be holy and without blemish"
(5:27). Horton reminds: "The church is always on the receiving end in its
relationship to Christ; it is never the redeemer, but always the redeemed;
never the head, but always the body."[76] As Ephesians recounts, the uniquely
glorious and ontologically distinct Christ graciously unites us to himself,
shares his glory with the church, and gives leaders to the church so that
the church will become increasingly mature and glorious, so that he can
present the church to himself as glorious.

While the nature of this glory we receive is not spelled out in precision,
it is related to the image of God. John Calvin notes this in his comments
on 2 Corinthians 3:18:

[75] See Peter T. O'Brien, *The Letter to the Ephesians*, Pillar New Testament Commentary (Grand
Rapids, MI: Eerdmans, 1999), 141.
[76] Horton, *People and Place*, 31.

Observe, that the design of the gospel is this—that the image of God, which had been effaced by sin, may be stamped anew upon us, and that the advancement of this restoration may be continually going forward in us during our whole life, because God makes his glory shine forth in us by little and little.[77]

Sinclair Ferguson agrees. That Adam was created as the image of God and his final condition was to be one of glory is indicated by Paul's statements in Romans related to our human refusal to glorify God, our exchange of God's glory, and our falling short of his glory (Rom. 1:21–22; 3:23). Ferguson explains:

In Scripture, image and glory are interrelated ideas. As the image of God, man was created to reflect, express and participate in the glory of God, in miniature, creaturely form. Restoration to this is effected through the Spirit's work of sanctification, in which he takes those who have distorted God's image in the shame of sin, and transforms them into those who bear that image in glory. . . .

The mark we were created to reach, but have missed, was glory. We have sinned and failed to attain that destiny. Against this background, the task of the Spirit may be stated simply: to bring us to glory, to create glory within us, and to glorify us together with Christ. The startling significance of this might be plainer if we expressed it thus: the Spirit is given to glorify us; not just to "add" glory as a crown to what we are, but actually to transform the very constitution of our being so that we become glorious. In the New Testament, this glorification is seen to begin already in the present order, in believers. Through the Spirit they are already being changed from glory to glory, as they gaze on/reflect the face of the Lord (2 Cor. 3:17–18). But the consummation of this glorification awaits the eschaton and the Spirit's ministry in the resurrection. Here, too, the pattern of his working is: as in Christ, so in believers and, by implication, in the universe. . . .

The image and image-bearers are one in Spirit to the end, so that when Christ appears in glory image-bearers are one with him in that glory (Col. 3:4). We are raised in Christ, with Christ, by Christ, to be like Christ.[78]

Horton adds:

---

[77] John Calvin, *Commentary on the Epistles of Paul the Apostle to the Corinthians* (repr. Grand Rapids, MI: Baker, 2003), 187.

[78] Ferguson, *The Holy Spirit*, 139–40, 249, 251. For insights related to cosmic glorification, see Ferguson, 252–55; Horton, *People and Place*, 14–16, 21, 27, 31, 62.

Through the Spirit, all that is done by Christ for us, outside of us and in the past, is received and made fruitful within us in the present. In this way, the power that is constitutive of the consummation (the age to come) is already at work now in the world. Through the Spirit's agency, not only is Christ's past work applied to us but his present status of glory in glory penetrates our own existence in a semirealized manner. The Spirit's work is what connects us here and now to Christ's past, present, and future. . . . [T]he Spirit shapes creaturely reality according to the archetypal image of the Son.[79]

God's sharing of God's glory with us does not elevate us beyond our humanity or our nature as creatures but actually enables us to live in full humanness as image-bearers of God.

In sum, from our vantage point, the story of our salvation as it relates to glory is this: as humans we all refused to acknowledge God's glory and instead sought our own glory. Through this we forfeited the glory God intended for us as his image-bearers. By his grace and through union with Christ, the perfect image, God restores us as full image-bearers to participate in and reflect the glory we longed for the whole time. Thus, we are recipients of glory, are undergoing transformation through glory, and will be sharers of glory. Our salvation is not merely from sin but it is also unto glory. What grace we have received: we who exchanged the glory of God for idols, we who rebelled against God's glory, have been, are being, and will be completely transformed by the very glory we despised and rejected. Even more, through union with Christ, together we are the church, the new humanity (Eph. 2:11–22; 4:11–16, 20–24), the firstfruits of the new creation, bearing God's image, displaying how life ought to be, and making known the manifold wisdom of God (Eph. 3:10–11).

From an even broader vantage point, salvation history is the story of the intrinsically glorious God graciously and joyfully communicating his fullness, chiefly through his creation, image-bearers, providence, and redemptive acts. As his people we respond by glorifying him, and in this God receives glory. Further, through uniting us to the glorious Christ, the perfect image of God, God shares his glory with us. And all of this redounds to his glory, as God in his manifold perfections is exhibited, known, rejoiced in, and prized. In this sense, the entire biblical plot—creation, fall, redemption, and consummation—is the drama of God's glory. Jonathan Edwards

---

[79] Horton, *People and Place*, 21; Horton, *Covenant and Salvation*, 302: "God did not become human so that humans might become God, or even supernatural, but so that humans who had fallen into sin and death could be redeemed, reconciled, justified, renewed, and glorified as the humanity that we were created to become."

captured it well: "the whole is *of* God, and *in* God, and *to* God; and he is the beginning, middle, and end."[80]

"To the only wise God be glory forevermore through Jesus Christ" (Rom. 16:27).

---

[80] Edwards, "The End for Which God Created the World," 247.

7

. . . .

A Pastoral Theology of the Glory of God

BRYAN CHAPELL

. . . .

W e had not meant to deceive, but that is how we were perceived. We taught the young women in our youth group that Jesus had died for them and, if they believed in him, then he would make them happy. They accepted our offer, accepted Jesus, and waited for the blessings. But, in the meantime, they fell in love and prepared to marry young men who did not believe in Jesus. Then we in the church made what could only be perceived as an ugly turn of face. We said to the young women, "You cannot marry these young men. You must separate from them because the Bible says that believers should not be 'unequally yoked' with unbelievers."

The young women responded, "But you said that God would make us happy, if we believed in Jesus. We believed in him and want him to bless these relationships that will make us happy. Why are you now changing your message?"

We responded weakly, "Because the Bible says living for the glory of God is more important than doing what you think will make you happy."

Who Gets the Glory

The young women did not listen to us, and it was hard to blame them, based on what we had told them. Our mistake was not recognizing the power of

Augustine's observation that life's most basic questions boil down to determining who gets the glory—God or his creatures.[1] If we encourage people to give loyalty to Christ with personal blessing as their primary motivation, then the purpose of their faith is self-satisfaction. God's glory takes a backseat to personal gain, and personal satisfaction is the inevitable idolatry of their hearts. On the other hand, if we command loyalty to God with no promise of blessing, then we seem to offer a faith devoid of good news. Is that the gospel? Does God's glory demand his people's unhappiness?

Guides to Glory

Such questions underscore the importance of understanding God's glory and its relationship to the pastoral task. Only when the pastor understands both the demands and delights of God's glory can God's people be well shepherded toward his purposes. Earlier essays in this work have laid the foundation for understanding a theology of God's glory; now we need to consider how this understanding informs the pastoral task.

Determining how God's glory guides the pastor demands a quick rehearsal of definitions already offered in this work. The Old Testament term for *glory* communicates the weight or significance of God's being and nature. The New Testament writers present God's glory as his self-revelation of his being, power, and presence. Both Testaments present God's glory as an expression of his intrinsic beauty and splendor, but no term or set of terms fully captures the scope of the glory revealed in both terminological and narrative revelations of our God's unfathomable magnificence.

Glory Defined by Fear

We gain some measure of understanding what God's glory is by the response expected in his people when they behold it: fear. When Moses hides his face before the burning bush, when the people of Israel cower below a thundering Sinai, when Isaiah wilts upon sight of the seraphim around the throne of heaven, and when the shepherds tremble as the glory of the Lord shone around them on the fields of Bethlehem—all respond in fear. But the fear is not simply terror. In each case, the Lord dampens that emotion with some disclosure of the purpose of his appearing. With the revelation of God's glory, Moses hears that he will deliver God's people; at Sinai, Israel learns that God will lead and protect; Isaiah receives the sweet burn of an atoning kiss; and the shepherds are calmed by an angel choir heralding the glory of peace on earth.

---

[1] Cited in Stephen Nichols's essay, "The Glory of God Present and Past," on p. 33 of this volume.

From these examples and many more in Scripture, we learn that biblical fear is not simply "alarm" or "fright," nor is it simply "dread"; and even "awe" does not fully capture the fear that is the beginning of wisdom (Prov. 9:10). Biblical fear—in its right and mature expression—is a humble and loving response to the character of God. Such fear rightly perceives the awesome and even terrifying power of God, but this perception is tempered with marveling that one so majestic is so concerned for his people.

God is infinite in power but intimate in love. He creates and sustains the universe and yet is present with us. As the earliest of biblical writers said, such knowledge is "too wonderful for me," and its glorious revelation always takes the blood from our faces and the strength from our knees (Job 42:3). These responses may mirror the human behaviors before a tyrannosaurus, but we would be quite mistaken to say that biblical fear is anything like that fear.

Glory Defined by the Son

Biblical fear is not merely concern for possible harm. Rather, biblical fear is proper regard for all God discloses about himself in his glory: lordship with love, infinitude with intimacy, an all-powerful hand with a redeeming heart.[2] We do not have a single word that adequately translates the term for biblical fear, but we do have a clear example to remove all questions as to its basic meaning. Isaiah prophesies of the coming Messiah, saying that "the fear of the LORD" will "rest on him" and "he will delight in the fear of the LORD" (Isa. 11:2, 3 NIV).

Jesus fears God, and he delights to do so. This means that the relationship of God the Father and God the Son ultimately exemplifies biblical fear. Since we know eternal and infinite love exists between the Father and the Son, we must understand that Christ's fear cannot simply be terror. Perfect love must drive out that kind of fear (1 John 4:18). Jesus' intimacy and humility with his heavenly Father reveals that his fear is proper regard for the full spectrum of divine attributes—including his wisdom, power, holiness, justice, goodness, truth, and love.

Thus, we learn from the response that God's glory elicits more of what his glory is. Since biblical fear is proper regard for the fullness of divinity, the glory that produces this fear must be revelation of all that defines divinity. This revelation occurs in various stages and degrees in Scripture. Sometimes we get glimmers of glory, as in the burning bush; and, some-

---

[2] John Piper summarizes nicely by saying that God's glory generally is "the visible splendor or moral beauty of God's manifold perfections" (as quoted by Tremper Longman, in his essay, "The Glory of God in the Old Testament," on page 78 of this volume).

times glory blinds, as in Saul's Damascus road encounter. Sometimes glory whispers, as in a still small voice for Elijah; and sometimes glory thunders, as at Sinai. But our clearest and most powerful revelation of the glory of God comes from the one who most experienced it.

Jesus is "the radiance of God's glory and the exact representation of his being" (Heb. 1:3 NIV). "In Christ all the fullness of the Deity lives in bodily form" (Col. 2:9 NIV). He "is the image of God" made incarnate "to give us the light of the knowledge of the glory of God in the face of Christ" (2 Cor. 4:4, 6 NIV). In Christ Jesus we have our most complete definition of the glory of God.

Glory Distinguished by Redemption

As the God-man, Jesus reveals not only God's supreme power, absolute holiness, and sublime wisdom, but also his surpassing love. Because it was the eternal intention of God to use Jesus to deliver his people (Eph. 1:4, 5; Rev. 13:8), Christ cannot be rightly considered apart from his redemptive purpose. And, since he is the most complete revelation of the glory of God, we learn that God's glory—while including power, holiness, and wisdom—also necessarily includes the qualities of redemption: mercy, grace, and love.[3]

Not only does God intend to shine his glory through Jesus but also to share his glory through his Son. Peter wrote that God "has granted to us his precious and very great promises, so that through them you [his people] may become partakers of the divine nature" (2 Pet. 1:4). Paul explicitly tells the Thessalonians that they have been called by the gospel so "that you might share in the glory of our Lord Jesus Christ" (2 Thess. 2:14 NIV).

Originally God shared his glory with humanity by creating it in his image (Gen. 1:26). Pre-fallen Adam reflected the glory of God in the man's ability to know, honor, relate to, and reflect the character of the divine. When Jesus came as the second Adam, he demonstrated the glory that God intended for original humanity and grants to restored humanity (1 Cor. 15:45–49). In this present age, God restores his glory in us through our union with Christ. By this union what is true of our sin and penalty was placed on him, and what is true of his righteousness and status is imputed to us (Gal. 2:20; Eph. 2:6; 2 Cor. 5:11).

---

[3] This understanding that the revelation of God's glory necessarily includes redemptive themes coheres with Geerhardus Vos's observation that God's self-revelation in Scripture is inseparably linked to redemption. In fact, revelation is the interpretation of redemption. See Geerhardus Vos, *Biblical Theology: Old and New Testaments* (Grand Rapids, MI: Eerdmans, 1948), 5.

In addition, we are equipped by the gifts and graces of Christ's Spirit to reflect his glory with increasing godliness. Echoing Moses' experience with the glory of God on Mount Sinai, Paul writes of the Christian's experience with Christ, "We all, with unveiled face, beholding the glory of the Lord, are being transformed into the same image from one degree of glory to another" (2 Cor. 3:18).

Glory Shared in Christlikeness

The ultimate transfer of glory occurs with our glorification. At that stage of our existence the imperfections of this world are left behind, and God's glory becomes fully radiant in us. But even this glory is scripturally defined as our Christlikeness. In one of his finest messages, entitled "The Weight of Glory," C. S. Lewis observes what our future glory entails:

> The dullest and most uninteresting person you talk to may one day be a creature which, if you saw it now, you would be strongly tempted to worship. . . . Next to the Blessed Sacrament itself, your neighbor is the holiest object presented to your senses. If he is your Christian neighbor he is holy in almost the same way, for in him also Christ *vere latitat* [Lat. "truly hides"]—the glorifier and the glorified, Glory Himself, is truly hidden.[4]

If these words of Lewis's sound too strong, then we need only to see how much more strongly the apostle John speaks: "When he [Christ] appears we shall be like him" (1 John 3:2).

Thus, we learn from the scope of biblical revelation that in the past we were created in Christlikeness, in the present we are restored and equipped for Christlikeness, and in the future we will have a perfected Christlikeness. Our purpose and end is the glory of God as it is revealed in Christ. Paul says this to the Ephesians, when he reminds them that the hope and purpose Christ provides them is "to the praise of his glory" (Eph. 1:12, 14).

The Westminster Shorter Catechism beautifully captures God's intention for our lives: "Man's chief end is to glorify God, and to enjoy him forever."[5] Still, this phrase is rightly understood in the context of what both glorifies God and enables our enjoyment of him: our Christlikeness.

---

[4] C. S. Lewis, "The Weight of Glory," in *The Weight of Glory and Other Addresses* (New York: HarperOne, 2001), 36, 46.
[5] Westminster Shorter Catechism, answer 1.

Glory Applied to Pastoral Theology

We are meant to glorify him who shares his glory with us. Glory comes to us through the generosity of Jesus (John 17:22), and glory returns to him through the faithfulness of his disciples (John 17:10). We find our greatest fulfillment, highest aim, and truest humanity in living for and as Christ. No area of life is excluded. Paul instructs, "So whether you eat or drink or whatever you do, do it all for the glory of God" (1 Cor. 10:31 NIV). This comprehensive command for living in Christlikeness forms the foundation for a pastoral theology. Not only does the apostle's imperative provide warrant for pastoral instruction, reproof, and encouragement that promotes living for God's glory (cf. 2 Tim. 3:16), but it also makes God's glory the proper motivation behind such pastoral endeavors.

Motivating Holiness

When Christlikeness is understood as living wholly for the one who gave himself for us, then Christian obedience cannot be defined as living unhappily for the sake of a selfish God. We do not tell persons such as the young women described at the beginning of this chapter that God delights in depriving them of their desires. Rather, we seek so to extol the glory of God in Christ that living for him *is* their chief desire. I do not by the simplicity of this statement mean to deny the difficulty of the pastoral task, but rather to establish its aims.

If the pastoral task gets defined as helping persons gain what they want apart from the glory of God, then they will discover neither his aid in their pursuits nor personal fulfillment in their gain. Preachers may promise that Jesus will bring health, wealth, and a "good life now" in order to attract crowds, but any who seek him primarily to serve their own interests will not find their soul's satisfaction. None made in the image of God can find true fulfillment in paths that deny first priority to God's glory.

We are most satisfied in lives that bring God the greatest glory. But how do we help people understand this? And how do we enable them to live with such motivation? The answer has already been given several times in this book. The glory of God is inextricable from the message of humanity's redemption in Christ. By relating God's glory to his gracious character, power, and presence as they are revealed in the ministry of Jesus, love for God grows in the Christian heart. This love is the compelling force of the Christian life.

The Bible clearly identifies the source of this love. We love God, because he first loved us and gave his Son as an atoning sacrifice for our sins (1 John 4:10, 19). Apprehension of the mercy of God in Christ stimulates love for the Savior and the one who sent him. Jesus also tells us the result of such love: "If you love me, you will keep my commandments" (John 14:15).

Setting His Agenda

Christlike living flows from the desire to honor the God we love. We simply love to glorify the one who loves us enough to share his glory with us despite our sin and through no merit of our own. This way that the human heart responds to the glory of God made known in the grace of Christ sets the agenda for pastoral ministry. Ministers of the gospel make the glory of God in Christ the chief end of believers' lives by making his grace the dominant message of ministry. When God's people grasp his surpassing love for them, glorifying him becomes their preeminent desire (see Eph. 3:19). Thus, the goal for pastors is to make the grace of God so overwhelm people's hearts that the glory of God becomes the priority of their lives.

Over the centuries many have objected that such an emphasis upon grace will create a disposition toward license rather than holiness. Honesty requires the acknowledgment that the message of grace apart from an emphasis upon the glory of God may cause people to reason that because they may sin with impunity, they might as well sin with abandon. Surely this is why the Reformers who resurrected the centrality of grace in church teaching also emphasized the glory of God as the chief end of man.

Hearts that are cold or hardened to the glory of God will take advantage of the truths of grace. Even in the apostles' time some knew to challenge an emphasis upon grace with the taunt, "Are we to continue in sin that grace may abound?" (Rom. 6:1). But the reasoning that uses grace to excuse sin is not the logic of the heart.

The apostles knew that a heart full of love does not seek to take advantage of its object. By its nature love "is not self-seeking" (1 Cor. 13:5 NIV). If the heart is full of love for Christ, then it desires nothing more than his glory. And the way to fill the heart with such love is to flood the soul with an awareness of the awfulness of sin, the mercy of the cross, and the sufficiency of grace. The kindness of God leads to repentance (Rom. 2:4). Thus, the believing heart is fueled for obedience when it is filled with the knowledge (intellectual and experiential) of grace.

Grace can be abused, but its abusers claim its safety without assurance of its application to them. Grace applies to those who love God (Rom. 8:28). Persons who use the truths of grace to excuse their sin and trample upon the blood of Christ have no assurance that its provisions apply to them. Though they may be among the elect who are rebellious for the moment, any certainty they express in the claims of grace is only speculation of the greatest risk.

In contrast to the risks of the arrogant are the assurances God makes to those who humbly and sincerely seek his mercy despite the severity and frequency of their sins (Isa. 1:18; Matt. 18:22). For such persons there is always mercy—abundant and free (Eph. 2:8–9; 1 John 1:9). And if such individuals fear that by their frequent petitions they will wear out the patience of God, then he assures them that his patience is greater than the persistence of their sin (Hos. 3:1; 1 Tim. 1:16). Our frequent confessions are God's means to sicken us of our sin so that we turn from it, rather than any rationale he will use to turn from us (Luke 15:21–24).

There were those in John Bunyan's day who challenged such declarations about the grace of God. The Anabaptists said, "If you keep assuring people of God's love, then they will do whatever they want." "No," was Bunyan's famous reply, "if you keep assuring God's people of God's love, then they will do whatever *He* wants." The glory of God is the chief priority of those who love him, and they will continually seek to renew their service to him when their hearts throb with the confidence of his grace.

Reflecting His Offices
The way that a pastor keeps others' hearts warmed toward the priorities of the glory of Christ is by consistent declaration of his gracious character and provision. These are historically represented in his divine offices of prophet, priest, and king—offices the pastor also reflects in ministering Christ to his people. Lest these claims seem unbiblical or immodest, we should consider the apostle Paul's reminder that those who minister the gospel are "Christ's ambassadors, as though God were making his appeal through us" (2 Cor. 5:20 NIV).

The pastor both declares the content of the gospel of grace and represents the Giver of that grace in faithful performance of this ambassadorship. Thus, by presenting and representing the glory of God made known in Christ's offices the pastor knows and fulfills the glory of ministry. As examples, consider how in preaching the pastor presents Christ's prophetic message but also represents his prophetic role; in forgiving, the pastor knows more of Christ's gracious provision while also reflecting his priestly office; and in leading, the pastor commends Christ's kingship over all of life while representing his authority. In each pastoral duty the minister of the gospel does not merely communicate the content of Christ's message but the reality of him.

The Glory of the Pastor's Prophetic Ministry

Nowhere is the glory of ministry more evident than in the proclamation of the Word of God. By proclaiming the Word the pastor reflects Christ's prophetic office both in speaking about the glories of Christ and in speaking with the glory of Christ's own voice.

Christ's Message

Since the glory of God is inextricable from his work of redemption, the message of the preacher necessarily includes a redemptive focus. This means that while a sermon may include obligations of duty and doctrine that enable listeners to glorify God, the Scriptures cannot be faithfully expounded without relating them to gracious aspects of God's glory.

Jesus gave his own interpretation of the scope of Scripture on the road to Emmaus after his resurrection. Luke records, "And beginning with Moses and all the Prophets, he explained to them what was said in all the Scriptures concerning himself" (Luke 24:27 NIV; cf. John 5:39). The assessment is striking and instructive. Jesus says that all the Scriptures are about him. Thus, to explain any text without relating it to him is to fail to say what Jesus himself said the text discloses. This does *not* mean that every text mentions Jesus or should be magically twisted with the touch of an allegorical wand to make it seem so to speak. Rather, preaching that rightly glorifies the intent that God has for every passage will indicate how the text (in context) discloses the gracious character of God that is ultimately and fully revealed in Christ.

The Bible's consistent revelation of God's grace enables the apostle Paul to write, "Everything that was written in the past was written to teach us, so that through endurance and the encouragement of the Scriptures we might have hope" (Rom. 15:4 NIV). By proclaiming the grace of all Scripture, the preacher gives people hope in a fallen world despite their fallen condition. This good news is not only a blessing to God's people; it is essential to giving God the glory that is his due in Scripture.

Christ's Voice

Jesus says that the role of the Holy Spirit is to testify of the Son (John 15:26). This same Spirit inspires all Scripture. Thus, the Word of God must testify of Jesus in whose face we see the glory of the Father. That glory shines in many different hues. Still, preaching and teaching true to the purposes of the Spirit fulfills the prophetic role not only of telling people how to glorify God, but also of speaking for God.

By the work of the Spirit with the Word we yet have the voice of God incarnate among us. Hearing this voice requires a foundation of belief in what the Bible says about itself. Paul says that Scripture is "God-breathed" (*theopneustos*, 2 Tim. 3:16 NIV). The Greek term actually refers to "expiration" (i.e., breath being breathed out as one speaks). When you speak, you feel your breath come out as the words are expressed. So Paul contends that when Scripture was written God was breathing out his Word.

Just as God breathed life into humanity at creation, so also Paul says that God breathes the message of eternal life into the Scriptures in order that those who receive it would be new creations. In theological academia we can abstract these words in mere reflection upon the doctrine of biblical inspiration, but in pastoral ministry the reality of Christ's inspiration is the glory of his present voice among his people.[6]

Exactly how words written by men are made by God into his own Word is a mystery. We do not entirely understand its intricacies, but elsewhere Scripture describes the process. The apostle Peter writes, "No prophecy of Scripture comes from someone's own interpretation . . . but men spoke from God as they were carried along by the Holy Spirit" (2 Pet. 1:20, 21). Paul states the consequence of this process when he commends believers at Thessalonica for receiving his message "not as the word of men, but as it actually is, the word of God" (1 Thess. 2:13 NIV).

Augustine understood well the import of these truths and could well be summarized as saying, "Where the Bible speaks, God speaks."[7] This is an amazing and precious truth: all that is Scripture is God-breathed, God's very Word to us. In the Scriptures pastors proclaim, God is yet speaking to his people. The thunder and smoke of God's glory at Sinai may not accompany our words, but his glory is no less present, because his voice still echoes. We need not speak with feigned authority nor fear others' opinions. God has left his voice in the church through his Word to correct, rebuke, and encourage (2 Tim. 4:2). When we speak his truth, he is present and we are not alone.

The leaders of the Reformation expressed these truths with powerful insight. Martin Luther said that the church is God's "mouth-house."[8] As faithful ministers proclaim inspired Scripture in the church, God is yet speaking to the church and the world. The Second Helvetic Confession of the Swiss Reformers made the point in stronger terms: "The preaching of the Word of God, is the Word of God."[9] To the extent that our preaching

---

[6] Some material in the following paragraphs of this section is excerpted from a message delivered to the April 2009 Gospel Coalition Conference in Chicago, IL.

[7] See how Luther summarized Augustine in *Weimarer Ausgabe*, 54, 263 and 34, I, 347; Cf. Augustine in *Epistles* 28.3–5 and 82.1.3; see also Westminster Confession of Faith I.4.

[8] *Luther's Works*, American Edition, ed. Jaroslav Pelikan and Helmut Lehmann (St. Louis: Concordia; Philadelphia: Fortress, 1955 ff.), companion vol. 63. See also *Weimar Ausgabe* 10, I, 48.

[9] Second Helvetic Confession, chap. 1.

is true to Scripture, God's words yet echo in the church. His voice is available to his people—even when it comes through our human mouths—as pastors preach the truths of God's Word.

No one was bolder in expressing the significance of biblical inspiration than John Calvin. Were it not Calvin who spoke, we might question if such things should be said. The French Reformer said, "God has chosen so to anoint the lips and tongues of his servants that, when they speak, the voice of Jesus yet resounds in them" (*Institutes* 4.1.5).

We are accustomed in preaching circles to thinking that Christ is the ultimate audience of all we proclaim. So we speak to glorify and please him. We are less accustomed to thinking that Jesus is the speaker as well as the audience. But when our words are true to his Word, Jesus yet comes and ministers to his people in the preaching of Scripture's truths. The human instrument is used, but Jesus speaks for his own glory.

A little plaque appears in many churches behind the pulpit for only the preacher to see. It quotes from the Bible, "Sir, we would see Jesus" (John 12:21 KJV). With a full understanding of the Spirit's work, we could well alter the plaque to say, "Sir, we would hear Jesus." God's voice is present to his people when pastors speak the truth of his Word in the pulpit, in Sunday school, in the counseling office, or in a child's bedroom.

What I am contending—because the Scriptures attest the same—is that when we speak the truths of the Word of God, we are not simply speaking about Jesus, nor are we simply speaking for Jesus. We are speaking as Jesus. By the work of the Holy Spirit, Christ and the glory that is his encounter his people in their hearts as preachers faithfully express his Word.

If we do not perceive the profound presence of Christ's glory in pastoral proclamation, we may not be prepared for its effects. Anticipating this need, in the same passage where Paul tells us how Christ's voice is present in faithful preaching, the apostle also tells what to expect when we so speak. The proclamation of the Word in some measure always demands or produces purity, persecution, and power. The first two are dimensions of Christ's priestly office and the last a feature of his kingly office—all of which are aspects of his glory represented in the pastoral task.

The Glory of the Pastor's Priestly Ministry
Purity
Since we are speaking as Jesus, we should be concerned for his glory in how we conduct ourselves. God is "making his appeal through us" (2 Cor. 5:20), so it *is* legitimate to ask, "What would Jesus do?" Paul answers that question for Timothy: "You . . . have followed my teaching, my conduct, my

aim in life, my faith, my patience, my love, my steadfastness. . . . Continue in what you have learned" (2 Tim. 3:10, 14). The words remind Timothy that he is to "desire to live a godly life in Christ Jesus" (v. 12) and that he is called to be a "man of God" (v. 17).

These instructions also remind us that pastors communicate the holiness God requires not only by what they say but also by how they live before God's people. As the priests of old were expected to communicate the holiness of God's Word by the purity of their lives, we who represent the glory of Christ's holiness are also to speak and live in exemplary ways. In this way we reflect Jesus' own priestly concerns for his people.

The quality of our lives is not necessary to make the Word of God true or endue it with spiritual power—the Word is inherently true and powerful—but by our lives we can either add static or provide clear channels to the Bible's instruction. We should not let present, legitimate demands for authenticity and transparency convince us that Christ's call to godliness is old-fashioned or ineffective. Since we are speaking "as Christ," we must take care not to put words in his mouth that are either untrue or impure. We reflect his glory by our own integrity, piety, and holiness.

Always those with priestly responsibilities teach God's people how their lives may be made pure. By preaching the imperatives of Scripture and the provisions of the Redeemer and administering the sacraments, pastors verbally and symbolically teach God's people of the holiness he requires and provides. But no lesson is more important than the life of the pastor. We who have the Word of Christ in our mouths are charged to commend it with the purity of our speech, habits, and motives. In this way we show that the truth of the Word is true in our lives.

We should not let anyone convince us that the people of God do not desire godliness from their leaders. Piety is not passé. While no one wants sanctimonious religiosity, God's people need to know the gospel is real and frees us from our sin. The leaders of God's people communicate the glorious hope of the gospel by speaking and living so as to honor the Jesus we voice. Pastors, who are the priests of his Word for his people, should faithfully represent the glory of his character by both the content of their instruction and the godliness of their lives.

Persecution
Christ fulfills his priestly office not only by instructing his people in holiness but also by sacrificing himself for the unholy (1 Pet. 3:18).[10] He suffers on our

---

[10] "Christ executeth the office of a priest, in his once offering up of himself a sacrifice to satisfy divine justice, and reconcile us to God, and in making continual intercession for us" (Westminster Shorter Catechism, answer 25).

behalf. Ministers, who are Christ's ambassadors and voice, should expect similar experiences. Paul appropriately warns Timothy: "You, however, have followed my teaching . . . my persecutions and sufferings that happened to me at Antioch, at Iconium, and at Lystra" (2 Tim. 3:10–11). These were the cities of riots and rocks, where crowds were stirred up against Paul and stoned him. Paul adds, "Indeed, all who desire to live a godly life in Christ Jesus will be persecuted" (v. 12).

Jesus suffered for the sins of others. When the divine Son offered himself as a sacrifice to satisfy divine justice and reconcile us to God, the glory of redemption shined brightly.[11] When we who pastor endure the persecutions of the world for the sake of safeguarding the purity of the church or promoting the holiness of her people, then we are suffering for the good of others and also reflecting Christ's redemptive glory.

More challenging is the realization that pastors are also called to suffer for the sins of those in the church. When our lives are made difficult by the faults, failures, and attacks of those within the church, and when those difficulties are endured, forgiven, and met with unabated love, then we reflect Christ's glory. Whenever pastors resist returning evil for evil, we are also suffering for the sins of others. In this Christlike service we also reflect the glory of his priestly office for the sake of his testimony.

Intercession

Priests also intercede for God's people. In his intercessory role, Christ advocates our cause and speaks for our needs while he is seated in glory at the right hand of God. This role is not entirely separate from his suffering. By his suffering for our sin, Jesus takes the penalty for our sin and gives us access to the Father (Eph. 2:14–18). We have boldness before the throne of heaven because Christ's blood purchased our right to petition the Father. Whenever pastors pray for the family of God, they echo Christ's priestly intercession with the glory of his status at God's right hand.

Pastoral intercessions most poignantly reflect our suffering Savior whenever we pray for those who persecute us, spitefully use us, and fail our Lord. In so interceding we give ourselves for the sake of sinners as our Great High Priest does for us in his intercessions. An old hymn asks about the path of suffering, "It is the way the master went, should not the servant tread it still?" If Christ experienced suffering in priestly service for us, then we should expect that we who represent that aspect of his glory now will also experience suffering for the sake of others.

---

[11] Westminster Shorter Catechism, no. 25.

Christ was made perfect through suffering that brought many sons to glory (Heb. 2:10), and we are perfected in his glorious likeness through suffering for others. The apostle Paul rejoiced that he could "fill up in [his] flesh what is still lacking in regard to Christ's afflictions, for the sake of his body, which is the church" (Col. 1:24 NIV). These words do not mean that Paul doubted the sufficiency of Christ's sacrifice for our sin, but rather that his priestly care for his people is made glorious and present in the church as Christ's servants give of themselves for the sake of the present generation.

From outside and inside the church persecutions will come against those who speak Jesus' words and represent his heart. The apostles write of such suffering not to frighten, but to forearm. When we face persecution for faithfulness, we often presume that we have done something wrong, or that our situation is strange. But God actually intends for such suffering to refine and reflect his glory in us. All pastors who are faithful in representing Christ should expect the challenges of his priestly office. As we endure for Jesus' sake, we more deeply understand and more brightly mirror the glory of his suffering on our behalf.

The Glory of the Pastor's Kingly Ministry

With wonderful pastoral wisdom Paul follows his warning about persecution with a promise of power. We are not alone *in* suffering for God's Word, and we are not alone *when* suffering for God's Word. Paul says to Timothy, "I charge you in the presence of God and of Christ Jesus, who is to judge the living and the dead, and by his appearing and his kingdom: preach the word" (2 Tim. 4:1–2).

Christ's Presence

We should be able to read the verse in the preceding paragraph with new understanding when we recognize that Christ is present in the preaching of his Word. The reason that Paul can charge Timothy to faithful proclamation of the Word in the presence of God and Christ Jesus is not simply because they superintend all human activity, looking down from heaven, but also because they are gloriously present in the Word preached.

Christ's Power

Since Christ is present, so also is the glory of his resurrection power. Though once he died, he speaks in his Word, indwells us, and will appear to judge the world. Christ is alive! He conquered the power of sin and death. Since such life-giving power is present in the preaching of the Word, Christ's glory surrounds the pastor and infuses ministry with divine authority. This does not spell an end to all worldly challenges; it does indicate that God's Word will accomplish what he intends as it is preached faithfully (cf. Isa. 55:11). Thus, the preacher speaks with the power of the One with sovereign power over his Word in the world. Christ's kingship reflects in the authority the pastor possesses in the preaching of the Word.

No one in this nation can launch an atomic weapon without orders from the president. The power is too great to leave to the discretion of any lower official. In comparison consider how powerful must be the force that requires a charge from God and Christ Jesus! Yet, this is precisely the power that is at work in us, when we preach God's Word. Eternity changes with the preaching of the Word. Its power is that great and glorious.

Christ's Authority

Because of this present power Paul urges Timothy to "be ready in season and out of season; reprove, rebuke, and exhort, with complete patience and teaching" (2 Tim. 4:2). The power of the Word warrants its expression in season and out with the expectation that it always has the right to an audience and the authority to perform God's purposes.

A king needs no invitation to speak and no permission to express his will. Similarly, the pastor who possesses the Word of the Lord has the authority of King Jesus to speak his will. For this reason we are to preach with boldness and without compromise. We do not have to apologize for speaking the Word that offends the rebellious, convicts the sinful, or pierces the heart of those in whom the Spirit is active. Nor do we need to fear proclamation of God's mercy, peace, and protection to the outcast, disgraced, and oppressed, regardless of popular opinion or societal opposition. With the glory of the King's Word in our mouths we have the authorization to condemn rulers and challenge the accepted order of a sinful world.

Christ's Care

The metaphors and figures that we use to express the power of the Word should not make us forget that preachers labor in a human world. The Word is not a bulldozer that allows pastors to crush God's people. Pastors are right to combine prophetic wisdom with priestly sensitivity when employing the kingly authority of the Word. For this reason Paul encourages Timothy to preach with "great patience and careful instruction" (2 Tim. 4:2 NIV). If the Word of God has the power of dynamite (*dunamis*), then like dynamite it should be handled with great care. We can afford to be "patient" and "careful" when we believe that the power of our preaching is not in our eloquence, volume, or zeal, but in the Word itself. With such words the apostle communicates not only the glory of the power of the Word but also the glory evident in the tenderness of God's heart.

We do not have to browbeat people into spiritual surrender. The Word is so powerful that we can afford to be compassionate in its expression. God does not need us to strong-arm or manipulate his truth in order to bring others' hearts into submission. We have the Word of Christ, so it is appropriate that we express its truths with the manner of Christ—with courage as required and with compassion as needed. In either case, we expect the power of Christ to be present because his voice resounds in the truth we speak, making the appropriate aspects of his glory known to all who have ears to hear.

Because the voice of Jesus is present in the proclamation of the Word, we are not alone when we preach, nor are we powerless. The one who brought creation into being when he spoke yet speaks with the power to make new creatures in Christ Jesus through the faithful proclamation of his Word. Such assurances are great comfort and strength to pastors called to "preach the word" (2 Tim. 4:2)!

The authority of Christ represented in the preaching of the Word pervades other aspects of the pastoral office. In church leadership, discipleship, instruction, and discipline the pastor brings the rule of Christ into the life of the church. The pastor not only serves Christ in this capacity but also represents Christ through the exercise of these responsibilities. To the church are committed the keys of the kingdom for the testimony and protection of the glory of Christ (Matt. 16:19). Leaders who steward these keys well bring glory to the one who indwells them and the ministry he entrusts to them. King Jesus parades with full glory into the church in which the pastor fulfills the requirements of his sovereign Redeemer with the courage and compassion of Jesus.

The Glory of Christ's Full Ministry

Through their leaders entire churches can come to embody the glory of Christ's prophetic, priestly, and kingly offices. In fact, certain personalities may become so concentrated in the congregation that individuals may press leaders to overemphasize one of these aspects of Christ's character. The intellectual and doctrinally astute may desire prophetic proclamation but have little patience for the priestly needs of the broken—and little tolerance for any authority that challenges their own wisdom. The emotionally needy may demand priestly care to the exclusion of prophetic instruction or authoritative leadership. Finally, those often fighting for control of their own urges, or zealous to control the lives of others, may demand the exercise of Christ's rule without priestly sensitivity or prophetic wisdom.

Though the varieties of church situations and personalities may require varying pastoral approaches, a ministry must to some degree reflect *all* of Christ's offices or it cannot adequately glorify God.[12] The glory of God is not fully expressed in any single dimension of Christ's ministry. The fear of the Lord demonstrates that the glory of God is the full array of his attributes that are ultimately revealed in the fullness of Christ's person and ministry. Similarly, the pastoral ministry dedicated to God's glory must reflect all the offices expressing Christ's character. Thus, the following summarize what the Scriptures teach about the glory of God as it relates to pastoral ministry:

- The fear of the Lord is the glory of God rightly apprehended.
- The glory of God is the character of Christ fully revealed in his offices.
- The glory of ministry is all of the offices of Christ faithfully represented.

These conclusions do not presume that any pastor can fully represent Christ. Yet, when that human weakness is freely acknowledged in the light of the grace of Christ, then the redemptive nature of God that is the best expression of his glory shines in the hope made plain by such pastoring.

In ministry that reflects the offices of our Redeemer, the glory of God yet shines. When God's Word is faithfully expressed from the pulpit, in the classroom, to a child in need, or to a widow in grief, then the *prophetic* voice of Jesus sounds and the glory of the Lord yet surrounds. When a pastor ministers Christ's peace through comfort of a child, administration of the sacraments, selfless intercession, Alzheimer's patient visitation, unconditional forgiveness, and personal suffering, then the *priestly* glory of the cross yet embraces God's people. And when the nature of the *kingly* rule of our Savior is made plain through servant leadership in the church, then the guiding light of the *shekinah* glory yet pervades meetings with leaders, the duties of office administration, the authoritative proclamation of the Word, the counsel given to those hurting, and the discipline exercised with the rebellious.

---

[12] For similar discussion see Calvin's comments on 1 Cor. 1:30, *The First Epistle of Paul the Apostle to the Corinthians*, vol. 9, ed. D. W. Torrance and T. F. Torrance and trans. John W. Fraser (Grand Rapids, MI: Eerdmans, 1960), 45–47.

Every ministerial duty is an opportunity to exhibit Christ's glory. For pastors who can see it, this light creates not only a great sense of obligation but also the joys of deepest fulfillment. In our labors Christ's glory shines. A pastor has no higher purpose or reward.

The Glory of the Church's Corporate Ministry

Before concluding this discussion of the glory of God in pastoring, we must consider the glory intended for the object of every pastor's ministry: the church. While there is much of Christ's glory reflected in a faithful minister's individual efforts, the goal of these efforts is for the church to bring glory to the Savior. The glories of personal ministry cannot be rightly considered or pursued without reflecting upon the glory God intends for the corporate ministry pastors foster.

The Agency of Glory

God calls the church to corporate ministry so that by her proclamation of Christ in word and deed her people will advance his kingdom in all the earth. The church is the primary instrument of the glory of Christ on earth (Eph. 1:23). In an individualistic culture we can forget this. We may talk about changing the culture, being salt and light, taking the message of Christ into the marketplace and, with the best of intentions, think almost entirely in terms of personal, autonomous efforts. In accord with our Western culture's habits and interests, even pastors may think primarily in egocentric terms: what I will do, how I will change a community, what contribution I will make to Christian thought, or what movement I will lead. While we do have individual responsibilities, we do not fulfill our calling if the churches we lead do not corporately bring glory to God.

Despite the church's flaws and failures God intends for her to glorify Christ. Those who pastor her can have no higher calling than helping the entire body fulfill this corporate calling in united understanding and efforts (Eph. 4:12–13). Our individual efforts ultimately glorify God only as they help the body of Christ fulfill its divine design of glorifying him. Pastoral sacrifice and service will not satisfy, bear fruit, or be sustainable if they are not buried in this greater purpose. Conversely, there is no greater reward for pastors than the knowledge that their efforts glorify the Savior and further his eternal kingdom. Such knowledge the Scriptures graciously and zealously supply.

As pastors lead bodies of believers in loving one another, helping and forgiving one another, praying for the work of Christ in their midst, supporting each other in joy and in sorrow, equipping disciples for unified ministry, showing mercy to outsiders, serving together in harmony, and praising the God who enables it all, then churches reflect Jesus' character and fulfill his calling. The cumulative effect of multiple churches so living is Christ's greatest glory in this world—for the glory of Christ himself pervades the world in the corporate life of the church. The immature and bruised can find many reasons to disparage the institutional church, but these complaints are inevitably personal and myopic. The glory of the church—with all the obvious faults of its human occupants—is that it is indwelt with the presence and purposes of the Redeemer.

With inspired vision, the apostle Paul teaches us to see Christ's church as a building of living stones gathered from every kind of people and indwelt as by the *shekinah* glory with the Spirit of God (Eph. 2:21–22). This spiritual temple rises to heaven on the foundation of the apostles and prophets with Christ Jesus himself as the chief cornerstone (Eph. 2:20). The image of such disparate and difficult people arranged on so grand a foundation for such heavenly purposes is so profoundly expressive of God's manifold wisdom that even the angels give glory to God for the design of Christ's church (Eph. 3:10).

Glory is due God "in the church" because he has chosen to use her as the instrument of his purposes on this earth and for eternity (Eph. 3:21a). Here his gospel is proclaimed, his Son is honored, and his people are nurtured in his grace and equipped for world transformation. Whatever the church accomplishes occurs because our God directs and enables us, and therefore its corporate glory also belongs to him.

We may readily understand what it means for there to be glory to God in the church, but Paul also takes care to say the glory to God is "in Christ" (Eph. 3:21b). What does that mean? The answer comes as we remember that the church is Christ's body (Eph. 1:23). So if there is glory in the church, the glory is his. This is not merely an abstraction but an affirmation of our corporate union with Christ.[13] Though he gifts us differently by his Spirit, our Lord shares his identity with each believer, who is united to all others in the body, and, thus, we also corporately possess his righteousness, purpose, and glory.

The Assurance of Glory

This corporate Christlikeness assures us that pastoral ministry is never in vain. Despite struggles and opposition we have the assurance that God will

---

[13] This union "in Christ" emphasized so often in Ephesians for individual hope is most often expressed corporately (e.g., Eph. 1:1, 3, 4, 7, 9, 10, 12, 13; 2:6, 7, 10, 13; 3:6, 11, 21; 4:21, 32). Individual believers are united to Christ, but in him they are also united to each other so that the whole church is consequently united to him.

ultimately bless faithful ministry. This assurance is not based on pastoral talents, and it does not guarantee fruit that the pastor will see in this life. Rather this assurance is based upon confidence in the love of a sovereign God for his eternal Son. Our God is passionate for the glory of the Son he loves. Those who bear Christ's image individually and corporately will be the recipients of the Father's favor in the time and ways that he knows are best.

Our God has no higher aim than the redemption of humanity by which his glory is most profoundly grasped by his people. We individually know and experience this redeeming work by a Savior fulfilling the offices of a prophet, priest, and king. Through these offices he reflects the glory of the Father as revealed to us by the Holy Spirit working by and with the Word in our hearts. This Word is from first to last a message of an eternal love incessantly, relentlessly, inexorably, and sometimes aggressively redeeming wayward children and renewing their world. No merit or achievement causes the love or maintains it. We tremble before such magnificent affection whose source is entirely outside of us and completely within him whose glory the heavens cannot contain. Those who perceive the splendor of such undeserved mercy from so glorious a sovereign are humbled with an overwhelming regard for God that is known from earth's perspective as fear, though it is provided from heaven through grace.

We sometimes mistakenly think of grace as some material blessing or privileged circumstance that God provides to us. But grace is simply an expression of his character. His grace is often most evident to us in the glory that Christ Jesus shares with us individually. That glory comes to us by the mercy, love, and compassion of the Son that are the glory of the Father. But as tender as these qualities are, they are equally an expression of the fierce resolve of the Father to honor his Son. The Father's ferocity of purpose is evident in the corporate nature of the church that proclaims the individual blessings of grace. God promises eternal glory to the church because his Son indwells it. The glory of the Son in the church that is his body is the assurance of every pastor that Satan cannot defeat Christ's purposes in us. Our guardianship of the church is the guarantee of the provision of God. Our ministries shall ultimately prevail in the purposes of the Father because he will glorify his Son.

8

A Missional Theology
of the Glory of God

J. NELSON JENNINGS

Cosmic restoration—nothing less adequately describes God's mission. In fact, God has committed himself not only to re-create his universe to its original, spectacular condition but also—as the Bible's apocalyptic literature attempts to convey—to display added, inexpressible magnificence in the coming new heaven and new earth. The God of the Bible is a big God, and his mission is a big mission.

God's mission also concerns micro needs and situations. What happens to an infant, an elderly woman, a child fending for his own in one of the world's countless urban slums, as well as any nonhuman creature, big or small, falls within God's deep love and concern. You and I are dependent on God as our provider, counselor, and king. It is in very personal ways that you and I serve God, participate in his mission, and experience his ongoing presence.

Setting the Stage
God's actual presence is a hallmark of both the initial and the final created orders. Genesis records how, like any monarch surveying his kingdom,

"The Lord God [was] walking in the garden in the cool of the day" (3:8). In the city to come, "Behold, the dwelling place of God is with man. He will dwell with them, and they will be his people, and God himself will be with them as their God" (Rev. 21:3). Throughout the eventful interim, during which the triune God acts to restore his beautiful but rebellious and curse-ridden cosmos, God's inescapable presence is often hidden from, unrecognized by, or even openly rejected by human beings. Even so, "day to day" and "night to night" (Ps. 19:2) the rest of creation cannot help but declare the Creator's "eternal power and divine nature" (Rom. 1:20). Starry nights, spring flowers, crawling bugs, and all sorts of sensory experiences give unflinching testimony to God's goodness and greatness.

Furthermore, by God's astonishing and gracious initiative a whole host of rebellious people are being "delivered . . . from the domain of darkness and transferred . . . to the kingdom of his beloved Son" (Col. 1:13). With God's final triumph in view, "not only the creation, but we ourselves, who have the firstfruits of the Spirit, groan inwardly as we wait eagerly for adoption as sons, the redemption of our bodies" (Rom. 8:23). While groaning in anticipation, those of us whose allegiance has been captured by Jesus' life, death, and resurrection now participate in his restorative mission as he "always leads us in triumphal procession, and through us spreads the fragrance of the knowledge of him everywhere" (2 Cor. 2:14). The triune God works through feeble but restored people to call other rebels to return to their Creator King, the one who is restoring the whole world to its proper state of his kingdom and palatial residence.

In light of God's cosmic mission, our task in this chapter is to spell out that mission's interconnectedness with God's glory. By definition a "missional theology" gives words (*logoi*) about God's (*theos*) mission; i.e., it describes God's cosmic restoration. How, then, can we describe how God's glory interrelates with his mission? Also, how might the often misconstrued character of that interrelationship between God's glory and mission be understood better? Another question that emerges is whether we can learn about God's mission and glory through religious traditions other than Christianity. Finally, how do we navigate the peculiarities of articulating in the English language "a missional theology of the glory of God"? For reasons that should become clearer along the way, we will take up these four questions in reverse order. Furthermore, it will take some hard and tedious work to make our way through these nuanced topics. The final payoff, well worth the effort, will be to impress upon ourselves most pointedly the glory of God in relation to his mission and, in related fashion, to Christian missions.

A Missional Theology of the Glory of God

The fact that we can use the English language to discuss God's glory—along the lines of this book, for example—is itself evidence of God's missional commitment to restore the entirety of his creation. A moment's reflection reminds us that the Bible was not originally written in English: hence this book has examined Hebrew and Greek terminology in order to understand more sharply God's originally intended meaning in his biblical revelation. Further investigation instructs us that there was no English language per se when the biblical canon was completed: Germanic-rooted "Old English" did not take shape until the fifth century (AD), and French-informed "Middle English"—like Old English very different from the still future sixteenth-century and multi-linguistically based modern English—did not develop until after the eleventh-century Norman invasion.[1] Moreover, it was not until the fourteenth century that the Bible was first translated into (Middle) English by Wycliffe.

The missional impact of this linguistic history hits home when considering Paul's first-century instruction to the Gentile Christians in Ephesus. Paul explained to them that they and their ancestors had been "separated from Christ, alienated from the commonwealth of Israel and strangers to the covenants of promise, having no hope and without God in the world" (Eph. 2:12). That separated, alienated, and hopeless condition was only accentuated for the geographically, culturally, and religiously removed ancestors of those of us today who are English speakers. That God has been "rich in mercy" and has exhibited "great love" (Eph. 2:4) toward English speakers starting many generations ago—just as he has shown to all the world—is a clear demonstration of God's missional commitment.

Christianity's Translatability

It is God's intention to restore all things that have been driving the translation of the Bible, the special good news of God's saving work, into the world's various languages. The ongoing translation of the Bible is due to the fact that the Christian faith is not hermetically sealed within a particular esoteric, religio-linguistic-cultural form. Translatability, one of Christianity's central traits, reflects God's missional commitment to come close to all people by interacting with us in our various heart languages. That same commitment lies behind the incarnation itself, by which "the Word

---

[1] "History of the English Language," http://www.englishclub.com/english-language-history.htm. Cf. "A Brief History of the English Language," http://www.anglik.net/englishlanguagehistory.htm (accessed June 29, 2009).

became flesh and dwelt among us" (John 1:14) and is "not ashamed to call [us] brothers" (Heb. 2:11).[2]

Together with the entrance of biblical faith and language into the stream of English-language currents and tributaries has come the challenge of expressing that faith by choosing appropriate English terminology. Such choices of new linguistic terms for the Bible's words are rarely clear and self-evident; as our small sample below demonstrates, the translation process into English has been no exception. "Appropriateness" of biblical terminology needs to account for various factors, including faithfulness to God's originally intended meaning, effectiveness in communication, and relevance to the receiving audience.[3] Appropriate communication of the Bible and of the gospel in English, then, involves God appropriately expressing to English-speaking people his missional commitment to cosmic restoration, or "making all things new" (Rev. 21:5). God's English-language communication of his missional commitment needs to be both consistent with how he originally communicated that commitment as well as clearly understandable by contemporary English speakers.

The Glory of God

To come to the specific topic at hand, then, is "God's glory" an appropriate biblical phrase? Do the terms *God* and *glory* appropriately convey biblical terminology and God's missional passion? While the following linguistic discussion might seem tedious at certain points, remembering that we are discussing how God has been communicating the gospel to English speakers should, I believe, prove both instructive and inspiring. I thus ask that you continue reading with care and a prayerful posture.

"Glory"

Earlier chapters in this book examined original biblical terms, particularly the Hebrew *kabod* and the Greek *doxa*, that in English have been translated as "glory." Those Hebrew and Greek terms connote (along with other nuances such as "heavy") an active and manifest presence. How did the English word *glory* come to be considered the most appropriate term for *kabod* and *doxa*?

---

[2] Andrew Walls, along with such renowned scholars as Lamin Sanneh and Kwame Bediako, has led the way in pointing out this central Christian characteristic of translatability, as well as its many implications.

[3] These three aspects of appropriate communication of the Bible form the structure of R. Daniel Shaw and Charles E. Van Engen, *Communicating God's Word in a Complex World: God's Truth or Hocus Pocus?* (Lanham, MD: Rowman and Littlefield, 2003).

As almost any English dictionary will indicate, the word *glory* stems from the French *glorie*, which in turn rests on the Latin *gloria*. In classical Latin, *gloria* could connote either "fame and honor" or "ambition and boasting," frequently in either case with regard to military or political achievement. Records indicate that as the Christian faith spread and Jesus' followers were scattered throughout various language groups, Latin-speaking worshipers came to use the term *gloria*. These Christians then added to the meaning "fame and honor" that of "transcendent," "supernatural splendor" and "light." Another important development (as implied earlier in this book) was that Jerome sometimes, but not always, translated *kabod* and *doxa* as *gloria* in the Latin Vulgate. We can conjecture that Jerome's inconsistency in using *gloria* for *kabod* and *doxa*—he sometimes used *majestete*, for example— was due to his hesitancy to risk attributing to God a negative connotation of ambitious boasting.[4]

In sum and stated in missional terms, God, through the Latin Bible and Christian liturgy, used Latin speakers' notions of the fame of Roman military and political heroes, along with an infused religious sense of transcendent light, to communicate what he had also intended to communicate to Hebrew and Greek speakers through the terms *kabod* and *doxa*. In that missional sense, then, English-speaking Christians have used *glory* in reference to God's fame and splendor associated with his manifest presence.

"god" ("God")

What about the designation *god* (or *God*)? It might seem odd to question whether *God* is an appropriately biblical term, but Christianity's translatability makes the question not only meaningful but in fact deeply instructive. Indeed the "risk" God has taken in communicating to people in our particular heart languages, as well as the extent of his missional intentions, are perhaps no more evident than in this matter of how he desires to be addressed.

As noted earlier, English has Germanic and Latin-French roots (along with input from several other languages, as well as terminology that has been invented over the years, decades, and centuries). With regard to expressing in English the Hebrew *elohim* and the Greek *theos*, the Germanic and Latin-French heritages rendered two options: one derived from a Germanic designation for a supreme being, *Gott* (and related terms), and the other *deity* or *Deus* (originally from *Zeus*?). The former option was selected as the appropriate English equivalent of *elohim* and *theos*, with an adjusted

---

[4] Nathan Bierma, "Glory," Calvin Institute of Christian Worship, http://www.calvin.edu/worship/lit_arts/word/words/glory.php (accessed June 30, 2009).

neuter-to-masculine form[5] (and in capitalized form when used with specific reference to the biblical Creator-Redeemer).

Perhaps the passage of time has shielded us later English-speaking Christians from any discomfort we might feel from using the term *God*; after all, it is the English transliterated form of the pre-Christian designation *Gott* that at least formerly bore the meaning of a religious being that was invoked or to whom libations were poured. At any rate, the Creator-Redeemer of the Bible has dared to come as close as possible by interacting with us in our heart languages, including in taking on existing pre-Christian designations. Using a foreign, non-English designation would have contributed to our rebellious desire to hold him at arm's length. Instead, the one whom we in English now call "God" has drawn so close as to both leave us without excuse and compel us to embrace him as *our* rightful king.

Just to utter the English phrase "glory of God," then, connotes the missional passion of the Creator to reclaim all people and the entire creation as he displays to us his fame and splendor. He has gone to the great lengths of interacting directly even with us English speakers.

A "Missional Theology"

The phrase "missional theology" is transliterated from the Latin *missio* and the Greek *theos* and *logoi*. This type of Latin and/or Greek *theological* phrase demonstrates the enduring legacy for English speakers of Latin and Greek Christian terminology. Also, the fact that the translatable Christian faith was first expressed in Greek, and soon after in Latin (and other tongues), demonstrates God's enduring commitment to communicate with all sorts of people.

In terms of content, *missio* is a translation of the Greek *apostellō* (to send).[6] Hence a "missional theology" is a verbalization of how God has sent his agents to accomplish his purposes. Jesus' words to his disciples quickly come to mind: "As the Father has sent [*apestalken*, a form of *apostellō*] me, even so I am sending you" (John 20:21). God has sent Jesus, who in turn has sent his followers. That sending or *missional* pattern interlocks, as we have just explored, with the English-language-expressed "glory of God." Just as he has done with all linguistic groups throughout the world, God has sent his agents to facilitate the display of his fame and splendor among English-speaking people, including you and me.

---

[5] See, e.g., the etymological explanation for "god" in Douglas Harper, "Online Etymology Dictionary," 2001, http://www.etymonline.com/index.php?search=god&searchmode=none (accessed July 1, 2009).

[6] See my related discussion in J. Nelson Jennings, *God the Real Superpower: Rethinking Our Role in Missions* (Phillipsburg, NJ: P&R, 2007), 17.

In a nutshell, God's passionate commitment is what is meant by the phrase "a missional theology of the glory of God." Review slowly each substantive, italicized term of that phrase: "A *missional theology* of the *glory* of *God.*" God's glory can shine through even a somewhat tedious etymological study like this one. Just think of it: the world's Creator-Redeemer has spoken in our mother tongue to communicate to us his presence, majesty, and character. His passion truly is undying, irresistible, and unable to be thwarted.

God's Glory and People's Religious Traditions

God thus speaks to people in our respective languages, using pre-Christian terms for the most vital of biblical vocabulary. What about other religions? Can we see God's mission and glory—his fame and splendor—there as well? While some Christians might feel that raising such a question borders on blasphemy, the fact that God (*Gott*) has chosen to assume to himself existing pre-Christian designations demands that we not skirt what for some can be uncomfortable.

Preexisting Designations

That God, through the translation of the Bible, has taken on designations already present in target languages is undeniable. The English *God* is but one example. West African Yoruba-speaking Christians address the Creator-Redeemer of the Bible as *Odolumare*, the name of the high and distant supreme spirit so common to primal religious traditions. Korean-speaking Christians call him *Hananim*, the single, all-powerful, and sovereign deity of traditional Korean religion. Arabic-speaking Christians use *Allah* (which, given the complexity of Muslim-Christian relations, can raise even further questions beyond the scope of our purposes here). All of these terms and many more like them were not invented when the Bible was translated and God's special revelation of himself came to people. Rather, they were existing terms that were deemed appropriate (i.e., faithful to the Bible's original meaning, effective for communicating, and relevant to the recipients) for the Creator-Redeemer of the Bible.

Even the original biblical designations themselves were preexisting terms; *elohim* and *theos* did not appear in the Scriptures out of thin air. The Holy Spirit–inspired biblical authors used designations that were most appropriate for Hebrew and Greek speakers to understand the one, true Creator-Redeemer. Put from the divine side, God communicated himself to Hebrew and Greek speakers using understandable terms that conveyed his character.

Religious Connections

One inevitable implication of the linguistic continuity between pre-Christian and biblical designations is at least some measure of religious continuity between them as well. Otherwise, there would have been no reason for selecting the particular translated terms for *elohim* and *theos* (e.g., "God," "Hananim") that have been used. Something about the religious meaning of those pre-Christian designations persuaded translators of the Bible—as well as, remember, the original biblical authors themselves—to use those terms in reference to the one, true, and living Creator-Redeemer.

To facilitate this nuanced discussion, allow me to set forth (without a great deal of supportive explanation) a couple of important frameworks for understanding religious traditions in general. First, the operative sense of "religion" I am using here is that of "people's responses to God's inescapable presence." There are almost as many definitions of "religion" as there are religious scholars, but I find that this simple and straightforward definition[7] acknowledges several key components, including: (1) God is real, alive, and active; (2) God has initiated dealings with people; and, (3) all people in turn must respond to him. Biblically we see God's dealings with the people of Canaan, for example, when he tells Abram that his descendants would move into Canaan several generations later, "for the iniquity of the Amorites is not yet complete" (Gen. 15:16). God was dealing with the inhabitants of Canaan quite independently of his still unformed people Israel, and those inhabitants' unfavorable response to God's dealings was going to cost them dearly. The Creator-Redeemer of the Bible has always been dealing with all people he has made, including Cain (Gen. 4:9–16[8]), the Ninevites (Jonah 4:11), Rahab (Josh. 2:8–14), the queen of Sheba (1 Kings 10:1–13),[9] ancient Chinese, the Incas, Bantu peoples, and everyone else.

A second important framework involves characterizing people's responses to God's inescapable presence as a threefold combination of sinful, satanic, and searching.[10] Religion involves rebellious hiding from God, satanic deception at work, and genuine and truthful searching for the

---

[7] The definition is my own and one that I use in teaching about world religions.

[8] After receiving the punishment of some sort of protective mark from God, Cain "went away from the presence of the LORD," v. 16 records. Instead of indicating that Cain had thus escaped God's "inescapable presence"—cf. David's words in Ps. 139:1–12, e.g.—these words point to Cain's sinful attempt to flee the ongoing reminder of God's uncomfortable righteousness and holiness.

[9] Without some measure of prior acquaintance with the one true creator, how else would Rahab and the queen of Sheba, e.g., have recognized the Yahweh of Israel as that same one true creator?

[10] Cf. Harold Netland, *Encountering Religious Pluralism: The Challenge to Christian Faith and Mission* (Downers Grove, IL: InterVarsity; Leicester, England: Apollos, 2001), 330–37. For a defense of exclusivism, see Christopher W. Morgan and Robert A. Peterson, eds., *Faith Comes by Hearing: A Response to Inclusivism* (Downers Grove, IL: InterVarsity, 2008).

Creator that the retained image of God in people longs to know. All three elements, I believe, are present in people's responses to God, i.e., in people's religious beliefs and practices. It is easy to reduce other religions to one or two of these elements, but one can always find evidence of all three at work. For example, Gautama Buddha's insight into the world's pervasive suffering evidenced true insight, yet his proposed solutions were off the mark. Even the horrific ritual of human sacrifice that has been practiced in various settings demonstrates a truthful sense of the high demands of deity to be satisfied.

Given these two frameworks for understanding people's religious traditions, it only makes sense that glimpses of the one, true Creator-Redeemer would show through. Thus while pre-Christian Germanic peoples would have been engulfed by sin, Satan, and thus false notions of the Creator-Redeemer, their invoking and pouring out libations to a particular *Gott* evidenced at least some notion of dependence on a higher power. The Hindu longing for union with ultimate reality, while vastly misconstrued in terms of what constitutes that reality's character as well as what it means to be united to it (him), still evidences the human need to be in relationship with the one who made us. The Qur'an's repeated ascriptions to Allah of being gracious and merciful are true glimpses of the Creator-Redeemer's qualities, mixed as those ascriptions are with skewed pictures of deity and with no acknowledgment of Jesus' accomplishments as Redeemer and Mediator.

God's fame and splendor—his glory—thus shimmer through people's various ways of responding to his inescapable presence. Indeed, the plurality of intertwined cultural-religious matrices within which all people respond to God can enable all of us to catch challenging glimpses of his glory that a different cultural-religious matrix accents better than what our own cultural-religious matrix might stress. Thus, for example, an "Eastern-Buddhist" epistemological approach can help shake a "Western-Christian" epistemological mindset free from confining God's self-revelation in Moses' day, "I AM WHO I AM" (Ex. 3:14), to an ontological claim. Contextually that self-revelation points to God's covenant faithfulness, a relational category perhaps more congenial to "Eastern" epistemological instincts.[11]

God is a big God, and his mission is a big mission. It should therefore not be surprising that glimpses of his glory can be seen in people's various responses to his ongoing and inescapable presence. The fact that the Cre-

---

[11] Hisakazu Inagaki and J. Nelson Jennings, *Philosophical Theology in East-West Dialogue*, Encounter Series (Amsterdam: Rodopi Bv Editions, 2000), 20–26.

ator-Redeemer of the world would affirm those shimmers by assuming to himself designations that non- and pre-Christian people have used serves to emphasize the extent of God's manifest presence, as well as of his missional intention to display his glory extensively throughout the earth and across all generations.

Reexamining the Relationship between Christian Mission(s) and God's Glory

We have seen the great testimony it is to God's missional passion that we English speakers can speak meaningfully and truthfully of "God's glory." There is additional testimony to God's missional passion in the fact that he displays glimpses of his glory through people's feeble, fractured, and even false responses to his inescapable presence. On top of all that, what an honor, privilege, and responsibility it is for those of us who know Jesus Christ to be used of God as participants in his mission. That mission of cosmic restoration includes a particular focus on reclaiming rebellious human beings through the person and work of Jesus Christ.

Basic to appreciating how we as Jesus' followers participate in God's mission is to distinguish between God's mission (singular) and Christians' organized missions (plural) initiatives.[12] God's mission is more fundamental; Christian missions are only part of God's more comprehensive mission. God in his mercy has chosen to work through his people; Jesus' followers are thus responsible to speak and live as witnesses to Jesus' person and work. Even so, God is the one ultimately responsible for restoring his cosmos, using whatever means he chooses. Those means center on his Son, Jesus, along with his serving and witnessing people.

While choosing to use his people, God also works throughout the world directly in displaying his glory and upholding the goodness of his created order. God's creatures everywhere have always found his cosmic-wide presence inescapable. We thus need to appreciate the somewhat nuanced tension between God's commitment to use his people and his presence and work apart from his people. To do that we must carefully examine how Christians can easily misconstrue certain aspects of that nuanced tension.

Some Well-intended Misconceptions

As a practitioner and missiologist, I can safely say that few subjects stir English-speaking evangelical Christians' hearts more deeply than missions. After all, what holier calling is there? What more passionate appeal can be made to God's people than to go to the mission field, or at least give and

---

[12] Cf. Jennings, *God the Real Superpower*, 16–19, 217–25.

pray for those who do in fact go? For what other purpose besides missions do churches collect "faith promise" pledges? What greater compliment can be paid a church than to call it "missions-minded"? Is not having a heart for missions a highly admirable trait for any Christian?

As a practitioner and missiologist who moved to the United States after living a substantial portion of my adult life elsewhere, I can also safely say that few words are used by English-speaking evangelical Christians in as commonly an assumed but undefined way as the term *missions*. All the talk of a "call to missions," "missions giving," or interest in "missions" assumes that we know what we are talking about. In discussing here the relationship between Christian missions and God's glory, we need to clarify different aspects of what we mean (and do not mean) by *missions*.

Reductions

Evangelical Christians' excitement about missions results in strong, impassioned appeals to go and to give. That excitement can be so compelling that involvement with what God is doing in the world can be equated with missions involvement. Missions speakers can even unintentionally employ guilt manipulation tactics to elicit interest and participation in missions activities so as to take part in God's work.

Aside from guilt manipulation, there are problems with reducing God's work in the world to missions activities. For one, as noted earlier the entirety of God's comprehensive mission of cosmic restoration is much broader than Christian missions. When he revealed to John, "Behold, I am *making all things new*" (Rev. 21:1–5), God pointed to himself as the one responsible for the new heaven and new earth, the new Jerusalem, and the elimination of pain and death. It is God, not Christian missions activities, who continues to display himself through the created order that Jesus upholds "by the word of his power" (Heb. 1:3). Confining God to missions work substantially limits God's passionate mission to restore his world.

In related fashion, reducing what God is doing in the world to missions emasculates how God, in his passionate mission, calls and uses his people in their various vocations. God's mission of restoration enlists people to carry out all sorts of redemptive tasks—from engineering to parenting, research, medical practice, politics, finances, agriculture, and countless other labors. All of Jesus' followers, no matter what their tasks assigned by God, can confidently labor in Jesus' name as those sent by God to make the world a better place and to display God's character, i.e., to glorify God.

Another problematic missions-related reduction is that of failing to see Christian missions that take place beyond organized and intentional initiatives. In Acts, and throughout subsequent Christian history, we see both organized and unorganized Christian missions occurring. An example of the former is recorded in Acts 13: "Now there were in the church at Antioch prophets and teachers.... While they were worshiping the Lord and fasting, the Holy Spirit said, 'Set apart for me Barnabas and Saul for the work to which I have called them.' Then after fasting and praying they laid their hands on them and sent them off" (Acts 13:1–3). The organized church in Antioch intentionally sent out Paul and Barnabas as cross-cultural missionaries. Later, when the pair "arrived [back in Antioch] and gathered the church together, they declared all that God had done with them, and how he had opened a door of faith to the Gentiles" (Acts 14:26–27). In contemporary terms, the church in Antioch had a missions conference, featuring reports from Paul and Barnabas. So today we have missions agencies, missionary orders, and all sorts of organizational and institutional support mechanisms that make up the organized Christian missions enterprise.

At the same time, cross-cultural missions also take place in unorganized fashion: "There arose on that day a great persecution against the church in Jerusalem, and they were all scattered throughout the regions of Judea and Samaria, except the apostles.... Now those who were scattered went about preaching the word" (Acts 8:1, 4). Later Luke records, "Now those who were scattered because of the persecution that arose over Stephen traveled as far as Phoenicia and Cyprus and Antioch, speaking the word to no one except Jews. But there were some of them, men of Cyprus and Cyrene, who on coming to Antioch spoke to the Hellenists also, preaching the Lord Jesus" (Acts 11:19–20). These cross-cultural missions were not organized Christian activities: they were refugee movements. Similarly, throughout history up until today it has been as immigrants, students and teachers, business people, political emissaries, and as those performing numerous other functions that Christians have been involved in cross-cultural gospel ministry, or missions.

The important summary point is that we understand Christian missions to be cross-cultural gospel ministries that (a) are carried out in both organized and unorganized ways and (b) are only part of God's overall, comprehensive mission of cosmic restoration.[13] God's missional work in the world must not be reduced to missions, no matter how passionate the appeal might be. As our continuing discussion will show, this point about

---

[13] Note that I think it is helpful to use Christian "missions" as a plural noun and God's "mission" in the singular. A fuller and more nuanced discussion of the entire matter is interwoven throughout ibid.

what missions are (and are not) is vital for appreciating the relationship between Christian missions and God's glory.

Acting out of the Past

One instinctive response that Christians (especially U.S. Christians) can make regarding our missions responsibilities comes out of a "go-send-pray" paradigm. The most honored and significant role in this paradigm is that of the missionary, the one who goes to "the mission field." In fact, it is sometimes asserted that all Christians should plan on going unless prevented otherwise, or that one is not fit to stay unless one is willing to go. The next level is that of sending, particularly by providing financial support. Those who give various forms of administrative support (missions agency personnel or local church missions committees, for example) also fit in this sending category. As for praying, everyone can and should do that, it is noted, with the added encouragement that prayer is actually the most important way of participating in missions.

At this point in our discussion, we are at last only one step away from making a direct connection between misconceptions about missions (which we have been discussing throughout this section) and the glory of God. That next step is a very important one, however, so we must not take it too quickly or carelessly.

Underlying the sense of missions as "going [plus sending/praying] to the mission field" is a centuries-old, deeply rooted, and thoroughly metastasized notion of "Christian nations" versus "non-Christian nations," or "Christendom" versus "heathendom." Simply put, the fourth-century Constantinian acceptance of Christianity was a double-edged sword that both signaled Christianity's increased influence in the Roman Empire and co-opted it as that empire's supportive servant. Even more influential was the subsequent centuries-long process of Europe's Christianization, through which the socio-religio-political amalgam of *une foi, une loi, un roi* ("one faith, one law, one king") crystallized. The isolation of the vast majority of Europeans from other peoples of the world contributed to the pervasive outlook that Europe—in a combined territorial and sociopolitical sense—was Christian and that the rest of the world was living in the darkness of heathendom. The migration of Europeans across the Atlantic did little to shake this bedrock worldview (even with the formal adjustments in church-state relations that were forged in the North American colonies): while Caucasian-European people and societies were Christian, other people and societies were not, were inferior, and had to be either willingly or forcibly instructed. From this deep-seated notion, then, modern Christian missions have involved going from Christian territory and societies to "the mission field" located overseas and "out there."

Of the various recent missiological criticisms of the development and ongoing effects (particularly racist and nationalistic[14]) of European Christendom, the most helpful are those analyses that cultivate an understanding of the past that equips us to navigate the present constructively.[15] What those analyses point out is that a fundamental adjustment needs to occur with respect to what Christian missions involve. That is because the past five-hundred–year modern missions movement—by nature activist and lacking self-critical awareness—has in large part consisted of initiatives taken in connection with Western economic, political, and military expansion out of allegedly Christian territory to dark areas of the world. Spreading God's glory has thus been intertwined with spreading the powerful influence— or glory—of Spain, Portugal, Holland, Britain, France, Russia, the United States, and other European-related countries. Where the Bible forecasts that "all the earth shall be filled with the glory of the LORD" (Num. 14:21), the accompanying *modus operandi* has been that God's glory was to spread to the non-Western world through Western-based Christian missions. In related fashion, God's glory to be spread through Christian missions has been understood exclusively in exalted terms, focused on God's majesty, might, and authority.

Missions Today

The needed adjustment is related to missions' no longer being a singular West-to-the-rest movement. Instead, missions need to be understood as various and multidirectional Christian involvements in God's worldwide project of restoration in all parts of the world, bar none. God's restorative mission is comprehensive in scope and is never complete anywhere until Jesus' second coming and the final consummation. A European-Christendom–based missions mentality assumed and assumes that missions is no longer needed in the Christian West.[16] However, God's comprehensive

---

[14] I address these strongly worded matters in ibid.

[15] Among the relevant works I would commend are Andrew F. Walls, *The Missionary Movement in Christian History: Studies in Transmission of Faith* (Maryknoll, NY: Orbis, 1996); Andrew F. Walls, *The Cross-Cultural Process in Christian History: Studies in the Transmission and Appropriation of Faith* (Maryknoll, NY: Orbis, 2002); Philip Jenkins, *The Next Christendom: The Coming of Global Christianity* (New York: Oxford University Press, 2002); and, Wilbert R. Shenk, *Changing Frontiers of Mission*, American Society of Missiology Series, no. 28 (Maryknoll, NY: Orbis, 1999).

[16] The out-of-date singular verb (missions *is*)—still predominant in evangelical circles—is intentional here. Many U.S. evangelicals no doubt will balk at the point made here, noting the present state of missions directed toward post-Christian Europe. But are U.S. evangelicals instinctively able to accept "missions" directed toward Caucasian America?

mission, and Christians' corresponding activities called "missions," are ongoing from everywhere to everywhere.

Crucial here is the recognition that Jesus' international people are more worldwide than ever before. The twentieth-century demographic shift of the Christian church to "the Global South" has been well documented.[17] Christianity is no longer situated primarily in Europe (and more recently North America). There is no single geographic center of the church—Rome's, Canterbury's, America's, or any other see's or political entity's claims notwithstanding. This demographic reality is in accord with Christianity's aforementioned cultural and linguistic translatability, whereby no people or language can claim preeminence within God's international and multilingual kingdom.

Moreover, every part of the world is still in need of further restorative work. No country, city, or region has been fully redeemed. Injustice on both structural and personal levels is present everywhere, as are unbelieving people. Additionally, the church needs maturing and growth wherever we find ourselves. God's comprehensive mission includes maturing his people along with redeeming societies and the people who comprise them. God in his mercy is thus orchestrating his ongoing restorative mission project for the entire world.

God's Glory, God's Mission, and Christian Missions

We have come a long way to the point of finally stating positively a missional theology of God's glory. We first needed to develop a self-awareness of God's missional initiative to express his presence and character in the English language. We then saw how God has not left himself without witness in and through the world's various religious traditions, which are simply different manifestations of how people have reacted to God's inescapable presence. We then needed to examine the still prevalent notion of how God's glory and Christian missions interrelate in the wake of the Western-based modern missions movement. At last we are in a position to speak constructively about the interrelationship between God's glory and Christian missions.

God's Glory

Key here is that part of the biblical corpus (particularly John's Gospel[18]) that ties God's glory to suffering, preeminently Jesus' death on the cross.

---

[17] The universally cited database is David Barrett, George Thomas Kurian, and Todd M. Johnson, eds., *World Christian Encyclopedia: A Comparative Survey of Churches and Religions in the Modern World*, 2nd ed. (Oxford: Oxford University Press, 2001).

[18] See Andreas J. Köstenberger's essay, "The Glory of God in John's Gospel and Revelation," on pages 107–26 of this volume.

Upon hearing the Passover-attending Greeks' desire to see him, Jesus ties his own glory, as well as that of his Father, to his impending suffering and crucifixion:

> The hour has come for the Son of Man to be glorified. Truly, truly, I say to you, unless a grain of wheat falls into the earth and dies, it remains alone; but if it dies, it bears much fruit. Whoever loves his life loses it, and whoever hates his life in this world will keep it for eternal life. . . . Now is my soul troubled. And what shall I say? "Father, save me from this hour"? But for this purpose I have come to this hour. Father, glorify your name. (John 12:23–28)

Soon afterward, after dismissing Judas from the Passover meal to do "what you are going to do" (John 13:27), Jesus declares to his disciples that "now is the Son of Man glorified, and God is glorified in him. If God is glorified in him, God will also glorify him in himself, and glorify him at once" (John 13:31–32). In his High Priestly Prayer Jesus prays, "Father, the hour has come; glorify your Son that the Son may glorify you. . . . I glorified you on earth, having accomplished the work that you gave me to do. And now, Father, glorify me in your own presence with the glory that I had with you before the world existed" (John 17:1–5). Clearly Jesus here is pointing to the majesty and honor he will be receiving as the risen and ascended Son of God. At the same time he is undeniably linking his and the Father's glory to the horror and suffering of the crucifixion, now that "the hour has come" to accomplish the redemption of the world through his cross and resurrection.

Paired with the Bible's message about God's glory as majestic and unapproachable light, John's depiction of God's glory displayed through the pain, foolishness, and humiliation of Jesus' cross gives a fuller picture of God's presence and glory. That picture conveys both strength and weakness, both wisdom and folly, as well as both triumph and loss. In Paul's words, "We preach Christ crucified . . . the power of God and the wisdom of God. For the foolishness of God is wiser than men, and the weakness of God is stronger than men" (1 Cor. 1:23–25). Jesus' cross and resurrection, both his suffering and his exaltation, display God's glory and presence for all to see.

Is it going too far afield to suggest that, while building on certain aspects of early Latin-speaking Christians' use of *gloria* (particularly those associated with military-political fame and with transcendent light), the recent centuries of Western Christianity's alliance with sociopolitical power have fixated our instinctive sensibilities of God's glory on its powerful and splendorous side at the expense of its biblical pointers toward humility and weakness?

God's Mission

God's mission of restoring the world is thus carried out through what is weak and despised, not only through what is strong and admired. God did not just destroy the universe when Adam and Eve rebelled, then proceed to create another world order out of his greatness and power. Neither did he simply overwhelm Adam and Eve with blinding light and immediately cast the tempter into eternal fire. Rather, God brought his promised curses upon humankind and the rest of creation, then over many generations patiently oversaw and dealt with the earth's developing peoples, "having determined allotted periods and the boundaries of their dwelling place, that they should seek God, in the hope that they might feel their way toward him and find him" (Acts 17:26–27). Having patiently developed a covenant people through whom the entire world's Redeemer would finally come, God "commands all people everywhere to repent, because he has fixed a day on which he will judge the world in righteousness by a man whom he has appointed; and of this he has given assurance to all by raising him from the dead" (Acts 17:30–31). Through a particular man who lived, was unjustly executed as a criminal, and rose again, God has decisively acted to restore the world. God has displayed his glorious presence—his love, mercy, patience, judgment, and grace—through the humble life, horrific death, and stupefying resurrection of Jesus.

The Islamic teaching about Jesus represents a natural recoiling from God's way of executing his mission through such a special man. According to Islam, God would never dishonor a prophet like Jesus by allowing him to suffer and die. Hence contrary to the Bible's allegedly corrupted message, the Qur'an teaches that Jesus did not in fact die but was taken up into heaven and will one day return to help complete the world's submission to Allah. While Allah is ever compassionate and merciful, he does not bring about peace and submission through a program of suffering and death.

The triune God of the Bible, however, has most definitely and decisively displayed his character and glory through suffering and death. His appearance to Abram as "a smoking fire pot and a flaming torch" foreshadowed the substitutionary suffering that Jesus would willingly undergo. In assuring Abram that his descendants would one day inherit the land of Canaan, God alone passed between the killed, divided animals as a pledge that he, not Abram or anyone else, would suffer the same fate if either party broke the covenant being sealed (Gen. 15:17–19). Jesus of course fulfilled that pledge, suffering the awful consequences of humanity's rebellion against God's gracious reign. Thus "in Christ God was reconciling the world to himself"

(2 Cor. 5:19), displaying before the entire world his grace, love, and mercy in the "glorious gospel of the blessed God" (1 Tim. 1:11 NIV).

Christian Missions

Connecting the dots between God's glory, God's mission, and Christian missions should not be that difficult at this point. As just described, God's glory and mission embrace both majesty and service, both praise and rejection. Christian missions—Christians' efforts to participate in God's overarching mission—likewise are to embrace weakness, suffering, and helplessness along with strengths, joy, and capabilities. Paul boasted that God's glorious "power is made perfect in weakness" (2 Cor. 12:9), and insofar as Christian missions contribute to the manifestation of God's glory and presence they will exhibit a humble weakness that helps the participants not to rely on their own ingenuity, strength, resources, and talents.

Missions have in fact born the inherent mark of weakness and suffering throughout Christian history. The early Christians who fled persecution and spread the gospel were scattered about, running for their lives (Acts 8:1–4). It was two young brothers, Frumentius and Aedesius, who in the fourth century AD were taken as slaves on the northeast coast of Africa, then were used by God for the conversion of the king of Axum (ancient Ethiopia) and the early establishment of church institutions. Early Syrian missionaries traveled far eastward, including China, often apart from the safety of political protection. Mendicant orders, such as the Franciscans and Dominicans, spread God's Word as they modeled Christ's poverty and suffering to medieval Europeans. In the sixteenth century Bartolomé de las Casas, Spanish colonist turned Dominican priest, opposed his fellow Spaniards in fighting for the human rights of native peoples in the West Indies and Latin America. In the early 1700s Moravian missionaries were willing to be sold into slavery if that meant reaching faraway people with the gospel. Nineteenth- and twentieth-century Western missionaries often opposed colonial authorities under whom they served, for example disobeying orders to stay away from designated non-Christian areas of Africa that the authorities wanted to protect from disruption and unrest. God's glory has thus often shone through Christian missions that have been aligned with the weak, the oppressed, and those who suffer deeply.

Yet in modern times the arrival of Western missionaries together with Western military, political, and economic might in the Americas, Africa, and Asia might inevitably have linked missions with strength and with the majestic side of God's glory. In the late-fifteenth and early-sixteenth centuries it was the conquering Spanish in the Americas and newly-named

Philippines, as well as the Portuguese in present-day Brazil and along the coasts of Africa and Asia, who were accompanied by Jesuit, Franciscan, and other missionary orders. Aggressive English and Dutch trading companies were not far behind, inevitably with their English and Dutch Protestant chaplains. French expansion soon reached the Americas, Africa, and Asia, bringing with it a fresh wave of Roman Catholic influence. Russian Orthodoxy spread eastward together with the expanding Russian Empire into northern China, northern Japan, as well as northwestern North America. By the middle or end of the nineteenth century the young and growing United States, as well as Belgium, a newly formed Germany, various Scandinavian countries, and other Western nations were expanding economically, religiously, and in many cases militarily throughout the rest of the world. That the non-Western peoples receiving all of these influences often associated Christianity, and the God it conveyed, with Western political, economic, and military power was unavoidable.

A Japanese Corrective

In a work he described as autobiographical, the renowned Japanese Catholic writer Shusaku Endo (1923–1996) wrestles poignantly with the contrast between God's glory as strength and weakness in his historical novel *The Samurai*.[19] This contrast had been brought to Endo and countless others through Western Christianity and missions, and his works are characterized by his agonizing attempt to sort through various elements of the resulting paradox with which he had to live. The protagonist in *The Samuari*'s gripping story is Hasekura Rokuemon (1571–1622), a devoted samurai sent in 1613 as chief envoy of a trade delegation from a *daimyo* (regional ruler) in northeastern Japan to whom Hasekura was unequivocally loyal. This *daimyo* in turn was aligned with the *shogun* consolidating his rule over Japan at the time, Tokugawa Ieyasu. The delegation was headed to *Nueva España* (Mexico) and was guided by an ambitious Spanish Franciscan priest named Valesco.

Hasekura's intense inner struggle throughout the story—reflecting Endo's lifelong struggle as a Japanese who found himself baptized into Catholicism at the age of twelve because of his mother's newfound faith—involves the stark contrast between the suffering, crucified Jesus and the majesty of Spanish rule and of the institutional Roman Catholic Church. After the delegation finally arrives in *Nueva España*, Hasekura encounters both the

---

[19] An English translation is available: Shusaku Endo, *The Samurai: A Novel*, trans. Van. C. Gessel (Tokyo: Charles E. Tuttle, 1982). See p. 272 for Endo's remarks about the autobiographical nature of the novel.

glitter of Spanish-built church edifices and the suffering of poverty-stricken indigenous peoples. Among the latter Hasekura meets a renegade Catholic monk who has voluntarily left his privileged role within ecclesiastical structures and found Jesus among the poor, weak native people he had come to know and love. Hasekura is left to ponder the stark contrast he sees between this monk and Valesco, his constant traveling companion.

When the delegation unexpectedly continues its travels to Spain and then on to Rome, Hasekura's turmoil only increases. He witnesses the contradictory juxtaposition between the Church's glorious majesty (frequently pointed out by Valesco) and the pitiful, bloody Jesus hanging on the ubiquitous crucifixes that Hasekura unavoidably sees all around him. The final ignominy occurs when Hasekura agrees, out of his undying loyalty to his *daimyo* and the prospects of resulting trade relations, to accept Christian baptism—only to return to Japan and find that persecution of Christians has progressed to the point where he himself must suffer as one who has been baptized. Within the larger history of events, the systematic persecution of Christians in early seventeenth-century Japan was largely for political reasons: the Tokugawas did not need powerful and ambitious Westerners threatening the still fragile consolidation of their rule throughout Japan. For Hasekura (and for Endo), the dilemma centered on whether God's glory, the object of ultimate loyalty, was to be found among the majestic and powerful or among the weak and helpless.

Endo attempts to give his own honest answer as a perceptive non-Western recipient of the modern missions movement's dominant message that had directed him more to the majestic and powerful side of that dilemma. He correctively steers us toward both sides of the Bible's depiction of how God has shown us his glory. Something in Endo's engrained Japanese religio-cultural makeup, with its instinctive (and partly Buddhist-cultivated) preference for quietness, humble deference to others, and suffering, helped him latch onto God's revelation of himself as the one who has come to us meekly and humbly, even as he reigns in unending splendor and majesty.

It bears repeating that not all Christian missions in modern times have skewed the depiction of God's presence among the world solely toward power and strength. As already noted many missionaries have gone against that grain as they have stood with the weak and powerless, all the while speaking clearly the truth of the Christian gospel. Nor is it the case that modern Christian missions have owned a historical monopoly of overstressing, through their alliance with political and economic strength, the majestic side of God's dealings with the human race. The medieval Crusades, with all their paradoxical origins and objectives, come quickly to mind, for example. Even so, the Western-based Christian missions movement over the past half-millennium both assumed a superior Western Christendom and was fueled by Western economic and military might. Non-Western recipients have thus had to sift through the confusing Christian message about God's glory that unavoidably has come into their settings together with irresistible Western expansion.

A Biblical Corrective

God has come to us as the humble, suffering servant who now reigns in majesty and before whom one day every knee will bow in unquestioning acknowledgment of his rightful place as king of the universe. The apostle John records Jesus' self-references to being "lifted up" on the cross (John 3:14; 12:32); John then connects those references to Isaiah's visions of Jesus being "lifted up" both in majesty (Isa. 6:1) and as the suffering servant (Isa. 52:13; cf. John 12:38–41).[20] We see God's glory, his presence, in both his dazzling holiness and his disarming weakness.

As noted previously, Christian missions—Christians' efforts to participate in God's overarching mission—in turn are to point to God's glorious presence shown to us in all of its splendor as well as in all of its humility. As we Christians know all too well, Jesus of Nazareth, the very Son of God, did not come to us as a mighty socioeconomic-political authority figure. Rather, he came to us in poverty, weakness, and humility. God in the incarnation has shown us his glorious presence in this sinful world, the world he is saving through a most improbable manner that he has carried out in Jesus Christ. In his continuing mission God displays his glorious character through all of his creation, not only the largest of galaxies but also the smallest of microbes and the humblest of helpless baby animals. Hence Christian missions, especially when tempted to rely on economic, political, and military strength, must always take God's humble course of action to heart.

The Continuing Drama

Christian missions are in as good a position as ever to convey to God's fallen world the full scope of his glory. The Christian movement, the panoply of Jesus' followers, is more worldwide than ever before. We speak—and hear God speaking to us about his character and glory—in literally thousands of languages used around the globe. Because the wide range of our languages conveys various nuances of God's character and glory, the "heaviness" of

---

[20] See again Köstenberger's essay, "The Glory of God in John's Gospel and Revelation," on pages 109, 116, 122 of this volume.

Yahweh's kabod, the praise due to the *Kurios* for his *doxa*, the light emanating from *Shu no eikou* (Japanese), and Christ's suffering announced at the heart of his glorious gospel all are being expressed throughout the world.

We as Christ's worldwide followers have been shaped by, have instinctive understandings of, and follow Jesus in relation to what are effectively all of the world's religious traditions. That means that collectively we have the advantage of knowing the full kaleidoscope of how we as human beings have been responding to God's inescapable presence throughout a multitude of contexts. Different ones of us, then, can witness in understandable ways to Muslims, Hindus, agnostics, Buddhists, and other fellow human beings with regard to our common Creator's character and glory. Collectively as Christians we have the linguistic capabilities and religious sensibilities to be used by everyone's Creator to speak to others about how he has uniquely and decisively displayed his glory in Jesus of Nazareth, the one who has achieved the world's redemption.

Moreover, with twenty-first-century technologies of communication and travel we can interrelate with each other—as a worldwide movement—more efficiently and effectively than ever before. Together we are learning from generations of Christian missions about mistakes, pitfalls, and best practices, and how God uses his people to display the whole spectrum of his glory. Some of us organize mission societies that require intentional financial and prayer support. Some of us move around as immigrants and refugees in search of work, safety, or both, witnessing as we go. Some of us struggle to live out our Christian lives in the midst of poverty, religio-political environments unfriendly to Christianity, religiously indifferent affluence, or contexts filled with the awareness of unseen spiritual forces at work. We who are Christians are in an unprecedented position to learn from each other about how God is displaying himself through our various lives and ways of serving him.

Multidirectional Missions

Because the Christian church with all its branches is in fact more worldwide than ever, the actual movement of Christian missions is more multidirectional than ever before. No longer can it responsibly be imagined that Christian missions can, or should, be managed by any particular geographic, linguistic, or sociopolitical sector of the worldwide Christian church. Nor is it the case that Christian missions either originate exclusively or are received exclusively by any particular geographic, linguistic, or sociopolitical sector of the world. North Americans continue to move out into other parts of the world both as "organized" missionaries and in such "unorganized" fields as business, education, government, and tourism. Koreans do the same. So do Brazilians. Various sub-Saharan Christians are migrating to the world's cities, accompanied by internationally focused ministerial staff. It is the same with Chinese Christians—plus there are significant organized missions efforts springing forth out of China itself. The world's second-largest missions organization is Indian, operating largely within India's vast number of peoples and languages. The list goes on and on.

Because God's restorative, multidirectional mission is comprehensive in scope, he is using all sorts of people who follow Jesus to carry out various facets of the Christian missions enterprise. As the Lausanne Movement's 1989 Manila Manifesto stated, "God is calling the whole church to take the whole gospel to the whole world."[21] All Christians everywhere—throughout the world—are thus involved in what has been termed "glocal" mission: we are to be used of God to display his glory in our own "local" spheres of life and ministry, and we are connected to the "global" network of Christians living and ministering throughout the world. One of the most important ways we can develop our "glocal" missions involvements is to cultivate the eyes to see how God is bringing global missionaries into our local areas. Often he does that through unorganized comings of Christian immigrants, refugees, students, educators, and businesspeople. Connecting with these brothers and sisters in Christ can require extra effort and moving out of one's comfort zone. But such connections can give fresh impetus into living and ministering prophetically—missionally—within our "glocal" settings.

Displaying the Full Scope of God's Glory
Part of what God's calling on the whole church means is that Christian missions are by no means exclusively tied to economic and military power. As is increasingly recognized, the majority of Christians today live in what is often called the "Global South," basically the Southern Hemisphere. The Global South includes large parts of the world that are relatively powerless economically and militarily. As Christians from parts of Latin America facilitate the spread of God's glory both in Latin America and elsewhere (including Europe and North Africa, for example), or as Indian Christians share God's glory throughout the Indian subcontinent, the full scope of God's glorious and gracious dealings with his world are on display. As Christians in sub-Saharan Africa display God's glory where he sends and uses them, accompanying economic and military might is usually not an issue. The humility and weakness of Christ's glorious gospel is easier to

---

[21] "The Manila Manifesto." Available at http://www.lausanne.org/all-documents/manila-manifesto. html (accessed August 24, 2009).

receive through those who have no tantalizing economic or military benefits to pass along.

Those of us originating in economic-military power centers must be
extra careful about how we use those resources. For example, it is easy to
mistake the economic ability to travel internationally for God's leading to
go on a missions venture, especially a short-term one. Also, we must be
aware of how we who have financial and related resources are perceived
by those receiving us. The reality of those whom Mahatma Gandhi called
"Rice Christians" is well known: people who convert to Christianity in order
to gain some sort of social, educational, economic, political, or military
advantage from gospel messengers connected to those benefits. Money and
power are not bad in and of themselves; indeed, they can be useful means
for gospel expansion. However, they can become stumbling blocks to how
the Christian gospel, and God's glory, is spread and perceived.

Related is how enthusiasm and zeal for Christian missions must be tempered by self-criticism, humility, a sincere posture of learning, and God's
unfailing grace and mercy. It will no doubt continue to be the case that,
at least in terms of organized initiatives, the majority of Christian missions will originate in areas of the world that have the economic means
to support those initiatives. Korea and North America will thus continue
to be pacesetters for short-term missions trips for the foreseeable future.
Christians who participate in such initiatives must repeatedly be called to
Jesus' own example of poverty and of distancing himself from sociopolitical power. Renaming missions trips along the lines of "service and learning
trips" might be of practical help.

Thankfully, God is orchestrating the full scope of how he is using all
his people to display his character. Our very real confidence is that, given
today's multifaceted Christian missions context, the world's peoples can
more clearly see that God's glory consists not only of power, splendor, and
blinding light but also of compassion, mercy, and humility.

The Tapestry of God's People

Furthermore, the variety of human personalities, cultural traits, and crea-
tive initiatives that is now characteristic of the worldwide Christian movement displays God's presence and glory more fully than ever before. Paul's
declaration that "through the church the *manifold* wisdom of God might
now be made known to the rulers and authorities in the heavenly places"
(Eph. 3:10; emphasis mine) is more evident today than ever, certainly than
in the great apostle's day. Paul knew that "the mystery hidden for ages in
God who created all things" (Eph. 3:9) had been unveiled in Christ; namely,

that all kinds of people were co-heirs and fellow citizens of God's glorious kingdom. Two millennia later we can experience even more extensively an amazing array of ethnicities, cultural contexts, and backgrounds within which God's glorious kingdom is being realized. Today's display of God's glory as the God of all nations is on an unprecedented scale.

Some U.S. Christians have mixed reactions when they hear that Western Christianity and Western missions no longer predominate. The negative side of those reactions is associated with the sense that Christianity has receded in the West, particularly in Europe but increasingly in the United States. Three factors can temper such negative reactions. (1) The recession of the Christian faith in nineteenth- and twentieth-century Europe is a complicated phenomenon, as well as one that has occurred regularly throughout Christian history. (2) The Christian story in the United States will not necessarily follow the same pattern as in Europe (whatever one's evaluation of that fact might be). How Christianity fares in the U.S. will be due to contributing features of the unique U.S. scene, all within God's own providential dealings. (3) That the Christian movement, including cross-cultural and international missions, is more worldwide and multidirectional than ever is cause for great rejoicing and encouragement. God truly is the God of all the nations, and he is displaying his great and humble glory throughout the earth in ways that should assure Christians of the tenacity of his missional commitment to his world.

The "Glorious Gospel" of our "Glorious God"
The drama of God's displaying himself, of showing us his glory, is thus continuing. There has never been a time when more types of Jesus' followers are displaying that glory. Nor has there ever been a time when more types of people are coming to embrace God in Jesus Christ for who he truly is, throughout the world. The glorious God's glorious mission of cosmic restoration is moving toward its eschatological climax through his glorious gospel. May he grant all his people the eyes to see, the lives to convey, as well as the words to articulate the full spectrum of a missional theology of God's glory.

Selected Bibliography

Aalen, Sverre. "*doxa.*" In *New International Dictionary of New Testament Theology.* Edited by Colin Brown. 2:44–48. Grand Rapids, MI: Zondervan, 1971.

Balthasar, Hans Urs, von. *Seeing the Form (The Glory of the Lord: A Theological Aesthetics).* Translated by Erasmo Leiva Merikakis. Edited by Joseph Fessio and John Riches. 3 vols. San Francisco: Ignatius Press; New York: Crossroad Publications, 1983–1991.

Beale, Gregory K. *The Temple and the Church's Mission: A Biblical Theology of the Dwelling Place of God.* New Studies in Biblical Theology 17. Downers Grove, IL: InterVarsity, 2004.

Burge, Gary M. "Glory." In *Dictionary of Jesus and the Gospels.* Edited by Joel B. Green and Scot McKnight. 268–70. Downers Grove, IL: InterVarsity, 1992.

Burns, Lanier J. *The Nearness of God: His Presence with His People.* Phillipsburg, NJ: P&R, 2009.

Caird, G. B. "The Glory of God in the Fourth Gospel: An Exercise in Biblical Semantics." *New Testament Studies* 15, no. 3 (1969): 265–77.

Collins, C. John. "kabod." In *New International Dictionary of Old Testament Theology and Exegesis.* Edited by Willem A. VanGemeren. 2:577–87. Grand Rapids, MI: Zondervan, 1997.

Cook, W. Robert. "The 'Glory' Motif in the Johannine Corpus." *Journal of the Evangelical Theological Society* 27, no. 3 (1984): 291–97.

Davies, G. H. "Glory." In *The Interpreter's Dictionary of the Bible.* 4 vols. 2:401–3. Nashville: Abingdon, 1962.

Edwards, Jonathan. *Ethical Writings.* The Works of Jonathan Edwards, vol. 8. Edited by Paul Ramsey. New Haven: Yale University Press, 1989.

_____. "The End for Which God Created the World." In *God's Passion for His Glory*. Edited by John Piper. Wheaton, IL: Crossway, 1998.

Gaffin, Richard B., Jr. "Glory." In *New Dictionary of Biblical Theology*. Edited by T. Desmond Alexander and Brian S. Rosner. 507–11. Downers Grove, IL: InterVarsity, 2000.

_____. "Glory, Glorification." In *Dictionary of Paul and His Letters*. Edited by Gerald F. Hawthorne and Ralph P. Martin. 348–50. Downers Grove, IL: InterVarsity, 1993.

_____. *Resurrection and Redemption: A Study in Paul's Soteriology*. 2nd ed. Phillipsburg, NJ: P&R, 1987.

Hamilton, James M., Jr. *The Center of Biblical Theology: The Glory of God in Salvation through Judgment*. Wheaton, IL: Crossway, 2010.

_____. "The Glory of God in Salvation through Judgment: The Centre of Biblical Theology." *Tyndale Bulletin* 57, no. 1 (2006): 57–84.

Hannah, John D. *How Do We Glorify God?* Basics of the Reformed Faith. Phillipsburg, NJ: P&R, 2008.

Harrison, Everett F. "Glory." In *International Standard Bible Encyclopedia*. 4 vols. Edited by Geoffrey W. Bromiley. 2:477–83. Grand Rapids, MI: Eerdmans, 1982.

Huttar, David K. "Glory." In *Evangelical Dictionary of Biblical Theology*. Edited by Walter A. Elwell. 287-88. Grand Rapids, MI: Baker, 1996.

Kaiser, Walter C., Jr. *The Majesty of God in the Old Testament: A Guide for Preaching and Teaching*. Grand Rapids, MI: Baker, 2007.

Kittel, Gerhard, ed. *Theological Dictionary of the New Testament*. Translated by Geoffrey W. Bromiley. Grand Rapids, MI: Eerdmans, 2006.

Kline, Meredith G. "Creation in the Image of the Glory-Spirit." *Westminster Theological Journal* 39, no. 2 (1977): 250-72.

_____. *Glory in Our Midst: A Biblical-Theological Reading of Zechariah's Night Visions*. Eugene, OR: Wipf and Stock, 2001.

_____. *Images of the Spirit*. Grand Rapids, MI: Baker, 1980. Repr. South Hamilton, MA: self-published, 1986.

_____. "Investiture with the Image of God." *Westminster Theological Journal* 40, no. 1 (1977): 39–62.

Lewis, C. S. *The Weight of Glory and Other Addresses* (1949). New York: HarperCollins, 2001.

McConville, J. Gordon. "God's Name and God's Glory." *Tyndale Bulletin* 30 (1979): 149–63.

Newman, C. C. "Glory." In *Dictionary of the Later New Testament and Its Developments*. Edited by Ralph P. Martin and Peter H. Davids. 394–400. Downers Grove, IL: InterVarsity, 1997.

_____. "Glory, Glorify." In *New Interpreter's Dictionary of the Bible*. 2:577–80. Nashville: Abingdon, 2007.

_____. *Paul's Glory-Christology: Tradition and Rhetoric*. Leiden, New York: Brill, 1992.

Owen, John. *The Glory of Christ: His Office and Grace* (1684). Repr. Fearn, Ross-shire, UK: Christian Heritage/Christian Focus Publications, 2004.

Packer, J. I. "The Glory of God." In *New Dictionary of Theology*. Edited by Sinclair B. Ferguson and David F. Wright. 271–72. Downers Grove, IL: InterVarsity, 1988.

Piper, John. *Desiring God: Meditations of a Christian Hedonist*, rev. ed. Portland, OR: Multnomah, 2003.

_____. *God Is the Gospel: Meditations on God's Love as the Gift of Himself.* Wheaton, IL: Crossway, 2005.

_____. *God's Passion for His Glory: Living the Vision of Jonathan Edwards (With the Complete Text of* The End for Which God Created the World*).* Wheaton, IL: Crossway, 1998.

_____. *Let the Nations Be Glad! The Supremacy of God in Missions*. 2nd ed. Grand Rapids, MI: Baker, 2003.

_____. *The Pleasures of God: Meditations on God's Delight in Being God.* Portland, OR: Multnomah, 1991.

_____. *The Supremacy of God in Preaching*, rev. ed. Grand Rapids, MI: Baker, 2004.

Ramm, Bernard L. *Them He Glorified: A Systematic Study of the Doctrine of Glorification*. Grand Rapids, MI: Eerdmans, 1963.

Ross, Allen P. *Recalling the Hope of Glory: Biblical Worship from the Garden to the New Creation*. Grand Rapids, MI: Kregel, 2006.

Ryrie, Charles C. *Transformed by His Glory*. Wheaton, IL: Victor Books, 1990.

Schreiner, Thomas R. *New Testament Theology: Magnifying God in Christ*. Grand Rapids, MI: Baker, 2008.

_____. *Paul, Apostle of God's Glory in Christ*. Downers Grove, IL: InterVarsity, 2001.

Author Index

Subject Index

Adam, 39, 135, 135n13, 136–40, 136n16,
142n28, 143, 147, 169n50, 170, 180, 182,
185, 192, 225. *See also* Jesus Christ, as the
"last Adam"
aesthetics. *See* beauty
angels, 67, 84–85, 86, 87–88, 93, 95, 106, 121,
122, 125, 126
ark of the covenant, 54, 60, 63, 74, 157, 165, 181
assurance, 52, 195, 207–8, 225

battle, 56, 57, 58, 62–63
beauty, 27, 29–30, 45, 46, 49, 67, 67n23, 161,
162, 164, 164n36; holiness as, 162–63n32
birth narrative, 81, 84, 85, 85n6, 87, 92, 93, 155

Christlikeness, 193, 194, 207
church, the, 27–28, 41, 43, 44, 46, 142, 174,
189, 201–2, 204–5, 207n13, 208, 227–28,
231, 232; centrality of grace in, 195; church
history, 44; corporate ministry of, 206, 207;
the early church, 30, 31, 34, 80, 83n3, 220;
and the glorification of God, 100, 103–4,
156, 159, 206, 207; as glorious, 173, 182n70,
184; mission of, 174–75; sanctification of,
150–51, 184; as the voice of God, 198–99
church fathers, 29, 30–31, 32, 33n23, 34, 38, 44
cloud, 55, 57, 60, 61, 62, 72, 77, 123n31, 131,
171–72; glory cloud, 53–54, 60n12, 74, 155,
157, 165
commission, 48, 162–63n32. *See also* Ezekiel,
prophetic commission of; Isaiah, prophetic
commission of; Moses, commission of
cosmic restoration. *See* new creation
creation, 29, 30–32, 62, 130–31, 130n4, 135n13,
136–37, 137n18, 146–47, 149, 149n39,

155n6, 159–60, 167, 179–80, 211, 214, 225,
229; God revealed in, 41, 47, 155, 172; and
God's glory, 63, 63n15, 184, 186, 210; and
redemption, 182. *See also* new creation
cross, 113, 114, 116, 120, 122, 144, 170, 182,
183, 224, 229; glory of, 108–9, 111, 112,
126, 143, 159, 205; theology of, 89n25,
107–8, 119, 125

Daniel, 76–77
David, 58–60, 64, 136n16
deification (*theosis*), 28, 29, 170n52
disciples, 46, 82, 83, 88, 89, 92n28, 110, 112,
178, 206–7, 224; faithfulness of, 194; mission of, 114
doxa (Greek: glory), 81, 82, 84n4, 108, 131,
156–57, 180, 212–13, 230
doxology, 94, 96–97, 100–101, 101n53, 104–5

Eastern Orthodox Church, 28–29, 34n26, 38
Eli, 19, 48, 49, 58, 73
Elijah, 88, 88nn17–18, 89n20, 90, 192
eschatology, 135, 137n18, 154
eternal life, 37, 109, 141, 159, 198, 224. *See also*
heaven
eternity, 82, 90, 104, 125, 152, 159, 160, 177,
207
Ezekiel, 71, 72–74; prophetic commission of, 72

fall, the, 135, 135n13, 136, 137, 137n18, 149n41,
160, 180, 186
Father. *See* God the Father
fear, 56, 85–86, 131, 205, 208; biblical, 121;
glory defined by, 190–91

Scripture Index

John